JBoss AS 5 Performance Tuning

Build faster, more efficient enterprise Java applications

Francesco Marchioni

BIRMINGHAM - MUMBAI

JBoss AS 5 Performance Tuning

First published: December 2010

Production Reference: 1291110

Published by Packt Publishing Ltd.
32 Lincoln Road
Olton
Birmingham, B27 6PA, UK.

ISBN 978-1-849514-02-6

www.packtpub.com

Cover Image by Duraid Fatouhi (duraidfatouhi@yahoo.com)

Credits

Author
Francesco Marchioni

Reviewers
Devon Hillard

Kushal Paudyal

Acquisition Editor
Sarah Cullington

Development Editor
Meeta Rajani

Technical Editors
Sakina Kaydawala

Kartikey Pandey

Manasi Poonthottam

Indexers
Hemangini Bari

Rekha Nair

Editorial Team Leader
Mithun Sehgal

Project Team Leader
Priya Mukherji

Project Coordinator
Shubhanjan Chatterjee

Proofreader
Kevin McGowan

Graphics
Nilesh Mohite

Production Coordinator
Adline Swetha Jesuthas

Cover Work
Adline Swetha Jesuthas

About the Author

Francesco Marchioni is a Sun Certified Enterprise Architect employed by an Italian company based in Rome. He started learning Java in 1997 and since then he has followed the path to the newest Application Program Interfaces released by Sun. Since 2000, he has joined the JBoss Community when the application server was running release 2.X.

He has spent many years as a software consultant, where he has created many successful software migrations from vendor platforms to the open source products like JBoss AS, fulfilling the tight budget requirements of current times.

In the past five years he has started authoring technical articles for O'Reilly Media and running an IT portal focused on JBoss products (`http://www.mastertheboss.com`).

In December 2009, he published the title, *JBoss AS 5 Development*, which describes how to create and deploy Java Enterprise applications on JBoss AS—`http://www.packtpub.com/jboss-as-5-development/book`.

I'd like to thank Packt Publishing for offering another opportunity to write about my favorite application server. I'd also like to thank my family for supporting me during the creation of this book, in particular my father for teaching me all the tricks of the glorious C-64 when I was a kid.

Also a special thanks to the people that collaborated to this book: my friend Luca Viola who lent me the hardware for these benchmarks. JBoss guys Carlo de Wolf and Alessio Soldano for their precious advices. And last but not least the technical reviewers - Devon Hillard and Kushal Paudyal—and all the Packt Pub staff for their competent cooperation.

About the Reviewers

Devon Hillard is a J2EE Architect with over 12 years of experience working on some of the largest e-commerce sites in the world including AT&T, Target, JCrew, and many more. Working with large-scale enterprise environments has led to a natural focus on performance and security.

Devon created `http://10MinuteMail.com`, a popular temporary e-mail service, which is one of the top 10,000 sites in the world (based on `http://www.alexa.com/` ranking). Devon is also a founding partner at Spark::red, a premier hosting company for Fortune 500 clients using ATG e-commerce software, and often consults in the e-commerce, performance, and security arenas. He has also reviewed several technical book manuscripts on topics such as JBoss, GWT, and JBoss Seam.

Kushal Paudyal has been a professional Software Engineer for over five years on the Java/J2EE platform. He currently works as a Technical Lead for one of the biggest companies in USA that provides warranty management software. Apart from design, development, testing, and global delivery of the software, Kushal has extensive experience of leading a team of support analysts in supporting the enterprise applications deployed to top notch automotive industries in USA and optimizing the performance of production applications deployed to JBoss and WebSphere application servers.

Kushal's domain of expertise is warranty, fleet, and service lifecycle management. He holds a masters degree in Computer Science and a bachelor's degree in Computer Engineering.

Apart from work, Kushal is a hobbyist photographer. He can be reached at kushalzone@gmail.com.

www.PacktPub.com

Support files, eBooks, discount offers and more

You might want to visit www.PacktPub.com for support files and downloads related to your book.

Did you know that Packt offers eBook versions of every book published, with PDF and ePub files available? You can upgrade to the eBook version at www.PacktPub.com and as a print book customer, you are entitled to a discount on the eBook copy. Get in touch with us at service@packtpub.com for more details.

At www.PacktPub.com, you can also read a collection of free technical articles, sign up for a range of free newsletters and receive exclusive discounts and offers on Packt books and eBooks.

http://PacktLib.PacktPub.com

Do you need instant solutions to your IT questions? PacktLib is Packt's online digital book library. Here, you can access, read and search across Packt's entire library of books.

Why Subscribe?

- Fully searchable across every book published by Packt
- Copy & paste, print and bookmark content
- On demand and accessible via web browser

Free Access for Packt account holders

If you have an account with Packt at www.PacktPub.com, you can use this to access PacktLib today and view nine entirely free books. Simply use your login credentials for immediate access.

"Quod non fecerunt barbari, Barberini fecerunt. Quod non fecerunt Barberini, fecit Berlusconi."

We're living in Italy the last days of Pompeii: defend our cultural heritage before it's too late!

Table of Contents

Preface

JBoss AS 5 Performance Tuning will teach you how to deliver fast applications on the JBoss Application Server and Apache Tomcat, giving you a decisive competitive advantage over your competitors. You will learn how to optimize hardware resources, meeting your application requirements with less expenditure.

The performance of Java Enterprise applications is the sum of a set of components including the Java Virtual Machine configuration, the application server configuration (in our case, JBoss AS), the application code itself, and ultimately the operating system. This book will show you how to apply the correct tuning methodology and use the tuning tools that will help you to monitor and address any performance issues.

By looking more closely at the Java Virtual Machine, you will get a deeper understanding of what the available options are for your applications, and how their performance will be affected. Learn about thread pool tuning, EJB tuning, and JMS tuning, which are crucial parts of enterprise applications.

The persistence layer and the JBoss Clustering service are two of the most crucial elements which need to be configured correctly in order to run a fast application. These aspects are covered in detail with a chapter dedicated to each of them.

Finally, Web server tuning is the last (but not least) topic covered, which shows how to configure and develop web applications that get the most out of the embedded Tomcat web server.

What this book covers

Chapter 1, Performance Tuning Concepts, discusses correct tuning methodology and how it fits in the overall software development cycle.

Chapter 2, Installing the Tools for Tuning, shows how to install and configure the instruments for tuning, including VisualVM, JMeter, Eclipse TPTP Platform, and basic OS tools.

Chapter 3, Tuning the Java Virtual Machine, provides an in-depth analysis of the JVM heap and garbage collector parameters, which are used to start up the application server.

Chapter 4, Tuning the JBoss AS, discusses the application server's core services including the JBoss System Thread Pool, the Connection Pool, and the Logging Service.

Chapter 5, Tuning the Middleware Services, covers the tuning of middleware services including the EJB and JMS services.

Chapter 6, Tuning the Persistence Layer, introduces the principles of good database design and the core concepts of Java Persistence API with special focus on JBoss's implementation (Hibernate).

Chapter 7, JBoss AS Cluster Tuning, covers JBoss Clustering service covering the low-level details of server communication and how to use JBoss Cache for optimal data replication and caching.

Chapter 8, Tomcat Web Server Tuning, covers the JBoss Web server performance tuning including mod_jk, mod_proxy, and mod_cluster modules.

Chapter 9, Tuning Web Applications on JBoss AS, discusses developing fast web applications using JSF API and JBoss richfaces libraries.

What you need for this book

A technical prerequisite for this book is knowledge of and expertise with the Java Enterprise API and the basics of the JBoss application server. Besides the technical skills, which are necessary to grasp the tuning concepts, no other requirements are necessary. As a matter of fact, all the software discussed in this book can be freely downloaded and used both in development and in production systems.

Who this book is for

This book is for Java architects who design and configure Enterprise applications. It is great for Java developers who want to get into the inner details of the application server and of the correct tuning methodology. Application testers will also find this book useful as they will learn how to monitor the performance of the middleware with the correct instruments.

Conventions

In this book, you will find a number of styles of text that distinguish between different kinds of information. Here are some examples of these styles, and an explanation of their meaning.

Code words in text are shown as follows: "If you then request the ordered items through the customer.getItems() method, this would also fill the collection of items ordered with another database hit."

A block of code is set as follows:

```
@NamedQueries(
{
  @NamedQuery(
    name = "listCustomers",
    query = "FROM Customer c WHERE c.name = :name"
  )
})

public class Customer implements Serializable    {

}
```

When we wish to draw your attention to a particular part of a code block, the relevant lines or items are set in bold:

```
Session session =HibernateUtil.getSessionFactory().openSession();
session.beginTransaction();
for (int index = 0; index <1000;index++) {
    Person person = new Person();
    book.setCountry("Usa");
    book.setCity("NY");
    person.setName("Inhabitant n." + index);

    session.save(person);
    // Flush every 50 records
```

```
    if (index % 50== 0) {
        session.flush();
        session.clear();
    }
}
session.getTransaction().commit();
session.close();
```

Any command-line input or output is written as follows:

```
export JAVA_HOME=/installDir/jdk1.6.0_20
```

New terms and **important words** are shown in bold. Words that you see on the screen, in menus or dialog boxes for example, appear in the text like this: "Then pick up the method you want to test and select **Configure** which automatically configures your web service properties".

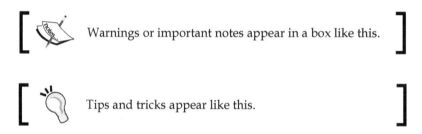

Warnings or important notes appear in a box like this.

Tips and tricks appear like this.

Reader feedback

Feedback from our readers is always welcome. Let us know what you think about this book—what you liked or may have disliked. Reader feedback is important for us to develop titles that you really get the most out of.

To send us general feedback, simply send an e-mail to feedback@packtpub.com, and mention the book title via the subject of your message.

If there is a book that you need and would like to see us publish, please send us a note in the **SUGGEST A TITLE** form on www.packtpub.com or e-mail suggest@packtpub.com.

If there is a topic that you have expertise in and you are interested in either writing or contributing to a book, see our author guide on www.packtpub.com/authors.

Customer support

Now that you are the proud owner of a Packt book, we have a number of things to help you to get the most from your purchase.

Downloading the example code for this book

You can download the example code files for all Packt books you have purchased from your account at http://www.PacktPub.com. If you purchased this book elsewhere, you can visit http://www.PacktPub.com/support and register to have the files e-mailed directly to you.

Errata

Although we have taken every care to ensure the accuracy of our content, mistakes do happen. If you find a mistake in one of our books—maybe a mistake in the text or the code—we would be grateful if you would report this to us. By doing so, you can save other readers from frustration and help us improve subsequent versions of this book. If you find any errata, please report them by visiting http://www.packtpub.com/support, selecting your book, clicking on the **errata submission form** link, and entering the details of your errata. Once your errata are verified, your submission will be accepted and the errata will be uploaded on our website, or added to any list of existing errata, under the Errata section of that title. Any existing errata can be viewed by selecting your title from http://www.packtpub.com/support.

Piracy

Piracy of copyright material on the Internet is an ongoing problem across all media. At Packt, we take the protection of our copyright and licenses very seriously. If you come across any illegal copies of our works, in any form, on the Internet, please provide us with the location address or website name immediately so that we can pursue a remedy.

Please contact us at copyright@packtpub.com with a link to the suspected pirated material.

We appreciate your help in protecting our authors, and our ability to bring you valuable content.

Questions

You can contact us at questions@packtpub.com if you are having a problem with any aspect of the book, and we will do our best to address it.

1
Performance Tuning Concepts

"All slow application abandon, ye who enter here." (Freely adapted from Dante's Divine Comedy Poem – http://en.wikipedia.org/wiki/Divine_Comedy*)*

Preface

One day like many, on a JBoss AS Forum:

> *"Hi*
>
> *I am running the Acme project using JBoss 5.1.0. My requirement is to allow 1000 concurrent users to access the application. But when I try to access the application with 250 users, the server slows down and finally throws an exception "Could not establish a connection with the database. Does anyone have an idea please help me to solve my problem."*

In the beginning, performance was not a concern for software. Early programming languages like C or Cobol were doing a decent job of developing applications and the end user was just discovering the wonders of information technology that would allow him to save a lot of time.

Today we are all aware of the rapidly changing business environment in which we work and live and the impact it has on business and information technology. We recognize that an organization needs to deliver faster services to a larger set of people and companies, and that downtime or poor responses of those services will have a significant impact on the business.

To survive and thrive in such an environment, organizations must consider it an imperative task for their businesses to deliver applications faster than their competitors or they will risk losing potential revenue and reputation among customers.

So tuning an application in today's market is firstly a necessity for survival, but, there are even more subtle reasons, like using your system resources more *efficiently*. For example, if you manage to meet your system requirements with fewer fixed costs (let's say by using eight CPU machine instead of a 16 one) you are actually using your resources more efficiently and thus saving money. As an additional benefit you can also reduce some variable costs like the price of software licenses, which are usually calculated on the amount of CPUs used.

On the basis of these premises, it's time to reconsider the role of performance tuning in your software development cycle, and that's what this book aims to do.

What you will get from this book?

This book is an exhaustive guide to improving the performance of your **Java EE** applications running on **JBoss AS** and on the embedded web container (Jakarta Tomcat). All the guidelines and best practices contained in this book have been patiently collected through years of experience from the trenches and from the suggestions of valuable people, and ultimately in a myriad of blogs, and each one has contributed to improve the quality of this book.

The performance of an application running on the application server is the result of a complex interaction of many aspects. Like a puzzle, each piece contributes ultimately to define the performance of the final product. So our challenge will be to teach how to write fast applications on JBoss AS, but also how to tune all the components and hardware which are a part of the IT system. As we suppose that our prime reader will not be interested in learning the basics of the application server, nor how to get started with Java EE, we will go straight to the heart of each component and elaborate on the strategies to improve their performance.

Should you be interested in learning more about the application server itself you can refer to the JBoss community at `http://community.jboss.org/` or you can have a look at my previous book: `https://www.packtpub.com/jboss-as-5-development/book`.

What is performance?

The term "performance" commonly refers to how quickly an application can be executed. In terms of the user's perspective on performance, the definition is quite easy to grasp. For example, a fast website means one that is able to load web pages very quickly. From an administrator's point of view, the concept needs to be translated into meaningful numbers. As a matter of fact, the expert can distinguish two ways to measure the performance of an application:

- Response Time
- Throughput

The **Response Time** can be defined as the time it takes for one user to perform a task. For example, on a website, after the customer submits one e-commerce form, the time it takes to process the order and for rendering and displaying the result in a new page is the response time for this functionality. As you can see, the concept of performance is essentially the same as from the end user perspective, but it is translated into numbers.

In practice, as shown in the following image, the Response Time includes the network roundtrip to the application server, the time to execute the business logic in your middleware (including the time to contact external legacy systems) and the latency to return the response to the client.

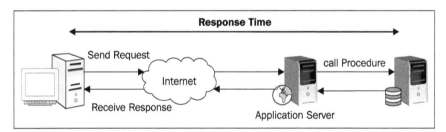

At this point the concept of Response Time should be quite clear, but you might wonder if this measurement is a constant; actually it is not. The Response Time *changes accordingly with the load on the application*. A single operation cannot be indicative of the overall performance: you have to consider how long the procedure takes to be executed in a production environment, where you have a considerable amount of customers running.

Another performance-related counter is Throughput. **Throughput** is the number of transactions that can occur in a given amount of time. This is a fundamental parameter that is used to evaluate not only the performance of a website, but also the commercial value of a software. The Throughput is usually measured in **Transactions Per Second** (**TPS**) and obviously an application that has a TPS higher than its competitors is also the one with higher commercial value — all other features standing equal.

The following image, depicts a Throughput comparison between a Linux Server and a Windows Server, as part of a complete benchmark (http://www. webperformanceinc.com/library/reports/windows_vs_linux_part1/index. html):

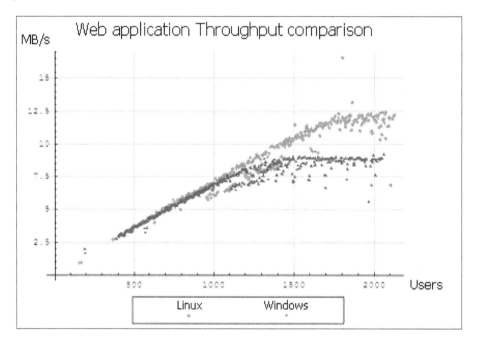

Scalability: the other side of performance

As we have just learnt, we cannot define performance within the context of a single user who is testing the application. The performance of an application is tightly coupled with the number of users, so we need to define another variable which is known as **Scalability**. Scalability refers to the capability of a system to increase total Throughput under an increased load when resources are added. It can be seen from two different perspectives:

- Vertical scalability: (otherwise known as scaling up) means to add more hardware resources to the same machine, generally by adding more processors and memory.

- Horizontal scalability: (otherwise known as scaling out) means to add more machines into the mix, generally cheap commodity hardware.

The following image is a synthetic representation of the two different perspectives:

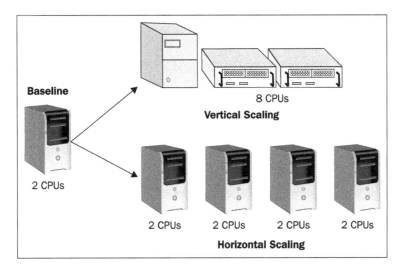

Both solutions have pros and cons: generally vertical scaling *requires a greater hardware expenditure* because it needs upgrading to powerful enterprise servers, but it's easier to implement as it *requires fewer changes in your configuration.*

Horizontal scaling on the other hand, requires *little investment on cheaper hardware* (which has a linear expenditure) but it *introduces a more complex programming model,* thus it needs an expert hand as it concerns configuration and might require some changes in your application too.

 You should also consider that concentrating all your resources on a single machine introduces a single point of failure, which is the case if you choose an extreme type of vertical scaling.

The tuning process

At this point you will have grasped that performance tuning spans over several components, including the application delivered and the environment where it is running. However, we haven't addressed which is the right moment for starting to tune your applications. This is one of the most underestimated issues in software development and it is commonly solved by applying tuning only at two stages:

- *While coding your classes*
- *At the end of software development*

Tuning your applications as you code is a consolidated habit of software developers, at first because it's funny and satisfying to optimize your code and see an immediate improvement in the performance of a single function. However, the other side of the coin is that most of these optimizations are *useless*. Why? It is statistically proven that within one application only 10-15 % of the code is executed frequently, so trying to optimize code blindly at this stage will produce little or no benefit at all to your application.

The second favorite anti-pattern adopted by developers is starting the tuning process just at the end of the software development cycle. For good reason, this can be considered a bad habit. Firstly, your tuning session will be more complex and longer: you have to analyze again the whole application roundtrip while hunting for bottlenecks again. Supposing you are able to isolate the cause of the bottleneck, you still might be forced to modify critical sections of your code, which, at this stage, can turn easily into a nightmare.

Think, for example, of an application which uses a set of JSF components to render trees and tables. If you discover that your JSF library runs like a crawl when dealing with production data, you have very little you can do at this stage: either you rewrite the whole frontend or you find a new job.

So the moral of the story is: *you cannot think of performance as a single step in the software development process*; it needs to be a part of your overall software development plan. Achieving maximum performance from your software requires continued effort throughout all phases of development, not just coding. In the next section we will try to uncover how performance tuning fits in the overall software development cycle.

Tuning in the software development cycle

Having determined that tuning needs to be a part of the software development cycle, let's have a look at the software cycle with performance engineering integrated.

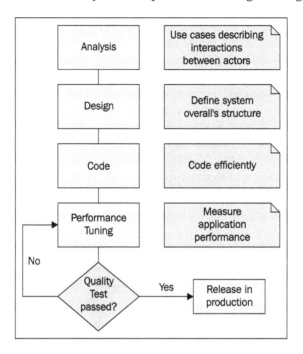

As you can see, the software process contains a set of activities (Analysis, Design, Coding, and Performance Tuning) which should be familiar to analyst programmers, but with two important additions: at first there is a new phase called Performance Test which begins at the end of the software development cycle and will measure and evaluate the complete application. Secondly, every software phase contains **Performance focal points**, which are appropriate for that software segment.

Now let's see in more detail how a complete software cycle is carried on with performance in mind:

- **Analysis**: Producing high quality, fast applications *always* starts with a correct analysis of your software requirements. In this phase you have to define what the software is expected to do by providing a set of scenarios that illustrate your functional domain. This translates in creating **use cases**, which are diagrams that describe the interactions of users within the system. These use cases are a crucial step in determining what type of **benchmarks** are needed by your system: for example, here we assume that your application will be accessed by 500 concurrent users, each of whom will start a database connection to retrieve data from a database as well as use a JMS connection to fire an action. Software analysis, however, spans beyond the software requirements and should consider critical information, such as the kind of hardware where the application will run or the network interfaces that will support its communication.

- **Design**: In this phase, the overall software structure and its nuances are defined. Critical points like the number of tiers needed for the package architecture, the database design, and the data structure design are all defined in this phase. A software development model is thus created. The role of performance in this phase is fundamental, architects should perform the following:

    ° Quickly evaluate different algorithms, data structures, and libraries to see which are most efficient.

    ° Design the application so that it is possible to accommodate any changes if there are new requirements that could impact performance.

- **Code:** The design must be now translated into a machine-readable form. The code generation step performs this task. If the design is performed in a detailed manner, code generation can be accomplished without much complication. If you have completed the previous phases with an eye on tuning you should partially know which functions are critical for the system, and code them in the most efficient way. We say "partially" because only when you have dropped the last line of code will you be able to test the complete application and see where it runs quickly and where it needs to be improved.

- **Performance Test:** This step completes the software production cycle and should be performed before releasing the application into production. Even if you have been meticulous at performing the previous steps, it is absolutely normal that your application doesn't meet all the performance requirements on the first try. In fact, you cannot predict every aspect of performance, so it is necessary to complete your software production with a performance test. A performance test is an *iterative* process that you use to identify and eliminate bottlenecks until your application meets its performance objectives. You start by establishing a baseline. Then you collect data, analyze the results, and make configuration changes based on the analysis. After each set of changes, you retest and measure to verify that your application has moved closer to its performance objectives.

The following image synthesizes the cyclic process of performance tuning:

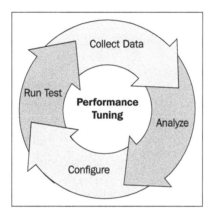

Building the performance test

You are now aware that performance tuning is an iterative process which continues until the software has met your goals in terms of Response Time and Throughput. Let's see more in detail how to proceed with every single step of the process:

Establish a baseline

The first part of performance tuning consists of building up a baseline. In practice you need to figure out the conditions under which the application will perform. The more you understand exactly how your application will be used, the more successful your performance tuning will be. If you have invested some days in an accurate analysis you should have already got the basis upon which you will develop your performance objectives which are usually measured in terms of response times, throughput (requests per second), and resource utilization level.

Plan for average users or for peak?

There are many types of statistics that can be useful when you are building a baseline, however one of your goals should be to develop a profile of your application's workload *with special attention to the peaks*. For example, many business applications experience daily or monthly peaks depending on a variety of factors. This is especially true for organizations like travel agencies or airline companies which expect great differences in workload in different periods of the year. In this kind of scenario, it doesn't make sense to set up a baseline on the average number of users: you have no choice but to use the worst case; that is the peak of users.

Collect data

In order to collect data, all applications should be instrumented to provide information for performance analysis. This can be broken down in a set of activities:

- Set up your application server with the same settings and hardware as the production environment and produce a replica of database/naming directories if you can't use the production legacy systems for testing.

- Isolate the testing environment so that you don't skew those tests by involving network traffic that doesn't belong in your tests.

- Install the appropriate tools, which will start the load test and the counterpart software that collect data from the benchmark. The next chapter will point you towards some great resources which can be used to start a session of performance tuning.

How long should data collection last?

If you surf the net you can find plenty of benchmarks affirming that X is faster than Y. Even if micro benchmarks are useful to quickly calculate the response of a single variable (for example, the time to execute a stored procedure), they are of little or no use for testing complex systems. Why? Because many factors in enterprise systems produce their effects after the system has been tested extensively: think about caching systems or JVM garbage collection tuning as a clue.

Investing a huge amount of time for your tuning session is, however, not realistic as you will likely fail to meet your budget goals, so your performance tests should be completed by a fixed timeline.

Balancing these two factors, we could say that a good performance tuning session should last at least 20-30 minutes (besides warm-up activities, if any) for bread-and-butter applications like the sample Pet Store demo application (`http://java.sun.com/developer/releases/petstore/`). Larger applications, on the other hand, require more functionality to test and engage a considerable amount of system resources. A complete test plan can demand, in this case, some hours or even days to be completed. As a matter of fact, some dynamics (like the garbage collector) can take time to unfold its effects; benchmarking these kinds of applications on a short-time basis can thus be useless or even misleading.

Luckily you can organize your time in such a way that the tuning sessions are planned carefully during the day and then executed with batch scripts at night.

Analyze data

With the amount of data collected, you have evidence of which areas show a performance penalty: keep in mind, however, that this might just be the symptom of a problem which arises in a different area of your application. Technically speaking the analysis procedure can be split into the following activities:

1. Identify the locations of any bottlenecks.
2. Think of a hypothesis which could be the cause of the bottleneck.
3. Consider any factors that may prove/disprove your hypothesis.

At the end of these activities, you should be ready to create a new test which isolates the factor that we suppose to be the cause of the bottleneck.

For example, supposing you are in the middle of a tuning session of an enterprise application. You have identified *(Step 1)* that the application occasionally pauses and cannot complete all transactions within the strict timeout setting.

Your hypothesis *(Step 2)* is that the garbage collector configuration needs to be changed because it's likely that there are too many full cycles of garbage collection (garbage collection is explained in detail in *Chapter 3, Core JVM Tuning*).

As a proof of your hypothesis *(Step 3)* you are going to add in the configuration a switch that prints the details of each garbage collection.

In definitive, by carefully examining performance indicators, you can correctly isolate the problem and thus identify the main problems, which must be addressed first. If the data you collect is not complete, then your analysis is likely to be inaccurate and you might need to retest and collect the missing information or use further analysis tools.

Configure and test again

When your analysis has terminated you should have a list of indicators that need testing: you should first establish a priority list so that you can first address those issues that are likely to provide the maximum payoff.

 It's important to stress that you must apply *each change individually* otherwise you can distort the results and make it difficult to identify potential new performance issues.

And that's it! Get your instruments ready and launch another session of performance testing. You can stop adjusting and measuring when you believe you're close enough to the response times to satisfy your requirements.

As a side note consider that optimizing code can introduce new bugs so the application should be tested during the optimization phase. A particular optimization should not be considered valid until the application using that optimization's code path has passed quality assessment.

Tuning Java Enterprise applications

One of the most pervasive myths about Java Enterprise applications is that they simply are slow. The notion of Java being "slow" in popular discussions is often poorly calibrated but, unfortunately, widely believed. The most compelling reason for this sentiment dates back to the first releases of Java Development Kit. In 1995, Java was much slower as the first implementations of the Java Virtual Machine didn't have a Just In Time complier, the garbage collector algorithms were not so refined and, generally speaking, lots of applications were written using classes with poor performance numbers (for example, Input/Output streams without buffering, or abuse of thread-safe collections classes like the `java.io.Vector`).

While the debate continues in many forums, featuring benchmarks generally with the "elder brother" C++, there is some truth in it; that is today (some time ago), many Java applications are still awfully slow. Why?

What happened is that, ironically, even if Sun engineers were able to deliver faster JVMs release after release, programming Java Enterprise applications became more and more complex, and therefore so did writing fast Java applications.

Not so long ago the archetype of a Java Application was made up of a *Front Layer* (usually developed with JSPs or Swing) and some *Middleware*, usually developed with a mix of Servlets and Data Access Objects (DAO) that contained the interfaces for the legacy system.

In such a scenario, the architect had to take care of fewer counters and there was only one, or perhaps two protocols involved in the communications (HTTP and RMI). With a minimal application and web server tuning along with some DBA tips you could bring home the desired result.

Today's enterprise applications are much more complex; take for example the input: it can come from HTML as well as a thick client or a web service, or even a mobile device. Also, lots of Java programming interfaces have been screened by other frameworks to simplify or enhance the productivity of the developer. For example, **Java Server Faces (JSF) specification** has been built on the top of **Servlet/JSPs** and then custom libraries (like **RichFaces**) have been built on the top of JSF. Another good example is the **Hibernate** framework, which has been built on the top of JDBC, and then **Entities** have been built on the top of Hibernate.

We might continue discussing other good examples, however the truth is that each of these extra layers inevitably carry some overhead, and have their own best practices which are usually unknown to the majority of developers.

Our conclusion is that today Java applications have a higher performance potential than they once did, but this needs expert hands and a solid tuning methodology to be allowed in the Eden where fast applications live.

Nevertheless, tuning Java Enterprise applications is more complex than standalone applications as it requires monitoring and configuring additional components like the application server, which acts as a container for the application, and all resources which are directly controlled by the application server. In the next section, we are going to explore all the single areas which have an impact on the performance of an enterprise application.

Areas of tuning

Configuration and tuning settings can be divided into four main categories:

- Java Virtual Machine (JVM) tuning
- Middleware tuning
- Application tuning
- Operating system / Hardware tuning

Let's enter more in detail in each area:

- **JVM tuning:** Every Java application runs in a Virtual Machine, so with proper configuration of JVM parameters (in particular those related to memory and garbage collection), it's possible to achieve better performance of your Java applications. The configuration of JVM has changed a lot since the first releases of Java, and most developers are not aware that the default JVM parameters are usually not optimal for running large applications. We will cover this topic in more detail in *Chapter* 3, *Core JVM tuning*, which is entirely dedicated to JVM tuning.

- **Middleware tuning** is managed to control how an application server provides services for running applications and their components. The application server is pretty complex stuff and at the same time, a fertile ground for optimizations for expert users. The application server contains a core configuration that is common to all applications (think about the pool of thread which is responsible for invoking other components), and also a set of Java EE services which are available for use (like EJB, the web container, JMS, and so on). Each of these services has a default configuration which can be just as good for average applications, but need to be tweaked in order to obtain superior performance.

- **Application tuning** requires that you write efficient code in your application, as well as adopt the best performing libraries to achieve the desired task.

  Most tuning experts agree that *application tuning accounts for about 75% of the overall tuning process*. This doesn't mean that hardware and correct administration configuration is useless. The truth is that even the best hardware and application server configuration will not provide dramatic performance numbers if you are running a poorly coded application. Just to mention a few:

    ○ Are you using queries without index on the where fields?

    ○ Are you gathering massive data in the HTTP session?

    ○ Are you issuing a select * and trying to cache all the data in the middle tier

  If you are performing any of these mistakes then there is little you can fix with proper JVM configuration or application server tuning alone.

- **Operating system tuning** relates to configuring your system and hardware resources so that they can efficiently run the software resources discussed previously. The most common hardware tuning is concerned with physical memory: if you determine that your application has a memory bottleneck, and it's not caused by inefficient coding, you have no other choice but to add more memory to your machine(s).

Another hot point for tuning hardware is CPU: each application that runs on a server gets a time slice of the CPU. The CPU might be able to efficiently handle all of the processes running on the computer, or it might be overloaded. By examining processor activity and the activity of individual processes including thread creation, thread switching, context switching, and so on, you can gain good insight into processor workload and performance. Again, if the CPU is the bottleneck and it cannot be solved by application tuning, you have to consider adding more CPUs or splitting the load on an array of servers.

- **Hardware tuning** also includes input/output tuning. Executing long-running file I/O operations, data encryption and decryption, or reading too much data from database tables can turn I/O operation into a serious bottleneck. A shortage of physical memory might also lead to an excessive input-output activity if the data cannot fit in the physical memory. Slow hard disks are another factor to consider and are the only possible solution if you still have disk I/O bottlenecks after optimizing all other factors.

The last hardware component we need to mention is the Network, which is the means by which different applications communicate. Tuning the network means shortening the number of hops your application needs to do in order to reach external systems. You also need to configure your protocol transmission in the most efficient way so that in turn your packets are routed in the most efficient way. Again, if you still have a bottleneck in this area, the last solution is to upgrade to a new set of network devices.

Is it possible to optimize all areas of tuning?

Theoretically yes, but in practice, optimization will generally focus on improving just one or two aspects of performance: for example execution time, memory usage, disk space, bandwidth, power consumption, or some other resource. This will usually require a trade-off where one factor is optimized at the expense of others. For example, increasing the size of cache improves runtime performance, but also increases the memory consumption. Other common trade-offs include code clarity and conciseness. In practice you have to define some priorities and code accordingly.

The following image synthesizes the concepts we have just covered:

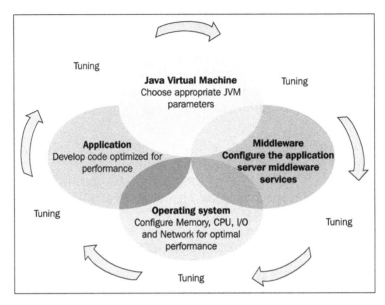

Summary

In this chapter, you have learnt the basics of the performance tuning process: let's shortly recap the most significant points:

- Performance can be evaluated with two main counters: The Response Time and the Throughput. The Response Time can be defined as the time it takes for one user to perform a task. The Throughput is the number of transactions that can occur in a given amount of time.

- In order to meet higher loads, applications need to be scalable. You can scale your applications vertically (that is switching to servers with higher capabilities) or horizontally (that is adding a line of servers).

- In order to improve the performance of your applications, you have to consider all resources which are around the application: the Java Virtual Machine, the middleware, the hardware, and how you code the application itself.

- Maximum application performance can be achieved only if performance tuning is considered to be a part of your overall software development plan.

In the next chapter, we are going to introduce a few essential tools, which you can freely download, and use in order to tune your Enterprise applications and your operating system as well.

Installing the Tools for Tuning

2

1st circle of Hell: The Limbo. Here reside virtuous programmers, who, though not sinful, did not use any instrument for tuning...

Welcome to scientific tuning

Today tuning has evolved to the rank of "science", first and foremost because it's supported by a vast collection of tools which can help you to systematically fix your performance issues.

So, before entering the tuning arena, we will install some nice software on your machine which will be used across the examples of this book. As we are embracing the open source philosophy, we have chosen to focus on high quality open source software, so your only investment will be the price paid for this book. You can still consider vendor alternatives, which often provide sales support and engineering staff trained to make the software have a less-daunting road to getting up and running.

In the first part of this chapter, we will learn about profiling the Java Virtual Machine (JVM), focusing on **VisualVM**, a powerful tool developed by Sun engineers.

In the next section of the chapter, we will learn about the **Eclipse Test and Performance Tools Platform** suite (**Eclipse TPTP**) which can be used to measure all critical parameters of your applications such as memory usage, CPU time, total threads used, and so on.

In order to do load testing on your applications we will then download and try **Jakarta JMeter**, a well-liked Java application which was originally built to test the performance of web applications. Since then it has expanded and can thus be used to test many type of protocols such as JDBC, JMS, web services, and so on.

We will then conclude our overview by looking at the most popular operating system tools and commands which can be used to complete our analysis.

As a picture is often better than many words, the following image will give you a better idea as to how the chapter is organized:

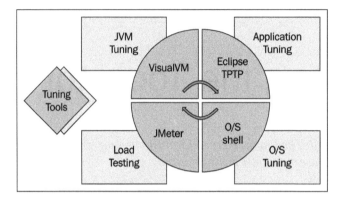

The rationale behind the choice of the tools

A small preamble is necessary before we begin. The list of tuning tools available today is quite bulky and most of the tools, originally built with one task in mind, have evolved to cover many aspects of the tuning process.

All the products introduced in this chapter can do, by any means, much more than we will reveal in a single section, so the competent reader might ask why don't we focus on just one tool and use it all around the book?

The reason behind our choice is certainly influenced by the author's personal tastes or programming styles; however we do believe that it's worthy to have more than one option available in your stock because a single tool might not be an appropriate solution for all scenarios. Specifically, even if all the software described here are excellent in many ways, maybe they lack ease or flexibility in some other ways.

So summing up, our suggested strategy will be to learn the best features of three tools, using the smallest learning curve. In the end, what will actually drive your performance tests is a solid tuning methodology and not the choice of the tool which is, after all, just an instrument to reach your goals.

Profiling the Java Virtual Machine

Profiling the JVM is an essential task to make sure the virtual machine is performing well and also to check the health of your application server.

Before we start profiling our applications it's a prerequisite that you have installed Java Virtual Machine v.1.6 on your computer: if you already have got one working you can safely skip the following section and move to the *Installing VisualVM* section.

Installing the JVM

In order to install Java, let's move to the Oracle/Sun download page:

`http://www.oracle.com/technetwork/java/javase/downloads/index.html`

Choose to download the latest JDK/JRE, which is, at the time of writing, the **JDK 1.6 update 20**. Once the download is complete, run the executable file to start the installation.

```
jdk-6u20-windows-i586.exe    # Windows
sh jdk-6u20-linux-i586.bin   # Linux
```

You can accept all the defaults given to you by the set up wizard. When the installation is completed, we need to update a couple of settings on the computer so it can interact with Java.

The most important setting is JAVA_HOME, which is directly referenced by the JBoss startup script. We recommend also including to the system variable PATH, the path to the new JDK/JRE so that you are guaranteed to use the same JDK across your scripts.

Windows users should right-click on **My Computer** and select **Properties** from the context menu. On the **Advanced** tab, click on the **Environment Variables** button. Then in the **System Variables** box, click on the **New** button. Give the new variable a name of JAVA_HOME, and a **Value** of the path to your JDK installation: for example, something like C:\Java\jdk1.6.0_20.

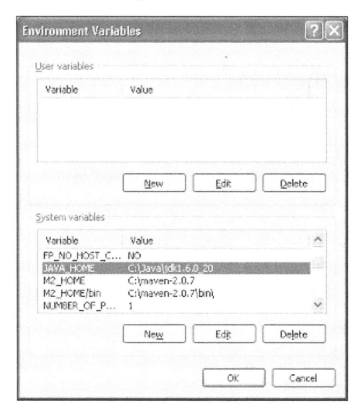

Now execute the same steps for the **Path** variable: double click on the Path System variable. In the box that pops up, navigate to the end of the **Variable Value** line, add a semicolon to the end, then add the path to your JDK. This will be something like C:\Java\jdk1.6.0_20\bin.

Unix/Linux users can add the following commands in the user's profile scripts.

```
export JAVA_HOME=/installDir/jdk1.6.0_20
export PATH=$JAVA_HOME/bin:$PATH
```

Installing VisualVM

One of the best JVM profilers available in the market is VisualVM. This great tool will allow you to generate and analyze heap data, track down memory leaks, monitor the garbage collector, and perform memory and CPU profiling; all this with a single tool!

What about JConsole ?

Some of you might argue why we have chosen VisualVM and not **JConsole** which has been included in the J2SE since release 5.0. As we said, the choice of the tool is often a matter of personal taste, however, we have chosen VisualVM because it provides all the nice functionalities that JConsole has, without the need to use additional utilities such as `jinfo`, `jmap`, `jstack`, `jstat` which are included in the JDK distribution.

At the same time, VisualVM can be extended to use all the plugins that have been added to JConsole, so we believe it's worth upgrading to VisualVM.

VisualVM comes out of the box if you have got a JDK 1.6 update 7 or later. As you can see from the following image, it is included in the JAVA_HOME/bin folder. Just click on the `jvisualvm.exe` icon if you are using Windows or simply `visualvm` for Linux OS.

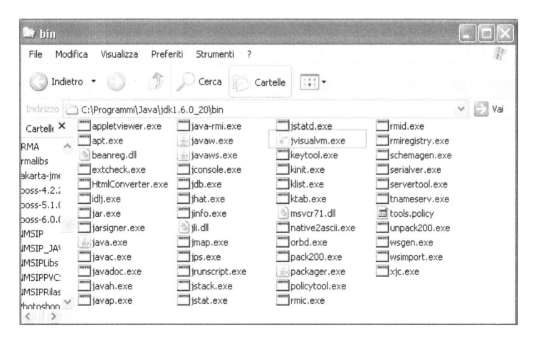

If you have got an earlier JDK 1.6 release then you can still download and install a fresh copy of VisualVM at the distribution main page: `https://visualvm.dev.java.net/`.

Connecting to a local server

When you start VisualVM, the **Applications** window is visible in the left side of the VisualVM window. The **Applications** window uses a tree structure to enable you to quickly view the applications that are running on local and remote JVM software instances.

In the following image, you can see the list of local Virtual Machines detected by VisualVM. The most relevant entry is the JBoss application server running with process id (**pid**) 2812:

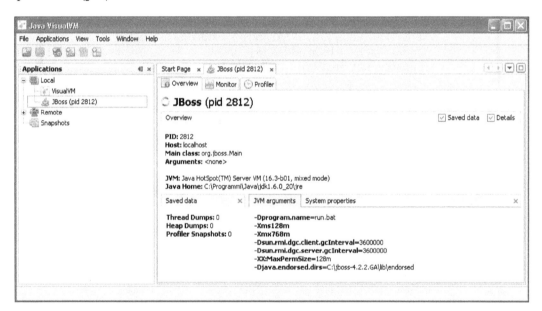

Connecting to a remote server

VisualVM can also reach a Java Virtual Machine that is running remotely. For this purpose, you need to use a tiny RMI service named `jstatd` to let VisualVM connect to your remote host. The advantage of this approach is that it doesn't require any change in the remote server's startup script, just start the service and connect to the remote JVM.

The `jstatd` RMI service is located in the `JAVA_HOME/bin` distribution folder.

Starting up `jstatd` requires setting up a security policy file for granting permissions to run `jstatd` and other JVM tools located in `tools.jar`:

Create the following `tools.policy` file in the `JAVA_HOME/bin` folder:

```
grant codebase "file:${java.home}/../lib/tools.jar" {
   permission java.security.AllPermission;
};
```

Then, you can start `jstatd` using the security policy contained in `tools.policy` and set an available port as TCP port (In our example, we will be using port 1234).

```
jstatd -p 1234  -J-Djava.security.policy=tools.policy
```

Now connect VisualVM to your remote server by right-clicking on the **Remote** icon on the **Applications** view. Choose **Add Remote Host...**.

In the pop up displayed, enter the **Host Name/Address** and select **Advanced Settings** where you will specify the port where `jstatd` is running and the **Refresh interval**.

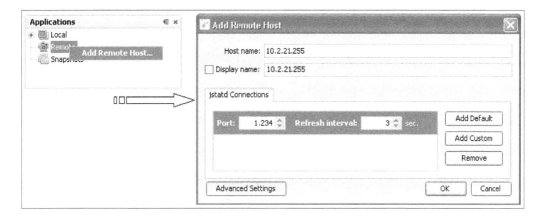

At this point, VisualVM should automatically detect both the `jstatd` Remote service and the JBoss AS running on the host 10.2.21.225. The following image shows how the **Applications** panel should look:

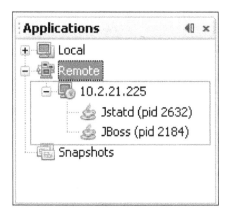

Monitoring your server

The central panel of VisualVM is the pulsing heart of the application. There you have access to all available profiler plugins. As a matter of fact, VisualVM is fully extensible and you can install additional plugins, which will monitor specific areas of your JVM. In the section, *Extending VisualVM*, we will show how to add some additional plugins to your VisualVM.

As shown in the following picture, you initially have the following tabs available:

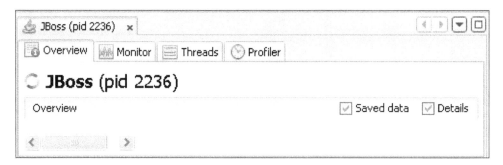

- **Overview**: This tab shows generic server info like JVM arguments and system properties.
- **Monitor**: This tab reveals a real-time set of graphs which collect data for the CPU, memory utilization, class loaded, and threads used.
- **Threads**: This tab provides a detailed view of all threads running in the JVM along with their state (Running, Sleeping, Wait, and Monitor).

- **Profiler**: This tab enables you to start and stop the profiling session of a local application. You can choose from the following profiling options:

    ◦ **CPU** Profiling: Choose this to profile the performance of the application.

    ◦ **Memory** Profiling: Choose this to analyze the memory usage of the application.

The Monitor tab

The **Monitor** tab plugin is useful to monitor the JVM in real-time. In the following image you can see how it looks like when you connect to a freshly booted JBoss AS 5.1.0 server:

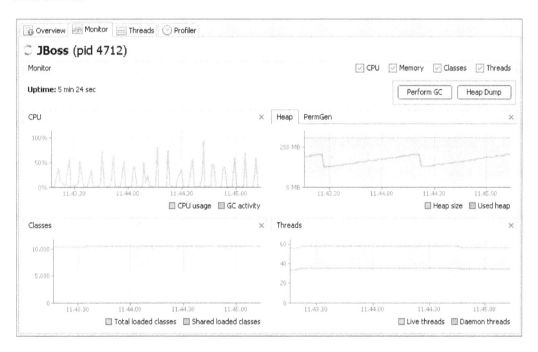

As we have anticipated, you can perform both a Garbage Collection and launch a Heap dump from this panel. Performing a garbage collection can be done by means of the **Perform GC** button; on the other hand, clicking on the **Heap Dump** button allows you to create a snapshot of your JVM Heap which can be saved and examined later.

By means of the Heap Dump, you can check the number of object instances created at any time and even inspect the content of the single instance fields thus making VisualVM a valuable option also for inspecting the status of applications deployed.

The Threads tab

The **Threads** tab displays a timeline of current thread activity. You can click a thread in the **Timeline** to view details about that thread in the **Details** tab:

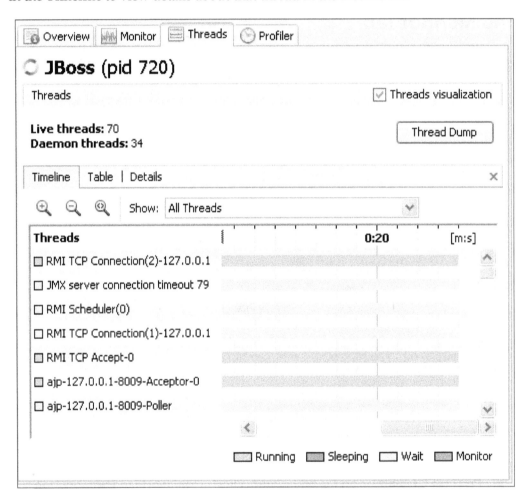

A **Timeline** for each thread provides a quick overview of the thread's activity. The drop-down list enables you to select which threads are displayed. You can choose to view all threads, live threads, or finished threads. You can also select a single thread or multiple threads to display a subset of the threads.

The **Details** tab displays more detailed information about individual threads. For each thread, the name, classname, and current status (alive/finished) are displayed. A short description of the thread is also provided.

As a side note you can also take a **Thread Dump** (stack trace) while a local application is running. Taking a **Thread Dump** does not stop the application. When you print the **Thread Dump** you get a printout of the thread stack that includes thread states for the Java threads. This can look a bit cumbersome compared to VisualVM simple statistics but it can be still useful if you have any console script which analyzes the output of the Java stack trace.

The Profiler tab

The **Profiler** option requires quite a lot of resources from your machine so it is not enabled by default. When you start a profiling session, VisualVM attaches to the local application and starts collecting profiling data. When profiling results are available they are automatically displayed in the **Profiler** tab.

You can choose from the following profiling options:

- **CPU** Profiling: Choose this to profile the performance of the application.
- **Memory** Profiling: Choose this to analyze the memory usage of the application. The results display the objects allocated by the application and the class allocating those objects.

The following image depicts a **Memory** Profiling session: start by clicking on the **Memory** button which will begin the Profiler Session. This activity is quite costly for your CPU so it's likely that your PC will freeze for a while until the initialization is complete.

When data profiling is started, you will see the first results in the **Profiling results** table which shows the impact on memory (or on CPU if you are profiling the CPU) of each class allocation:

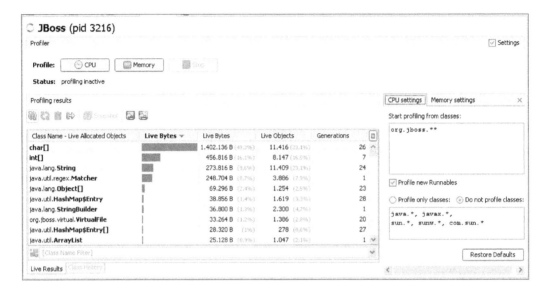

If you are not interested in knowing the details of all the objects created, then you can filter by package (or Classes too) in the lower section of the table.

Collecting snapshots

A Snapshot is a handy feature of VisualVM which allows you to capture application data and save it to your local system for later use. The advantage of using Snapshots is that the target application does not need to be running so that they can be viewed by any user.

VisualVM distinguishes between two types of snapshot:

- Profiler Snapshot
- Application Snapshot

Profiler snapshots, as the name implies, are generated when you are running a Profiler session. A Profiler snapshot either contains data for allocated objects (if you are running a Memory profiler session) or application performance data (if you are running a CPU profiler session).

To take a snapshot, simply click the **Snapshot** button in the **Profiler** tab.

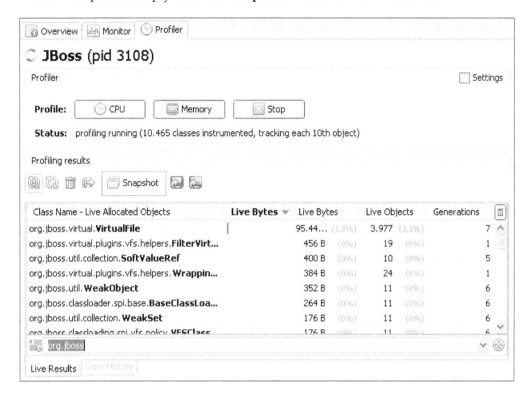

Once taken, the collected snapshot will be included within the application server tree, as shown by the following image:

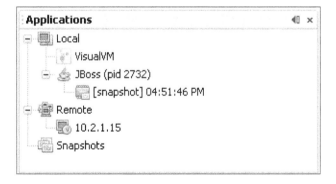

An application snapshot is a bit more complex as it contains all the collected Heap Dumps, Thread Dumps and profiler snapshots of an application at the moment the snapshot is taken. An application snapshot also captures general information about the Java Virtual Machine (JVM).

You take an application snapshot by right-clicking an application node in the **Applications** window and choosing **Application Snapshot** from the pop up menu. In the following image, we are gathering a Thread Dump and a Heap Dump in an application snapshot:

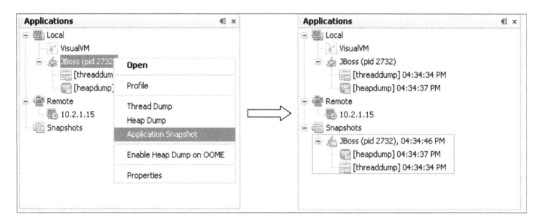

Using Snapshots to detect potential memory leaks

One nifty feature not known by all developers is the ability to compare snapshots. Provided that you have collected two snapshots in a different timeline (for example, before and after one core procedure), then you can compare them by selecting **Compare Snapshot** on the right-click selection.

This will add one more tab to your main window titled **Snapshot comparison** which contains the difference in allocated memory objects or time execution. On the basis of this comparison you can pinpoint which objects are potential memory leaks or bottlenecks of the application.

Extending VisualVM

With VisualVM you are not restricted to the basic functionalities we have covered here but you can expand them by downloading extra plugins.

In order to install new plugins, from the main menu choose **Tools | Plugins**; the **Plugins** dialog is opened. Switch to the **Available Plugins** tab and select the plugin you want to install.

There are quite a bit of available plugins: for the purpose of this book, you will need to install the **Visual GC** plugin, which can be used to collect and graphically display the garbage collector dynamics.

Installing a new plugin can be done by means of the **Tools | Plugins** menu option. The following image resumes the suggested selection. Click on **Install** and restart VisualVM to allow the changes to take effect.

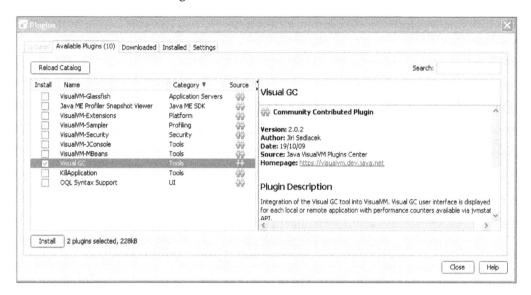

Profiling your applications with Eclipse Test and Performance Tools Platform (TPTP) Project

In the first chapter, we have stated that the application code is responsible for about 75% of the performance of the application itself; that way we should consider adding a specific tool which is able to pinpoint hot points and bottlenecks in your code.

The choice of the tool for application profiling was not an easy one for me, mostly because there are actually many good products available in the market. One in particular, JProfiler (an evaluation version is available at: `http://www.ej-technologies.com/company/profile.html`), has a very intuitive GUI that helps you find performance bottlenecks, pin down memory leaks, and resolve threading issues.

However, in the last few years a new open source profiler platform became popular across Eclipse developers: the Eclipse Test and Performance Tools Project. This project addresses the entire performance life cycle and can be considered the most valuable alternative to commercial profilers. Should you need a product which provides quality support and customer care strategy, you can still switch to JProfiler which requires a small learning curve once you have acquired the correct tuning methodology.

Installing the TPTP suite

In order to use TPTP suite, you need to have **Eclipse 3.5.0** (Galileo) or later installed on your PC. If you don't have Eclipse available you can download it from the following link:

```
http://www.eclipse.org/tptp/home/downloads/.
```

Now choose the distribution that's appropriate for your OS. Once the download is complete, Windows users can simply unzip the `eclipse-jee-galileo-win32.zip` file, while Linux users can use the `tar` command to uncompress the `.tar.gz` archive.

```
tar -zxvf eclipse-jee-galileo-linux-gtk.tar.gz
```

Unzipping the archive will create a root directory named `eclipse`. In that folder, you will find the Eclipse application (a big blue dot). We recommend you create a shortcut on the desktop to simplify the launching of Eclipse. Running Eclipse is simply a matter of executing the following command from the root directory of eclipse:

```
eclipse
```

Updating Eclipse

At this point you can proceed to install the TPTP suite. Our suggested procedure is by means of the **Eclipse Update Manager** facility. This has the advantage of avoiding common mistakes when manually installing the packages and also will automatically manage the dependencies by loading all required plugins.

Select from the Eclipse menu from **Help | Install New Software**. In the next panel, select **Galileo** from the **Work with** drop-down list:

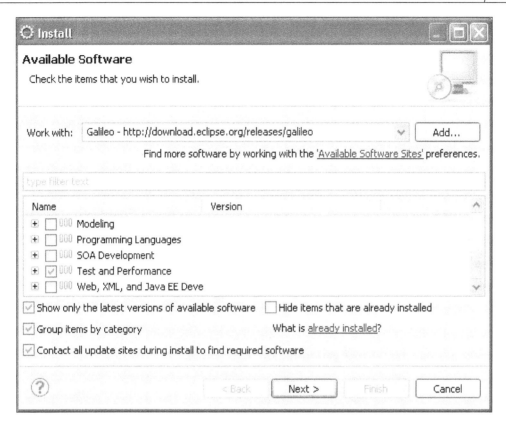

Enable **Test and Performance** and click on the **Next** button to verify the installation details.

In the **Install** dialog, click on the **Next** button to start the installation. Accept the license agreement(s) and click on the **Finish** button to end the installation. You need to restart Eclipse to acknowledge the changes made so far.

How to profile an application

If the installation was successful you should notice the new "Profiler" icon in the Eclipse toolbar, as shown in the following screenshot:

Profiling an application is pretty intuitive: either select the main class from the Profiler button or simply right-click on a Class and select **Profile as | Java Application.**

In order to profile components running on the application server, at first define a new server from the **File** menu: **File | New | Server** and add a new JBoss or Tomcat server instance.

Then, from the toolbar, launch the profile on the available server, as shown in the following screenshot:

As you start the Profiler, a configuration pop-up will open, which allows you to select which criteria you are profiling your application for:

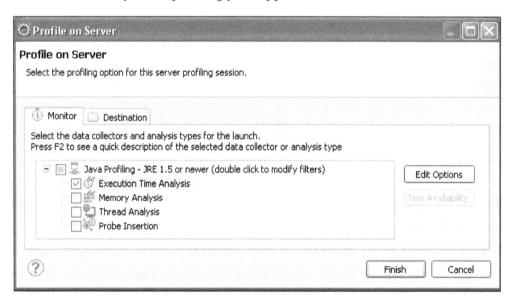

The current profiler version allows only mutually exclusive analysis types. Therefore only a single analysis type (among **Execution Time Analysis**, **Memory Analysis**, and **Thread Analysis**) is available per profiling session.

At this point, Eclipse will suggest to switch to the perspective **Profiling and Logging**. Each profiler analysis contains a set of reports exhibiting different levels of detail on the monitored feature. For example, this is a **Summary view** of an **Execution Time Analysis** related to a web application:

Highest 10 base time

Package	<Base Time (s...	Average Base ...	Cumulative Tim...	Calls
com.arjuna.ats.internal.arjuna.recovery	214,539327	21,453933	218,676123	10
com.icesoft.jasper.xmlparser	81,872822	0,000401	82,972826	204210
antlr	29,440438	0,000329	32,229411	89438
EDU.oswego.cs.dl.util.concurrent	14,934852	0,000560	14,934852	26655
com.icesoft.faces.webapp.http.servlet	8,231754	0,005063	158,638513	1626
(default package)	6,719593	0,003207	44,525342	2095
com.icesoft.faces.webapp.parser	6,154452	0,001523	93,858511	4041
oracle.jdbc.ttc7	3,628655	0,000660	5,769841	5497
antlr.collections.impl	2,796365	0,000627	2,796365	4460
com.icesoft.util	2,255263	0,020882	4,157094	108

Here there are a few statistics about the packages/classes that are displayed in the preceding report. In particular, we are informed about:

- **Base Time**: The amount of time (in seconds) the method has taken to execute. Not including the execution time of any other methods called from this method.

- **Average Base Time**: The average base time required to execute this method once.

- **Cumulative Time**: The amount of time (in seconds) this method took to execute. Including the execution time of any other methods called from this method.

- **Calls**: The number of times this method was invoked. In order to restrict the area of your analysis, you can set a filter on package/class names.

Profiling the JVM Memory will produce a detailed report about the objects created. The following report shows the **Memory Statistics** for the same web application:

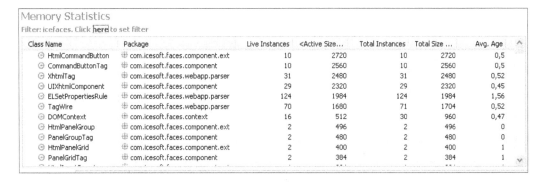

Notice the information provided in the preceding report:

- **Live Instances:** The number of instances of a class that are alive (the instances that were not collected by the garbage collector).

- **Active Size (bytes):** The size of an instance associated with a specific type.

- **Total Instances**: The total number of instances of the class.

- **Average Age**: The number of young generation collections survived by the objects (garbage collection is explained in detail in *Chapter 3, Tuning the Java Virtual Machine*).

All the Profiler resources created can be saved for later analysis by right-clicking on the server in the Profiling monitor window and then clicking on **Save**. You can also generate a report in various different formats (CSV, HTML, XML) by choosing the **New Report** option in the same menu.

Going beyond the basics of TPTP

The TPTP platform addresses the entire test and performance lifecycle, from early testing to production application monitoring, including test editing and execution, monitoring, tracing and profiling, and log analysis capabilities. In this section, we have covered the basics to get introduced quickly to application profiling. However, to learn more about this great tool you can visit the platform homepage at : `http://www.eclipse.org/tptp/`

Load testing your application with JMeter

Unless you plan to hire a few hundreds guys to set up a benchmark for your applications, you need to install some tools to automate your testing.

Automated load testing tools became popular in the late 90s to benchmark web applications. Today there's a vast choice of tools available, most of them are equipped with similar features: our favorite choice is the well known Jakarta JMeter which can be downloaded at the following location: `http://jakarta.apache.org/site/downloads/downloads_jmeter.cgi`.

Jakarta JMeter is delivered as a Java standalone application so it requires a JVM installed (1.4 or higher). In order to start JMeter, run the `jmeter.bat` (for Windows) or `jmeter` (for Unix) file. These files are found in the `bin` directory.

Once the JMeter GUI has loaded, you'll notice two elements in the left pane: the **Test Plan** and **WorkBench**:

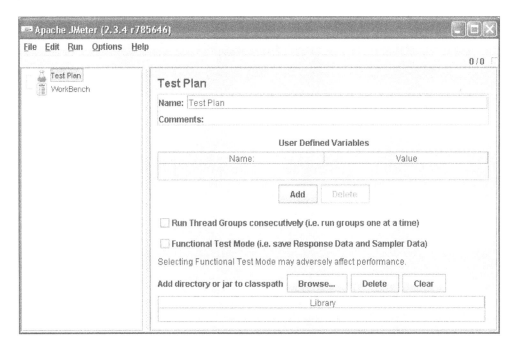

The **Test Plan** is a container for running tests. The **WorkBench** functions as a temporary workspace to store test elements. When you are ready to test what you have designed in the **WorkBench**, you can copy or move the elements into the **Test Plan**.

Building a Test Plan

The **Test Plan** is the main container where you will run your tests. It is basically made up of a minimal set of components:

1. You need to define the number of Threads running your test so you need to define a **Thread Group.**

2. Then you need to define the format of the request which will be used to run the test, so you need to define a **Sampler**. Even though JMeter has been originally built for web applications now you can also send FTP, SOAP/ XML, JDBC, or LDAP requests.

3. Finally you need an interface (named **Listener**) which is able to save the benchmark to a file or illustrate the results with a chart.

Step 1: Create a Thread Group

Let's begin by creating a **Thread Group** which will contain sub elements like the **Sampler**. Right-click on the **Test Plan** icon to see the context menu and choose **Add | Thread Group**. The **Thread Group** GUI will be displayed:

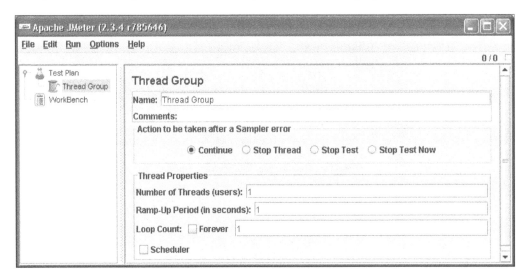

The fields in this window allow you to define:

- **Number of Threads** (that is the number of users)
- **Ramp-Up Period** (that is how long it takes to start each user)
- Number of times to execute the test

If you enable the **Scheduler** field, in the lower part of the GUI, you will be able to define a startup time and a stopping time for your test, which can be thus deferred to a later time.

Step 2: Create a Sampler

Once you are done with the **Thread Group** GUI we will move to the **Sampler**. From the **Thread Group** element right-click and choose **Add | Sampler | HTTPRequest**. The **HTTP Request** Sampler control panel looks like the following figure:

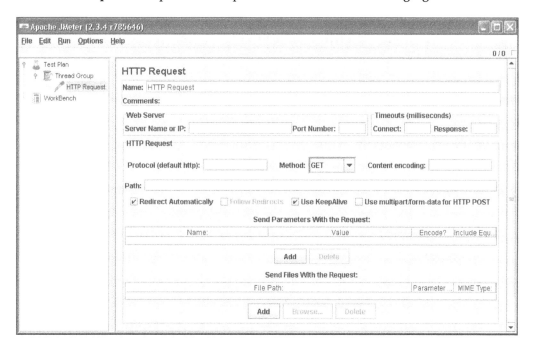

At first, define a meaningful name for the HTTP Request like "Homepage". Then in the **Web Server** section you need to define the server name and the port where the web application is running

If you plan to add several HTTP Requests to your Project then you should consider adding **HTTP Request Defaults** (this option is reachable from the menu **Add | Config Element | HTTP Request Defaults**).

By setting HTTP Request Defaults you can avoid entering elements multiple times (like the **Server Name** or the **Port**), which are common to every request.

Finally, you need to define the **Path** of the HTTP Request which can carry additional parameters/files as well. In our example, we will set the path field to "/" which means to load the default welcome page.

Step 3: Create a Listener

Finally, we will add a simple Listener like the Aggregate Graph. This element will store all results of your HTTP Requests and will display the statistical information in table and graph format.

From the **Thread Group** element select **Add | Listener | Aggregate Graph**. The only field we will populate is the **Write results to a file** section which will select where to save the graph data.

Before running the test, JMeter requires us to save a **Test Plan**: click on the **Save Test Plan** button from the **File** menu and then, from the **Run** menu, select **Run**.

The following screenshot shows how your **Aggregate Graph** panel should look at the end of a profiler session. In case you have selected to run benchmark forever, then you need to manually stop the run by selecting **Stop** from the **Run** menu.

The column headings are explained briefly as follows:

Column	Description
Label	The label of the sample
# Samples	The number of samples for the URL
Average	The mean time of a set of results
Median	The time in the middle of a set of results
90% Line	The maximum time taken for the fastest 90% of the samples
Min	The lowest time for the samples
Max	The longest time for the samples
Error %	Percent of requests with errors or failures
Throughput	Throughput measured in requests per unit of time
Kb/sec	The throughput measured in kilobytes per second

The preceding fields can be used to generate a graph in the lower section of the GUI: choose one meaningful field like **Average** and click on the **Display Graph** button. A tiny portion of the graph will be displayed in a panel which can be saved in graphical format by clicking on **Save Graph** or in CSV format if you choose **Save Table Data**.

Use Listeners with parsimony!

As you can see from the Listener menu, there are many other available listeners besides the Aggregate Graph. You might be tempted to add every kind of listener to improve your analysis: don't do it! JMeter will considerably slow down if you have many listeners active. Therefore, use a minimum set of the most appropriate listeners.

Making your test plan a bit more realistic

By default, JMeter sends one request immediately after the other: this could potentially saturate the server and also produce a test which is not close to real world cases. As a matter of fact user requests are usually separated by a variable amount of time, which can be thought as constant or following a statistical pattern like a gaussian curve.

In order to introduce a delay between requests you can introduce **Timers** in your **Test Plan**. Choose **Add | Timer** from the **Thread Group** context menu and select one timer from the available. In the following screenshot, we have added a **Constant Timer** to our **Thread Group**, which introduces a constant delay of **300** ms between requests:

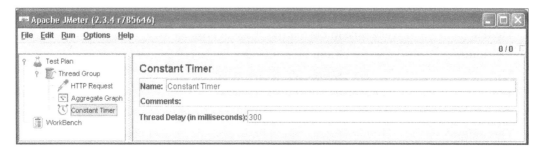

How to create a complex Test Plan

With the notions you have learnt until now you are able to create a simple web load test. In theory, you could build a more complex one by including a set of HTTPRequest, each one targeted at a different URL and carrying the appropriate parameters.

In practice, that would require quite a lot of time and would also be prone to human error (ironically you would end up testing the composition of the test too!). Luckily, there's a handy option which allows for using JMeter as proxy server, thus recording every request made to the application.

A proxy server can be added by right-clicking on **Workbench** and select **Add | Non Test Elements | HTTP Proxy Server**. As shown in the following image, JMeter proxy server sits in between the client (browser) and the web server:

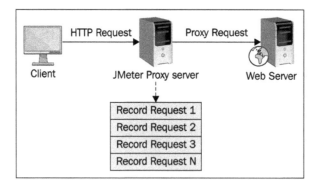

In order to configure the proxy server, you need to specify the **Port** on which the proxy will be started.

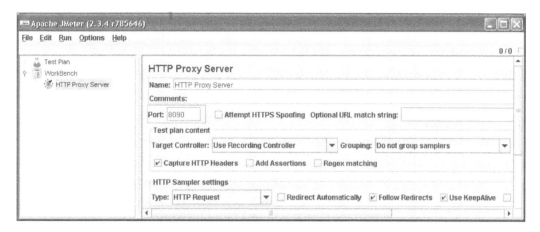

As in this example we have started the proxy server *on the same machine* where the web server is running, we cannot use the default port 8080 which is already engaged. So we will start the proxy on port **8090**.

Now you need to configure your browser so to that the proxy server will actually direct the proxy request to the web server. The following screenshots depict how to set up a proxy on your favorite browser (Internet Explorer/Firefox);

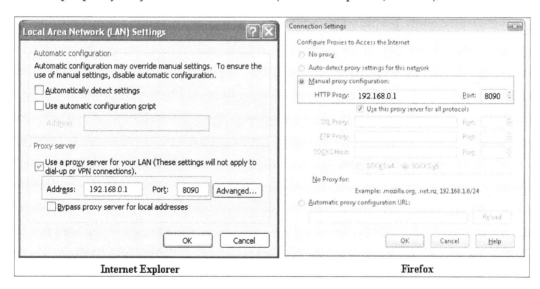

Internet Explorer   **Firefox**

Now start up JBoss AS, taking care to bind it to the available network interfaces (starting it with localhost might not work if you have configured the browser not to use the proxy for localhost):

```
run -b 0.0.0.0          #Windows
run.sh -b 0.0.0.0       #Unix
```

Finally start the HTTP Proxy Server by clicking on the **Start** Button in the lower part of the panel and start surfing on your JBoss AS.

In the following example we are pointing our browser to the JBoss AS's **jmx-console**:

```
http://192.168.0.1:8080/jmx-console.
```

When you enter this information in the navigation bar, the browser understands that the request needs to be proxied to the address 192.168.0.1.8090 first. There, JMeter HTTP Proxy records the request which will be finally forwarded to the original address where JBoss AS is running (port 8080).

That is what the **Workbench** contains after you have navigated through the JBoss AS **jmx-console**:

When you have completed your recording, click on the **Stop** button in the **HTTP Proxy Server** panel. The HTTP Request items created in **WorkBench** can be eventually dragged into your test plan.

How to create a stateful Test Plan

By default, when you queue up several HTTP Requests, every single request will be considered as stateless, this means that *a new HTTP Session will be created for every request*. Just like if you open a browser window, issue the request and close the browser.

If you want every user's request to hold Session data, you can simply instruct JMeter to use cookies to persist the HTTP Session. From the menu select **Add | Config Element | Http Cookie Manager**. The **Http Cookie Manager** needs to be added just below the **Thread Group** element, so that it will be shared among all HTTP Requests.

Running JMeter as a shell

Your hardware's capabilities will inevitably limit the number of threads you can effectively run with JMeter. If you need to set up a large scale test and you cannot afford to execute the JMeter GUI, you can consider launching JMeter using a command line.

You can use the following parameters in order to run JMeter from the command prompt:

- -n: This specifies JMeter is to run in non-GUI mode.
- -t: Name of JMX file that contains the Test Plan
- -l: Name of JTL file to log sample results to
- -r: Run all remote servers specified in JMeter properties.
- -H: Proxy server hostname or IP address, if run using firewall/proxy
- -P: Proxy server port, if run using firewall/proxy

For example:

```
jmeter -n -t test1.jmx -l logfile.jtl
```

JMeter will then execute the test plan contained in the test1.jmx file, logging the sample results to the file logfile.jtl.

Operating system tools and commands

The last (but not the least) element which influences the performance of the application is the kind of hardware on which it is running. If you want to check how much a single hardware resource is used by your application, you can use some common tools and utilities which are usually installed on your machine. Generally speaking, Unix systems have a greater set of built-in commands which are available to monitor your host. Windows users can, however, get an adequate amount of utilities with a simple search on the net and we will guide the reader to some good choices.

Windows users

One of the most useful applications is the **Performance Monitor**, which can be used to track a wide range of attributes of your machine and give it a real time graphical display of results. The performance monitor can be run by opening the control panel and clicking **Performance and Maintenance | Administrative Tools | Performance** (Windows XP).

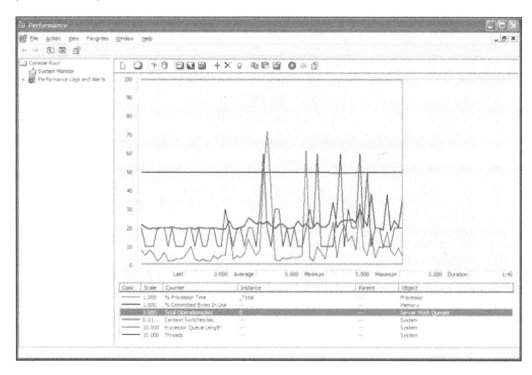

There you can add new counters on your graph by selecting the (**+**) button on the toolbar. As you look at the output, you can see that the lines on the graph correspond to the counters that you've installed. Once you have hunted which are the system bottlenecks of your machine, you can further restrict your analysis by looking at the **Task Manager** application.

From the **Task Manager** application, first select the **Processes** tab to view the list of processes that are running on your machine. Next, choose the **Select Columns** command from the **View** menu. You'll now see a list of all of the resources that you can monitor through the **Task Manager**.

For example, the following image illustrates a monitoring session which is observing the system input-output:

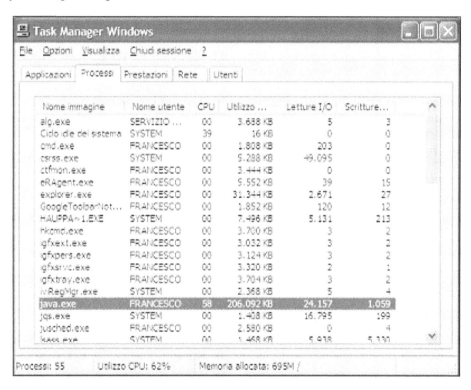

The **Windows Performance Monitor** and the **Task Manager** are functional but basic tools for keeping an eye on what your computer's up to. If you want to go beyond the built-in tools and for more in-depth information and control, check the following alternatives:

Tool	URL
Process Explorer	http://technet.microsoft.com/en-us/sysinternals/bb896653.aspx
System Explorer	http://systemexplorer.mistergroup.org/
Manage Engine Windows monitor	http://www.manageengine.com (Commercial)

Unix users

Unix and Linux users have a great number of tools available for monitoring the basic system activities, usually available as a shell executable command.

The most popular utility is top, which provides an ongoing look at processor activity in real time. It displays a listing of the most CPU-intensive tasks on the system and provides an interactive interface for manipulating processes. It can sort the tasks by CPU usage, memory usage, and runtime. See the following example:

```
load averages:  0.47,  0.15,  0.16
226 processes: 224 sleeping, 2 on cpu
CPU states: 73.1% idle, 25.0% user,  1.1% kernel,  0.8% iowait,  0.0%
swap
Memory: 4096M real, 1921M free, 2218M swap in use, 3111M swap free

   PID USERNAME THR PRI NICE  SIZE   RES STATE   TIME    CPU COMMAND
  1996 jboss     24   0    0  371M  103M cpu/2  5:35 20.75% java
  2001 jboss      1  55    0 2176K 1304K cpu/1  0:00  0.14% top
  2000 nms        1  48    0 2552K 1848K sleep  0:00  0.07% bash
  1622 oracle     1  58    0    0K    0K sleep  1:29  0.02% oracle
   498 oracle     1  58    0    0K    0K sleep  1:02  0.02% oracle
  1998 root       1  38    0 1848K 1344K sleep  0:00  0.02% in.telnetd
```

The upper highlighted lines describe the statistics about the machine, including CPU and Memory real time data. In the lower section, you can read per-process information: for example, you can understand that there's one java process, run by the user jboss, which occupies 103 MB of *resident set size memory* (the non-swapped physical memory that a process uses) and is using about 20% of the CPU time.

Topping for Solaris

Solaris users can use the `prstat` utility instead of top which can be used mostly the same way as top to provide views of a system's activity and resource consumption

Another useful tool, available in most Unix flavors is **vmstat**. As its name suggests, this utility reports virtual memory statistics. It shows how much virtual memory there is, CPU, and paging activity. This is extremely useful.

To monitor the virtual memory activity on your system, it's best to use vmstat with a delay. A delay is the number of seconds between updates. (If you don't supply a delay, vmstat just reports the averages since the last boot). Five seconds is the recommended delay interval.

To run vmstat with a five-second delay, type:

```
vmstat 5
```

Here's an example of system activity:

procs			memory				swap		io		system	cpu			
r	b	w	swpd	free	buff	cache	si	so	bi	bo	in	cs	us	sy	id
0	0	0	29232	116972	4524	244900	0	0	0	0	0	0	0	0	0
0	0	0	29232	116972	4524	244900	0	0	0	0	2560	6	0	1	99
0	0	0	29232	116972	4524	244900	0	0	0	0	2574	10	0	2	98

The output from this command is divided into five sections:

- `procs`: The number of processes waiting for run time (`r`), those in uninterruptable sleep (`b`) and the number of processes swapped out but otherwise runnable(`w`).

- `memory`: The amount of virtual memory used (`swpd`). The amount of idle memory (`free`). The amount of memory used as buffers (`buff`). Figures in KB.

- `swap and io`: The amount of memory swapped in (`si`) and to disk (`so`). The blocks sent (`bo`) and received from a block device (`bi`).

- system: The number of interrupts per second, including the clock (in) and the number of context switches per second (cs).

- cpu: The percentage of CPU usage among user time (us), system time (sy), and idle time (id).

These instruments provide an invaluable source of information to discover bottlenecks in your system caused by your applications or by your hardware. However, once you have evidence of a problem with your system, how do you apply the necessary corrections?

Dealing with low CPU utilization

Having too much idle time on your CPU is not necessarily a good thing. In particular, you should be suspicious if you have a high idle time in conjunction with the following symptoms:

- High idle time across all CPUs with a no unusual input/output or network activity.

- High idle time, which does not decrease with increased load.

- Response times degrade too rapidly with increased load.

If you are experiencing any of these symptoms it's likely that your application server is *waiting for some resources to be freed*. A fundamental instrument to find the source of the problem is the application server's Thread Dump, which can be obtained from the VisualVM monitor tab or by means of JBoss AS jmx-console.

For example, supposing that you have many Threads with the following stack trace:

```
"Thread-1" prio=6 tid=0x02a99c00 nid=0xee0 waiting for monitor entr...
   java.lang.Thread.State: BLOCKED (on object monitor)
       at SimpleDeadLock$Thread2.run(SimpleDeadLock.java:37)
       - waiting to lock <0x229bd238> (a java.lang.Object)
       - locked <0x229bd240> (a java.lang.Object)
```

Then, it's likely that you have a **deadlock** in your application caused by some of your threads. Definitive proof can be obtained by means of the jstack [pid] command line utility, which is part of the Java Development Kit distribution. Jstat will provide a full stack trace for the application along with a diagnostic about deadlocks.

Dealing with high CPU utilization

One of the most pervasive myths among IT technicians is that a high CPU usage is an obvious indicator of a system bottleneck. The following extract from vmstat output is a clear example:

procs					memory		swap		io			cpu			
r	b	w	swpd	free	buff	cache	si	so	bi	bo	in	cs	us	sy	id
0	0	0	29232	116972	4524	244900	0	0	0	0	0	0	45	45	10

Here the CPU is busy at 90% (45% user + 45% system) but there's no CPU bottleneck in this machine: simply the machine is working at full potential. As a matter of fact UNIX internal dispatchers are designed to keep the CPUs **as busy as possible**. This maximizes task throughput, even if it can be misleading for a neophyte. Even a 100% CPU usage is not generally a problem and can rather indicate an optimal state.

The only cause for a concern is *when the run queue* (r value under the procs column) *exceeds the number of CPUs* on the server.

procs					memory		swap		io			cpu			
r	b	w	swpd	free	buff	cache	si	so	bi	bo	in	cs	us	sy	id
12	0	0	56834	257452	4261	435600	0	0	0	0	0	0	30	65	5

In the preceding example, taken from a six CPU machine, it's clear that there's a CPU constraint because of the high run queue. As a next step, examine the cpu column to understand how the machine consumes CPU time. In this sample, having a high system time (65%), you are obviously performing *a large amount of system calls*.

This can happen if you are executing lots of input/output, socket or timestamp creation. You should find out, along with your performance tools, the modules that cause excessive or inefficient input/output. One potential candidate is, for example, a class, which perform lots of unbuffered input/output. Replacing it with a buffered one could greatly reduce the problem.

A special case is when only *one or a few* CPU experience a peak of usage. This scenario is usually caused by the fact that your system uses *a single thread* to manage some resources. Your checklist should include, at first, garbage collection configuration (see *Chapter 3, Tuning the Java Virtual Machine* for an in-depth discussion about it). If garbage collection is correctly configured, you should then verify if you have any contention for getting access to some resources. We will see this in a minute.

Dealing with high resource contention

One kind of issue, related to abnormal CPU utilization (high and low), happens when you have a single shared resource (think of an Object cache for example), which is shared among many users.

You can have a proof of it by using the shell command `mpstat`, which indicates your *thread's spin on mutex values*. In short this is s a measure for kernel contention (if a thread can't acquire a lock, it spins). Here's a sample of output for a machine with a high spin on mutex value:

```
cpu       smtx     sys usr
0         2632     55  40
```

The `smtx` measurement shows the number of times a CPU failed to obtain a mutex immediately. Depending upon CPU speed, a reading of more than 500 may be an indication of a system in trouble. If the `smtx` is greater than 500 on a single CPU and `sys` dominates `usr` (that is, system time is larger than user time, and system time is greater than 20%), it is likely that mutex contention is occurring.

You should further inspect through a Thread Dump what is the source of the problem. For example, in such a dump you have definitive evidence that your threads are locked waiting on a Queue:

```
"WorkerThread-8" ... in Object.wait() ...... - locked <0xf14213c8> (a
Queue) ...

"WorkerThread-10" ... in Object.wait() ...... - locked <0xf14213c8> (a
Queue) ...

"WriterThread-3" ... in Object.wait() ...... - locked <0xf14213c8> (a
Queue) ...
```

In order to mitigate this effect, you should introduce additional shared resources; for example, you might distribute your cache through a larger set of JVMs. *Chapter 7, JBoss AS Cluster Tuning* dedicates a wealth of information about partitioning your application across a set of JVMs.

Dealing with high disk utilization

Excessive disk utilization is a frequent bottleneck for Enterprise applications. The command `iostat` is commonly used by system administrators to detect input/output statistics. Here's an example:

```
Device    kr/s kw/s svc_t    %w    %b
Ssd1      1.6  69.6  8.5      0     4
```

Here, the first two columns indicate the KB read per second (kr/s) and KB writes per second (kw/s). The average service time is indicated by svc_t. The %w indicates the percent of time there are transactions waiting for service while the %b is percent of time the disk is busy.

You should pay attention if you find excessive values for these values:

- High service time (svc_t) (generally above 30s of ms).
- High %b (above 5).
- A consistently high reads/writes values.

You should evidently find out which is the module that is causing the excessive disk utilization. Some possible causes for a Java Enterprise application are:

- Excessive logging. See *Chapter 4*, *Tuning the JBoss AS* section *Logging* for Performance.
- Stateful Session Bean Passivation. See *Chapter 5*, *Tuning the Middleware Services* section *Session Bean*.
- Poorly configured database cache. See *Chapter 6*, *Tuning the Persistence Layer* section *Evaluate using caches to speed up your queries*.

If the bottleneck is not caused by your application, then you should consider spreading the file system of the disk on to two or more disks. As an alternative, move the file system to another faster disk/controller or replace the existing disk/controller with a faster one.

Summary

In this chapter, we have introduced some of the most popular tools available in the market for monitoring the JVM, the application server, its application deployed, and the operating system. These are the essential points covered:

- VisualVM is a monitoring tool developed by Sun, which can be used to analyze JVM heap data, track down memory leaks, monitor the garbage collector, and perform memory and CPU profiling.
- The Eclipse TPTP Platform covers the entire performance lifecycle so it can be used also as an all-in-one solution for your projects. In this chapter, we have learnt how to use it to profile and test your server applications.
- JMeter is a well-known application, which can be used to set up benchmarks of your web applications but can be equipped for a variety of tests as well.

- Each operating system has built-in tools, which can monitor your hardware resources.

- Windows users can opt for the Performance Monitor and the Task Manager as well as many freely available utilities.

  ○ Unix/Linux users have a great number of tools available, the most popular being the shell commands `top` and `vmstat`.

In the next chapter, we will review the first area of tuning introduced, that is the Java Virtual Machine, showing some concrete application use cases.

3
Tuning the Java Virtual Machine

2nd Circle of Hell: Lust. Here lies programmers overcome by lust, that created objects over 500 KB in size.

In this chapter, we will begin our performance tour with the Java Virtual Machine (JVM) tuning. As you know, every Java application requires a JVM environment to be executed and the JBoss application server is no exception.

With every new release of Java, many improvements have been made at all levels of the runtime system including in the garbage collector, in the code, in the VM handling of objects and threads, and in the compiler optimizations.

We have now got a much faster Virtual Machine but at the price of enhanced complexity due to the increase of the available algorithms and options. Therefore, our primary goal will be to simplify the management of the Virtual Machine and concentrate our efforts on the fixes that will surely pay good dividends such as Java heap and garbage collector settings.

Summing up, this chapter is organized into the following sections:

- The first section introduces the basics of Java Virtual Machine
- The next section discusses optimal JVM settings, focusing on the most appropriate memory and garbage collection settings
- The last section shows how to put in practice the theoretical concepts, just learnt, with a concrete use case

The starting point

So every Java program runs in a Virtual Machine environment, but how is a Virtual Machine made up? Essentially, there are two areas of memory which are used by Java programs. These are commonly known as the stack and the heap.

The **stack** is the memory set aside as scratch space for a thread of execution. When a method is called, a block is reserved on the top of the stack for local variables and some bookkeeping data. When the method returns, the block becomes unused and can be recycled the next time a function is called. The stack is always reserved in a LIFO (Last In First Out) order, which means that the most recently reserved block is always the next block to be freed. This makes it really simple to keep track of the stack meaning that freeing a block from the stack is nothing more than adjusting one pointer.

The **heap** is the area of memory set aside for dynamic allocation. Unlike the stack, you can allocate a block at any time in your code and free it as well at any time. This makes it much more complex to handle, as variables on the heap must be destroyed manually and never fall out of scope. If you don't keep track of your objects allocated on the heap, there can be memory leaks in your application.

One of the strengths of the J2SE platform is that it shields the developer from the complexity of memory allocation and garbage collection. As a matter of fact, the JVM handles these complex issues. However when memory management and garbage collection becomes a bottleneck in your applications, it is worth learning more about the internals of the JVM.

As you can see from the next picture, the Java heap is basically divided into two main parts. These are known as the **old generation** which is sometimes called the tenured space, and the **young generation** which is known as the new space. There is also a third generation which appears in the picture named as *the permanent space*. The permanent space is the area of the JVM that is used to store data structures and class information. We will deal with this area later on in this chapter, in the *Making good use of memory* section.

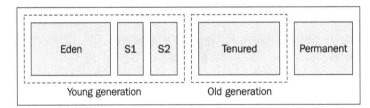

The young generation is further subdivided into three partitions. These are **Eden** and two **Survivor spaces**, called the *From space* (S1) and the *To space* (S2).

Objects are initially allocated in Eden. One Survivor space is empty at any time, and serves as a destination of the next, copying the collection of any live objects in Eden and the other Survivor space. Objects are copied between Survivor spaces in this way until they are old enough to be tenured, or copied to the Tenured generation.

In short, as depicted in the next picture, all objects that survived multiple garbage collections are finally moved from the young generation to the old generation.

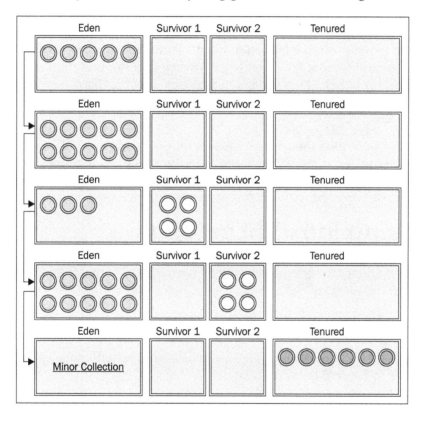

When is an Object eligible for garbage collection?

An object is considered garbage when it can no longer be reached from any pointer in the running program. The most straightforward garbage collection algorithms simply iterate over every reachable object. Any objects left over are then considered garbage.

You might wonder why the structure of Java heaps matter to the user. The answer is that these two partitions named young and tenured, are collected using two different algorithms. When the young generation is full, a **minor collection** is triggered, while the tenured generation can only be freed with a **major collection**.

As the name implies, a minor collection has a low impact on performance since it's targeted on a smaller area of memory where most of the objects are quickly reclaimed (that is have *died*). A major collection, on the other hand, involves the entire Java heap where lots of live objects are piled. This means that it is a lot more expensive.

Consequently, by setting the appropriate size for the young and old generation, you can reduce the time spent in garbage collections. In particular, this can decrease the need for costly major collections.

Choosing the JVM settings

You can control the JVM heap settings using a set of parameters known as non-standard options, which are prefixed by the –x flag. Our analysis will be split into three main areas:

1. At first, we will review the parameters that define the minimum and maximum heap sizes.
2. After that, we will inspect the flags which can be used to fine-tune the Young / tenured generation ratio.
3. Finally, we will examine the most complex part, which concerns the garbage collector behavior and that can be further optimized by choosing the optimal garbage collector algorithm.

Setting the correct heap size

You can configure the desired heap size using two switches: the -Xms option lets you decide the initial heap size. On the other hand, the -Xmx option is where you can set the maximum memory granted to the heap. If JVM tries to reclaim more memory when the maximum heap size is reached, a message saying java.lang. OutOfMemoryError: Java heap space is issued.

For example, the following command launches the MyApplication class using 128 MB as starting heap memory. This allows it to grow up to 512 MB.

```
java -Xms128m -Xmx512m MyApplication
```

If you don't specify a value for the initial and maximum heap size, JVM will choose some defaults. Prior to J2SE 5.0, the default values were 4 MB for the initial heap size, and 64 MB for the maximum allowed heap size.

Prior to J2SE 5.0 Settings	
Heap setting	**Default value**
-Xms	4 MB
-Xmx	64 MB

You might imagine that these values are grossly inadequate for most server applications. Moreover, since the 1.5 release of JVM, the default selection values have changed due to the introduction of *Ergonomics* self-tuning strategies.

In practice, the default values for the Java heap and garbage collector algorithms are calculated based on the hardware capabilities of your machine. If your machine has got two or more processors, or at least 2 GB of memory available, it's considered as a **server class machine**. Therefore it has higher default settings.

For server-class machines, the default value for the initial heap size is 1/64 of physical memory up to 1 GB. The maximum heap size is one-fourth of physical memory up to 1 GB. The most notable exception to this rule is JVM for Windows (32 bit), which always uses the older default values.

The following table summarizes the default values for the Java heap in both scenarios:

J2SE 5.0 Settings		
Heap setting	Not Server machine (or Windows 32 bit)	Server machine
-Xms	4 MB	1/64 of physical memory (up to 1 GB)
-Xmx	64 MB	¼ of physical memory (up to 1 GB)

So drawing some sums, if your machine is qualified as a server class machine and has got 2 GB available, it will use 32 MB as the initial heap size and 512 MB as the maximum size. That's the fairest configuration default. However for an application server, it can be still considered insufficient.

The correct amount of memory to grant your application

So you know, because of the nature of the beast of the application server, you cannot rely on the default values for the heap size; furthermore if you make a poor choice, the JVM can't compensate for it without a restart.

Luckily, setting the correct heap values is quite simple and requires just some trials.

Step # 1: Finding the maximum heap (-Xmx)

Finding the maximum size allowed for the Java heap is just a matter of observing the application under a consistent load. Suppose that your application has reached a peak load of 768 MB as depicted by the following screenshot:

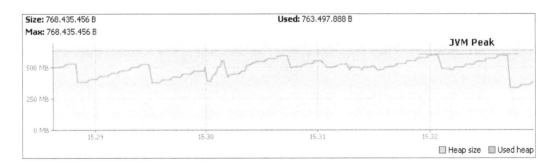

Then, you can add a bonus of 25-30% so that the JVM can handle an additional burst of request. This would turn out to a suggested maximum heap size of around 1024 MB

```
java -Xmx1024m . . .
```

For the best performance, it's important to make sure that no more than 70-80% of the heap is occupied, otherwise *the frequency of the garbage collector would be too great* and your application would freeze until the amount of memory drops down consistently.

Also consider that the maximum amount of memory is limited by the operating system limits (see next tip *I cannot allocate enough memory for JVM*) and applications running on the machine. As a general rule, it is wise to consider as an upper limit for JVM, the amount of physical memory available on the machine, minus about 1 GB which should be left to the operating system.

Translating this to numbers, *if you have got 3 GB of RAM*, this is the maximum amount of memory you should allocate.

```
java -Xmx2048m . . .
```

Assigning over 2 GB of RAM to your application server is, anyway, considered a bad practice because with extra large heaps the time spent in major garbage collection grows up accordingly. So, if you want fast and robust applications consider 2 GB as the maximum amount of memory for the Java heap.

Step # 2: Finding the initial heap size (-Xms)

Setting the amount of initial memory for your heap is generally a bit more controversial. We will soon see why. As for the maximum heap size, the strategy stays the same; that is you should observe your application when it's consistently loaded.

In many cases, you should just aim at a different target. Consider the following screenshot:

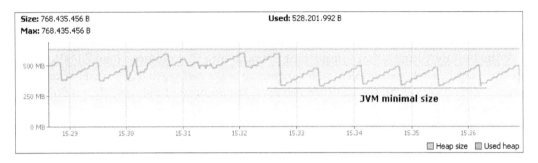

Almost all applications, which are developed without memory leaks, exhibit a heap graph bouncing around a constant amount of memory. In the preceding screenshot, the application bounces around a minimal value of 320 MB which should be apparently considered the optimal initial size.

```
java -Xms320m -Xmx1024m . . .
```

We said apparently because in real world Enterprise applications, you will hardly find a minimal or maximum size with such a difference. This is because most tuning experts agree that it is worthy to set the initial size of the JVM *at the same level* as the maximum heap size; Furthermore, by using a fixed size for your heap, it reduces the overhead of computing a new heap size as new memory is reclaimed by the JVM.

The critics say that this would lead to a potential waste of memory, especially in the initial stages of the application execution. In addition, this introduces delays in the start of garbage collection, which will be a very expensive operation the first times it is triggered.

Even if there's some truth in this criticism, in a long-term perspective the application will gradually reach 70-80% of the maximum memory (in our example 768 MB) and the garbage collector will stabilize as well. So, if you figure that you are going to get to the maximum heap anyway, then growing the JVM memory can be considered as pure overhead, which we should avoid.

The hardware resources available on the machine can have the last word in this contest. If your JBoss AS is running on a dedicated machine, then you should wisely set the initial size equal to the maximum heap size.

On the other hand, if your JBoss AS is competing with other applications for the same hardware (this typically happens on development machines) then it makes sense to set the initial size to the JVM minimal size, as pointed out by the preceding screenshot

I cannot allocate enough memory for the JVM!

A common issue that developers sometimes meet is that they are not able to allocate enough memory for server Java applications running on 32-bit machines.

The issue is not specific to the JVM: on a 32-bit machine, a process cannot allocate more than 4 GB (2^32 possible memory locations).

Unfortunately, that's just the beginning; part of the 4 GB address space is reserved for the OS kernel. On normal consumer versions of Windows, the limit drops down to 2 GB. On Linux the limit is 3 GB per process.

Finally, of the remaining memory available you are allowed to use only the biggest contiguous chunk of memory available. That's because the JVM needs to grab an unfragmented virtual space of memory.

That's an issue for the Windows platform where optimizations aimed to minimize the relocation of DLL's during linking, make it more likely for you to have a fragmented address space.

As a proof to our affirmations, examine the following picture taken from the **VMMap** utility (http://technet.microsoft.com/en-us/sysinternals/dd535533.aspx) which shows the largest chunk of virtual memory available on a 2 GB of RAM XP Machine.

As you can see in the following screenshot, barely 1.4 GB is left for a single process:

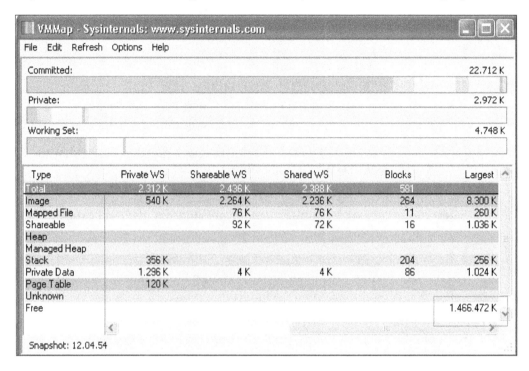

In the end, on a 32-bit Windows machine, you will hardly be able to allocate more than 1.5 GB. On a 32-bit Linux, you are a bit luckier and you can allocate about 2 GB. On Solaris, the limit is set to about 3.5 GB.

What are your alternatives if you need to allocate a larger set of memory? Actually, there are a few options:

- The most obvious one is to move to a 64-bit machine. On a 64-bit machine, the problem is nonexistent because you have 2^64 possible locations and you can allocate up to 16 Exabytes (An Exabyte equals to 1 billion GB).

- If you cannot afford to switch to 64-bit machines but you would just be fine with a little bit more of heap (let's say 2 GB for Windows), then you can consider switching to Oracle's **JRockit Virtual Machine** which introduced support for split heaps. This means that you don't need to allocate a contiguous chunk of memory, which is particularly restrictive on Windows platforms (you can download JRockit here: http://www.oracle.com/technology/products/jrockit/index.html).

- The last option available for Enterprise applications, which we strongly suggest to consider, is scaling your system configuration horizontally. By defining a cluster of application servers, the load will be split on several JVMs thus reducing the need to use very large heaps. If you still need to use a very large heap size (over 2 GB), (because of the inherent characteristics of your application), do remember that the time to complete a garbage collection cycle grows in direct proportion to the size of the heap. So, if you have to deal with a huge 64-bit heap size, a good rule is to keep the heap size as large as needed, but no more.

Where do I configure JVM settings in JBoss AS?

If you need to change the default JVM settings for your application server you should find the start-up script and search for the environment variables containing the Java options.

In JBoss application server, the start-up script is contained in the `JBOSS_HOME/bin` folder of your distribution. The thing that is slightly different is the default location, which contains the JVM default settings.

In earlier JBoss releases (JBoss AS 4.X) Virtual Machine's options were contained in the application server's start-up script (`run.sh` for Linux and `run.cmd` for Windows machines)

```
. . . .
set "JAVA_OPTS=-Xms128M -Xmx512M -XX:MaxPermSize=256M"
```

Since JBoss AS 5, the environment variables and Java options were configured in a separate file named `run.conf.sh/run.conf.bat`. You can customize your JVM settings in this file.

Sizing the garbage collector generations

The second most influential knob is the amount of the heap dedicated to the young generation. You can set the initial amount of memory granted to the young generation with the `-XX:NewSize` flag which can be coupled with `-XX:MaxNewSize`. For example the following configuration starts a JVM with 448m reserved to the young generation, out of the 1024m available.

```
java -Xmx1024m -Xms1024m -XX:MaxNewSize=448m -XX:NewSize=448m -
XX:SurvivorRatio=6 . . .
```

The last parameter, -XX:SurvivorRatio, specifies how much space will be granted to the survivor spaces compared to the whole young generation. In this example, setting the survivor ratio to 6 means that Eden receives 6 units of space while each of the two survivor spaces receives 1 unit, so each survivor space receives 1/8 of the young generation. A ratio of 8 equates to 1/10, and so on.

This may be a little complicated, however just remember you should stick to a range between 6-10. The higher the ratio, the smaller the survivor spaces.

Which is the correct ratio between the young and old generations?

The theory says that you should grant plenty of memory to the young generation for applications that create lots of short lived objects and, on the other hand, reserve more memory to the tenured generation for applications making use of long-lived objects such as pools or caches.

So, provided that you have decided the maximum heap size you can afford to give the JVM, you can plot your performance metric against different young generation sizes to find the best setting.

In most cases, you will find that **the optimal size of the young generation ranges from 1/3 of the total heap up to 1/2 of the heap**. Increasing the young generation becomes counterproductive over half of the total heap or less since it negates its ability to perform a copy collection and results in a full garbage collection. This is also known as the **young generation guarantee**.

What is the young generation guarantee?

To ensure that the minor collection can complete even if all the objects are live, enough free memory must be reserved in the tenured generation to accommodate all the live objects arriving from the survivor spaces. When there isn't enough memory available in the tenured generation to accommodate all these objects, a major collection will occur instead.

Also, the survivor spaces settings should be shaped for optimal performance. Therefore if you don't provide any value for them, they are only allocated 1/34 of the young generation, which turns into a survivor space segment of 1-2 MB. This means, in practical terms, that if you unwisely allocate a large object, it will transition to the tenured space in a few garbage collector cycles.

The suggested size for survivor spaces should range between 1/8 and 1/12 of the size of Eden. Things will get easier with practical examples so there is no need to worry.

The image below shows an example of Java Heap configuration with a young generation space too little. What happens here is that, since the young generation is filled up quickly, short-lived objects are tenured prematurely. They will be collected with a costly major collection, whereas with a larger young collection a minor collection could have reclaimed them.

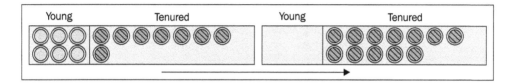

In the next case, we have set a young space over half of the total heap. Since there is not enough space to accommodate all the live objects promoted to the tenured generation, there will be frequent major collections.

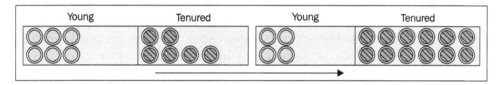

At the end of this chapter we have included a use case, which will show how you can find the correct balance between the two generations with some simple trials.

The garbage collector algorithms

The third important knob, which can influence the performance of your JVM, is the garbage collector algorithm, which determines how the garbage collection process is executed. There are three kinds of garbage collectors which can be used:

- Serial collector
- Parallel collector
- Concurrent collector

Actually there's a fourth one available since release 1.6.14 of J2SE called the **G1 collector**. We will discuss it in a while.

The serial collector performs garbage collection using a single thread, which stops other JVM threads. While it is a relatively efficient collector, since there is no communication overhead between threads, it cannot take advantage of multiprocessor machines. So it is best suited to single processor machines.

The following image resumes how the serial collector works, by stopping all other threads until the collection has terminated.

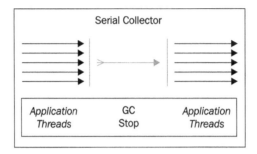

The serial collector is selected by default on hardware and operating system configurations not elected as server class machines, or can be explicitly enabled with the option -XX:+UseSerialGC.

The parallel collector (also known as the throughput collector) performs minor collections in parallel, which can significantly improve the performance of applications having lots of minor collections.

As you can see from the next picture, the parallel collector still requires a so-called *stop-the-world* activity. However, since the collections are performed in parallel, using many CPUs, it decreases garbage collection overhead and hence increases the application throughput.

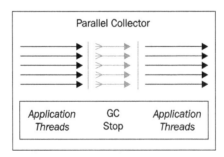

The parallel collector is selected by default on server class machines, or can be explicitly enabled with the option -XX:+UseParallelGC.

> Since the release of J2SE 5.0 update 6 you can benefit from a feature called **parallel compaction** that allows the parallel collector to also perform major collections in parallel. Without parallel compaction, major collections are performed using a single thread, which can significantly limit scalability.
>
> This collector includes a compaction phase where the garbage collector identifies the regions that are free and uses its threads to copy data into those regions. This produces a heap that is densely packed on one end with a large empty block on the other end. In practice this helps to *reduce the fragmentation of the heap*, which is crucial when you are trying to allocate large objects.
>
> Parallel compaction is enabled by adding the option -XX:+UseParallelOldGC to the command line.

The last collector we will cover, the **concurrent collector** (CMS), performs most of its work concurrently (that is, while the application is still running) to keep garbage collection pauses short.

Basically, this collector consumes processor resources for the purpose of having shorter major collection pause times. This can happen because the concurrent collector uses a single garbage collector thread that runs simultaneously with the application threads. Thus, the purpose of the concurrent collector is to complete the collection of the tenured generation before it becomes full.

The following image gives an idea of how the trick is performed:

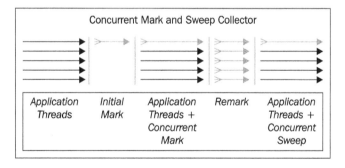

At first the collector identifies the live objects, which are directly reachable (initial mark), then the collector marks all the live objects reachable while the application is still running (concurrent marking). A subsequent phase named remark is needed to revisit objects modified in the concurrent marking phase. Finally the concurrent sweep phase reclaims all objects that have been marked.

The reverse of the coin is that this technique, which is used to minimize pauses, can reduce overall application performance. Hence, it is designed for applications whose response time is more important than overall throughput.

The concurrent collector is enabled with the option `-XX:+UseConcMarkSweepGC`.

Choosing the right garbage collector for your application

Once you have learnt the basics of garbage collector algorithms, you can elaborate a strategy for choosing the one which is best suited to your application.

The best choice is usually found after some trials. However, the following matrix will guide the reader to the available alternatives and their suggested use:

Collector	Best for:
Serial	Single processor machines and small heaps.
Parallel	Multiprocessor machines and applications requiring high throughput.
Concurrent	Fast processor machines and applications with strict service level agreement.

As you can see, by excluding the serial collector, which is fit for smaller applications, the real competition stands between the parallel collector and the concurrent collector.

If your application is deployed on a multiprocessor machine and requires completing the **highest possible number of transactions** in a time window, then the parallel collector would be a safe bet. This is the case of applications performing batch processing activities, billing, and payroll applications.

Be aware that the parallel collector intensively uses the processors of the machine on which it is running, so it might not be fit for large shared machines (like SunRays) where no single application should monopolize the CPU.

If, on the other hand, you have got the fastest processors on the market and you need to **serve every single request by a strict amount of time**, then you can opt for the concurrent collector.

The concurrent collector is particularly suited to applications that have a relatively large set of long-lived data since it can reclaim older objects without a long pause. This is generally the case of Web applications where a consistent amount of memory is stored in the HttpSession.

The G1 garbage collector

The **G1 garbage collector** has been released in release 1.6 update 14 of Sun's JDK. The G1 collector is targeted at server environments with multi-core CPU's equipped with large amounts of memory and aims to minimize delays and stop the world collections, replacing with concurrent garbage collecting while normal processing is still going on.

In the G1 Garbage collector there is no separation between younger and older regions. Rather the heap memory is organized into smaller parts called **Regions**. Each Region is in turn broken down into 525 byte pieces called **cards. For each card, there is one entry in the global card table, as depicted by the following image:**

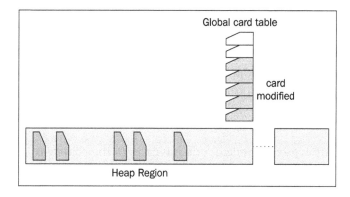

This association helps to track which cards are modified (also known as "remembered set"), concentrating its collection and compaction activity first on the areas of the heap that are likely to be full of reclaimable objects, thus improving its efficiency.

G1 uses a pause prediction model to meet user-defined pause time targets. This helps minimize pauses that occur with the mark and sweep collector, and should show good performance improvements with long running applications.

To enable the G1 garbage collector, add the following switch to your JVM:

```
java -XX:+UnlockExperimentalVMOptions -XX:+UseG1GC . . .
```

In terms of GC pause times, Sun engineers state that G1 is sometimes better and sometimes worse than the CMS collector.

As G1 is still under development, the goal is to make G1 perform better than CMS and eventually replace it in a future version of Java SE (the current target is Java SE 7). While the G1 collector is successful at limiting total pause time, it's still only a soft real-time collector. In other words, it cannot guarantee that it will not impact the application threads' ability to meet deadlines, all of the time. However, it can operate within a well-defined set of bounds that make it ideal for soft real-time systems that need to maintain high-throughput performance.

In the test we have performed throughout this book, we have noticed frequent **core dumps** when adopting the G1 garbage collector algorithm on a JBoss AS 5.1 running JVM 1.6 u. 20. For this reason, we don't advise at the moment to employ this GC algorithm for any of your applications in a production environment, at least until the new 1.7 release of Java is released (expected between the last quarter of 2010 and the beginning of 2011).

Debugging garbage collection

Once you have a solid knowledge of garbage collection and its algorithms, it's time to measure the performance of your collections. We will be intentionally brief in this section, as there are quite a lot of tools that simplify the analysis of the garbage collector, as we will see in the next section.

Keep this information as reference if, you haven't got the chance to use other tools, or if you simply prefer a low level inspection of your garbage collector performance.

The basic command line argument for debugging your garbage collector is -verbose:gc which prints information at every collection.

For example, here is output from a server application:

```
[GC 335414K->123000K(765444K), 0.2411273 secs] - Minor Collection
[GC 313425K->93236K(696456K), 0.2743125 secs]  - Minor Collection
[Full GC 307616K->95367K(826757K), 1.5439247 secs] - Major Collection
```

Here we see two minor collections and one major one. The first two numbers in each row indicate the size of live objects before and after garbage collection:

335414K->123000K (in the first line)

The number in parenthesis (765444K) (in the first line) is the total available space in the Java heap, excluding the space in the permanent generation. As you can see from the example, the first two minor collections took about half a second, while the third major collection required alone about one second and half to reclaim memory from the whole heap.

If you want additional information about the collections, you can use the flag -XX:+PrintGCDetails which prints information about the single areas of the heap (young and tenured).

Here's an example of the output from -XX:+PrintGCDetails:

```
[GC [DefNew: 125458K->15965K(119434K), 0.0657646 secs] 246024K-
>164635K(291148K), 0.1259452 secs]]
```

The output indicates, in the left side of the log, that the minor collection recovered about 88 percent of the young generation:

```
125458K->15965K(119434K)
```

and took about 65 milliseconds.

The second part of the log shows how much the entire heap was reduced:

```
246024K->164635K(291148K), 0.1259452 secs
```

and the additional overhead for the collection, calculated in 12 milliseconds.

The above switches print collection information in the standard output. If you want to evict your garbage collector logs from the other application logs, you can use the switch -Xloggc: which redirects the information in a separate log file.

In addition to the JVM flags, which can be used to debug the garbage collector activity, we would like to mention the **jstat** command utility, which can provide complete statistics about the performance of your garbage collector. This handy command line tool is particularly useful if you don't have a graphic environment for running VisualVM garbage collector's plugins.

Jstat is located in the JAVA_HOME/bin folder of your JDK distribution and needs as a parameter the statistic we are interested in (-gc), the process identifier (pid) and the interval between each statistic. For example:

```
jstat -gc 6564 5000
S0    S1    E    O    P  YGC  YGCT FGC   FGCT    GCT
```

```
0.00 99.99   4.20 84.56 0.15 2093 3.653 416 13.998 17.651

0.00 99.99   0.00 97.66 0.15 2100 3.665 417 14.023 17.688

0.00  0.00   0.00 71.25 0.15 2106 3.674 419 14.090 17.764
```

This reports the garbage collector activity for the pid 6564, adding a new line every 5000 ms. Notably useful are the attributes YGC and YGCT, which bear out the count for young collection events and their elapsed time, and the attributes FGC and FGCT which are the corresponding events and time spent for the tenured generation.

Check the jstat documentation page for additional info:

http://java.sun.com/j2se/1.5.0/docs/tooldocs/share/jstat.html

Making good use of the memory

Before showing a concrete tuning example, we will add a last section to alert you to the danger of creating large Java objects in your applications. We will also give some advice regarding what to do with OutOfMemory errors.

Avoid creating large Java objects

One of the most harmful things you could do to your JVM is allocating objects which are extremely large. The definition of a large object is often ambiguous, but objects whose size exceeds 500KB are generally considered to be large.

One of the side effects of creating such large objects is the increased heap fragmentation which can potentially lead to an OutOfMemory problem.

Heap fragmentation occurs when a Java application allocates a mix of small and large objects that have different lifetimes. When you have a largely fragmented heap, the immediate effect is that the JVM triggers long GC pause times to force the heap to compact.

Consider the following example:

```
<%
// 1 MB object
HugeObject obj = new HugeObject();
session.setAttribute(java.util.UUID.randomUUID().toString(),obj);
%>
```

In this small JSP fragment, you are allocating an Object named `HugeObject`, which occupies around 1 MB of memory since it's holding a large XML file flattened to a text String. The object is stored in the HttpSession using an unique identifier so that every new request will add a new item to the HttpSession.

If you try to load test your Web application, you will see that in a few minutes the application server will become irresponsive and eventually will issue an `OutOfMemory` error. On a tiny JBoss AS installation with `-Xmx 256`, you should be able to allocate about 50 Huge Objects.

Now consider the same application, which is using a smaller set of Objects, supposing a 0.2 MB object referencing a shorter XML file:

```
<%
// 0.2 MB object
SmallerObject obj = new SmallerObject();
session.setAttribute(java.util.UUID.randomUUID().toString(),obj);
%>
```

This time the application server takes a bit more to be killed, as it tried several times to compact the heap and issue a full garbage collection. In the end, you were able to allocate about 300 Smaller Objects, counting up to 60 MB, that is 10 MB more than you could allocate with the Huge Object.

The following screenshot documents this test, monitored by VisualVM:

Case 1: Allocating 1 Mb Objects   Case 2: Allocating 0.2 Mb Objects

Summing up, the best practices when dealing with large objects are:

- Avoid creating objects over 500 KB in size. Try to *split the objects into smaller chunks*. For example, if the objects contain a large XML file, you could try to split them into several fragments.

- If this is not possible, try to *allocate the large objects in the same lifetime*. Since these allocations will all be performed by a single thread and very closely spaced in time, they will typically end up stored as a contiguous block in the Java heap.

- Consider adding the option `-XX:+UseParallelOldGC` which can reduce as well the heap fragmentation by compacting the tenured generation.

Handling 'Out of Memory' errors

The infamous error message, `OutOfMemory`, has appeared at least once on the console of every programmer. It seems a very descriptive error and so you might be tempted to go for the quickest solution that is increasing the heap size of the application server. In some circumstances that could be just what you need, anyway the `OutOfMemory` error is often the symptom of a problem which resides somewhere in your code. Let's first analyze the possible variants of this error message:

- `Exception in thread "main": java.lang.OutOfMemoryError: Java heap space`

  The message indicates that an object could not be allocated in the Java heap. The problem can be as simple as a configuration issue, where the specified heap size (or the default size, if not specified) is insufficient for the application. In other cases, and in particular for a long-lived application, the message might be an indication that the application is holding references to objects, and this prevents the objects from being garbage collected. This is the Java language equivalent of a **memory leak**.

  The following screenshot depicts an example of memory leak. As you can see, the JVM is not able to keep a steady level and keeps growing both the upper limit and the lower limit (A):

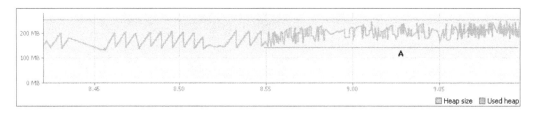

- Exception in thread "main": java.lang.OutOfMemoryError: PermGen space

  The detail message indicates that the permanent generation is full. The permanent generation is the area of the heap where class and method objects are stored. If an application loads a very large number of classes, then the size of the permanent generation might need to be increased using the `-XX:MaxPermSize` option.

> Why is the Perm Gen Space usually exhausted after redeploying an application?
>
> Every time you deploy an application, the application is loaded using its own classloader. Simply put, a classloader is a special class that loads `.class` files from `jar` files. When you undeploy the application, the class loader is discarded and all the classes that it loaded, should be garbage collected sooner or later.
>
> The problem is that Web containers do not garbage collect the classloader itself and the classes it loads. Each time you reload the webapp context, more copies of these classes are loaded, and as these are stored in the permanent heap generation, it will eventually run out of memory.

- Exception in thread "main": java.lang.OutOfMemoryError: Requested array size exceeds VM limit

  The detail message indicates that the application (or APIs used by that application) attempted to allocate an array that is larger than the heap size. For example, if an application attempts to allocate an array of 512 MB but the maximum heap size is 256 MB then an OutOfMemory error will be thrown with the reason, **Requested array size exceeds VM limit**. If this object allocation is intentional, then the only way to solve this issue is by increasing the Java heap max size.

Finding the memory leak in your code

If you find that the OutOfMemory error is caused by a memory leak, the next question is, how do we find where the problem is in your code? Searching for a memory leak can sometimes be as hard as searching for a needle in a haystack, at least without the proper tools. Let's see what VisualVM can do for you:

1. Start VisualVM and connect it to your JBoss AS, which is running a memory leaked application in it. As we will see in a minute, detecting the cause of a memory leak with VisualVM is a simple three-step procedure.

2. At first you need to know which classes are causing the memory leak. In order to do this, you need to start a **Profiler Memory** session, taking care to select in the settings **Record allocations stack traces**.

3. Start profiling and wait for a while until a tabular display of different classes, its instance count, and total byte size are displayed. At this point you need to take two snapshots of the objects: the first one with a clean memory state and the second one after the memory leak occurred (the natural assumption is that the memory leak is clearly reproducible).

4. Now we have two snapshots displayed at the left side pane:

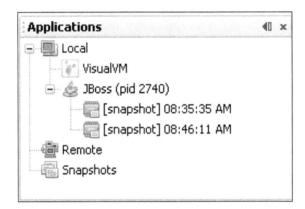

5. Select both of these snapshots (in the left side pane, by using the *Ctrl* key we can select multiple items), right click, and select **Compare**. A comparison tab will be opened in the right side pane. That tab will display items that have increased during the interval of the first and second snapshot.

As you can see from the screenshot, the class **sample.Leak** is the suspect for the memory leak.

6. Now that you have a clue, you need to know where this class has been instantiated. To do this, you need to go to the **Profiler** tab again. Add a filter so that you can easily identify it among the others and right click and select **Take snapshot and show allocation stack traces**.

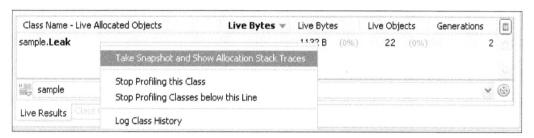

7. One more snapshot is generated. This time in the right side pane, an additional tab is available, named **Allocation Stack Trace**. By selecting it, you can check the different places where this particular item is instantiated and it's percentage of the total count. In this example, all memory leaks are caused by the **leak.jsp** page:

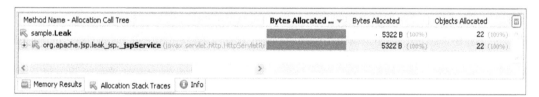

8. Good. So now you know the Class that is potentially causing the leak and where it has been instantiated. You can now complete your analysis by discovering which class is holding a reference to the leaked class.

9. You have to switch to the monitor tab and take a heap dump of the application. Once the dump is completed, filter on the **sample.Leak class** and go to the **Classes** view. You will find there the objects that are holding references to the leaked objects.

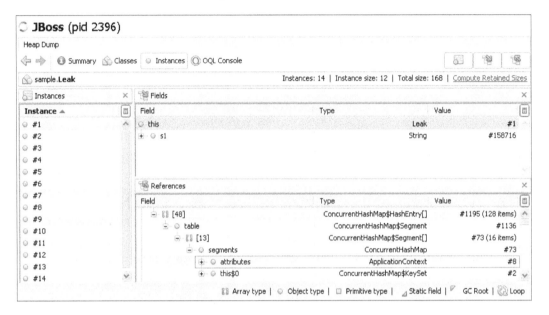

In this example, the **ApplicationContext** of a web application is the culprit as the unfortunate developer forgot to remove a large set of objects.

A practical example

Until now we have discussed many aspects of JVM tuning. All the concepts that you have learnt so far need a concrete example to be truly understood.

We will introduce here a complete JVM analysis use case, which can be used as pathfinder for your tuning sessions. In the first part of the example we will choose the correct amount of memory that needs to be allocated, then, we will try to improve the throughput of the application by setting the appropriate JVM options.

It is clearly intended that the optimal configuration differs from application to application so there is no magic formula which can be used in all scenarios. You should learn how to analyze your variables correctly and clearly find the best configuration.

Application description

You have been recruited by Acme Ltd to solve some performance issues with their web application. The chief analyst reported to you that, even if the code has been tested thoroughly, it's suspected that the application has got some memory leaks.

The Acme Web Computer Store is a quintessential web application, which is used to keep an on-line store of computer hardware items. The application lets the user log in, query the store, insert/modify orders, and customize the user's look and feel and preferences.

The application requires a Java EE 5 API and it is made up of a front-end layer developed with JSF Rich Faces technology and backed by Session Beans, and Entities.

Most of the data used by the application is driven through the **Servlet Request**, except for user settings, which are stored in the user's **HttpSession**.

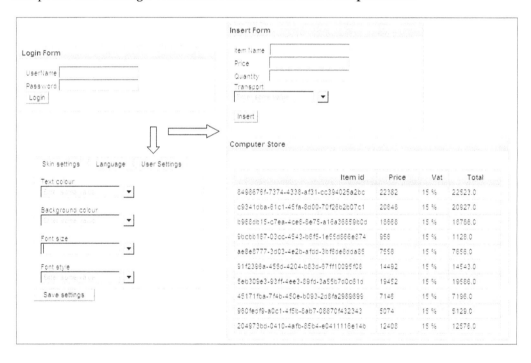

The application is deployed on a JBoss AS 5.1.0, which is hosted on the following hardware/software configuration:

- 4 CPU Xeon dual core
- Operating System: Linux Fedora 12 (64 bit)
- JVM 1.6 update 20

Setting up a test bed

The application has an average of 400 concurrent users navigating once through every page of the Web application (which are four in total). Since we require to keep running this benchmark for about 30 minutes, we have calculated that the test need to be repeated for about 250 times. We have allowed a 200ms time interval to make the test more realistic.

In total, that's 1000 pages for each user and a total of 400,000 total pages requested. Here's our Thread configuration on JMeter:

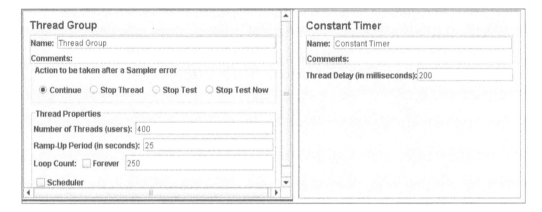

The amount of loops which need to be performed in a test bed

It depends mostly on the response time of the application and the hardware we are using. You should experiment with a small repeat loop and then multiply the loop to reach the desired benchmark length. In our case we tested that with 400 users and 50 repeats, the benchmark lasted around 6 minutes, so we have increased the repeats to 250 to reach a 30 minute benchmark.

Once we are done with the JMeter configuration, we are ready to begin the test.

As first benchmark, it's always best to start with the default JVM settings and see how the application performs. We will just include a minimal JVM heap configuration, just to allow the completion of the test:

```
set JAVA_OPTS=%JAVA_OPTS% -Xmx1024m -Xms1024m
```

Benchmark aftermath

Here's a screenshot of the JVM heap taken from the VisualVM monitor:

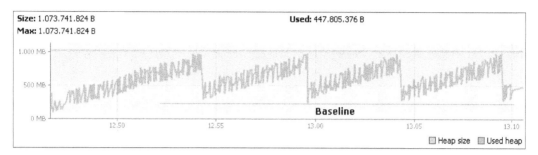

There are two elements, which draw your attention immediately:

Consideration #1

At first, you disagree that the application has got a memory leak. The heap memory grows up at regular interval with high crests. However, after each garbage collection, the memory dips to the same baseline, around 300 MB. Also the peak memory stays around 800 MB.

However, the fact that the application's heap grows steadily and can recover memory just at fixed intervals is a symptom that, for some time, lots of objects are instantiated. Then, a bit later, these objects are reclaimed and memory is recovered. This issue is well shown by the typical *mountains top's* heap trend.

What is likely to happen is that the application uses the HttpSession to store data. As new users kick in, the HttpSession reclaims memory. When the sessions expire, lots of data is eligible for garbage collector.

Consideration #2

Second, the impact of major collections is too high—the JVM spent an average of 1.7 seconds for each major collection because of the amount of objects that needed to be reclaimed. The total time spent by the application in the garbage collection is about 1 min. 46 sec. (of which 1' spent in minor collections and 46'' in major collections).

The following screenshot is taken from the VisualGC tab (See *Chapter 2* to install the VisualGC plugin):

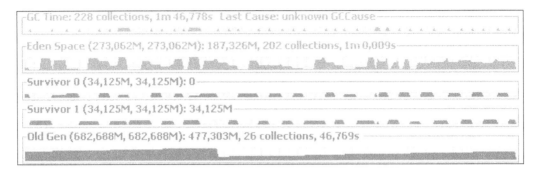

Action

The first fix we need to add will be increasing the size of the young generation. As it's evident from the graph, lots of objects are created. Both short-lived and medium-lived. If we let all these objects flow in the tenured generation, it will be necessary for a frequent evacuation of the whole JVM heap.

Let's try to change the JBoss AS's default JVM settings, increasing the amount of young generation to 448 MB:

```
set JAVA_OPTS=%JAVA_OPTS% -Xmx1024m -Xms1024m -XX:MaxNewSize=448m
-
XX:NewSize=448m -XX:SurvivorRatio=6
```

 As we have stated in the first chapter, it's important to introduce a single change in every benchmark, otherwise we will not be able to understand which parameter caused the actual change.

So let's run again the benchmark with the updated heap configuration. This is the new graph from the monitor tab:

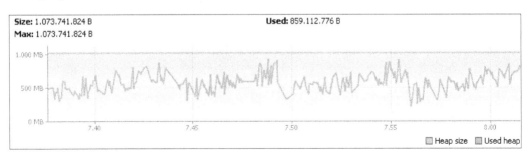

It's easy to guess that things got a lot better: the new heap's trend looks rather like a sore tooth now, which is a symptom that the memory is regularly cleared in the early stages of the objects' lives. The VisualGC panel confirms this visual estimate:

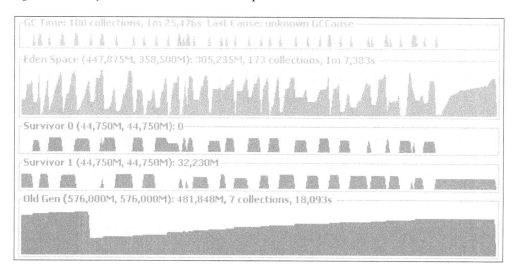

The total amount of time spent in garbage collection dropped down for over 20 seconds, especially because the number of major collections was drastically reduced.

The time spent for each major collection stays a bit too high and we ascribe this to the fact that the application uses about 10KB of Objects in the HttpSession. Half of this amount is spent to customize each page Skin, adding an HTML header section containing the user's properties.

At this stage, the staff of Acme Ltd does not allow major changes in the architecture of the web application, however by removing the block of text stored in the HttpSession and substituting with a dynamically included HTML skin, the amount of data stored in the HttpSession would drop down significantly, as shown by the following graph, which shows how an ideal application heap should look like.

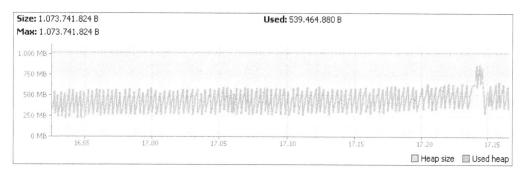

Further optimization

The Acme Ltd representative is quite satisfied with the throughput of the application; nevertheless, we are asked to pursue an additional effort in reducing the occasional long pauses, which happen when major collections kick in. Our customer would like to keep a maximum response time of no more than 2.5 seconds for delivering each response; with the current configuration, there's a very little amount of requests, which cannot fulfill this requirement.

The following picture, taken from JMeter's aggregate report, shows that a group of HTTP Request pages report a maximum response over the 2.5 limit.

Label	# Samples	Average	Median	90% Line	Min	Max	Error %	Throughput	KB/sec
HTTP Requ...	100000	316	311	595	143	2121	0,00%	38,9/sec	1,0
HTTP Requ...	100000	472	463	750	145	2396	0,00%	39,0/sec	1,0
HTTP Requ...	100000	556	556	815	238	2839	0,00%	38,0/sec	,8
HTTP Requ...	100000	556	556	815	238	2939	0,00%	38,8/sec	,8
TOTAL	400000	448	442	745	155	2256	0,00%	154,4/sec	3,6

Since we are running the application on a server class machine, the default algorithm chosen by the JVM for garbage collection is the parallel collector, which is particularly fit for applications requiring a high throughput for example, a financial application or a data warehouse application performing batch processing tasks.

We would need, however, an algorithm, which can guarantee that GC pauses will not take that long, at the price of an overall little performance degradation. The **concurrent collector** is particularly fit for application like ours, where latency takes precedence over throughput. In order to enable the concurrent collector we use the flag -XX:+UseConcMarkSweepGC, so this is our new set of Java options:

```
set JAVA_OPTS=%JAVA_OPTS% -Xmx1024m -Xms1024m -XX:MaxNewSize=448m
-
XX:NewSize=448m -XX:SurvivorRatio=6 -XX:+UseConcMarkSweepGC
```

Following here, is the VisualGC tab resulting after benchmarking the application with the concurrent collector:

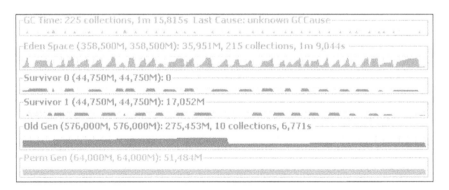

As you can see, the time spent in garbage collection has been further reduced to 1'15" seconds This is generally because the Old Generation collection dipped just to 6.7", even if the number of collection events increased. That's because the garbage collection pauses with the concurrent collector are short and frequent.

The aggregate report from JMeter shows that the application throughput has slightly dropped, while remaining still acceptable, but no single request was server over 2.1 seconds:

Label	# Samples	Average	Median	90% Line	Min	Max	Error %	Throughput	KB/sec
HTTP Requ...	100000	318	311	615	140	1211	0,00%	38,0/sec	1,0
HTTP Requ...	100000	489	463	760	145	1496	0,00%	38,7/sec	1,0
HTTP Requ...	100000	586	556	895	258	2045	0,00%	37,0/sec	,8
HTTP Requ...	100000	576	556	885	238	2039	0,00%	37,4/sec	,8
TOTAL	400000	488	442	755	145	2123	0,00%	151,1/sec	3,6

While there are still margins for improving the application, for example by analyzing what's happening on the persistence layer, at the moment we have applied all the fixes necessary to tune the JVM. If you check the Oracle/Sun JVM docs there are a pretty good number of other parameters which you can apply to tune the heap (`http://java.sun.com/javase/technologies/hotspot/vmoptions.jsp`), however we suggest you not to specialize too much your JVM configuration, because the benefits you could gain, might be invalidated in the next JDK release.

Summary

JVM tuning is an ever-evolving process that has changed with each version of Java. Since the release 5.0 of the J2SE, the JVM is able to provide some default configuration (Ergonomics), which is consistent with your environment. However, the smarter choice provided by Ergonomics is not always the optimal and without an explicit user setting, the performance can fall below your expectations.

Basically, the JVM tuning process can be divided into three steps:

- **Choose a correct JVM heap size.** This can be divided into setting an appropriate initial heap size (-Xms) and a maximum heap size (-Xmx).
    - ° Choose an initial heap size equal to maximum heap size for production environment. For development environment set up the initial heap size to about half the maximum size.
    - ° Don't exceed the 2GB limit for a single application server instance or the garbage collector performance might become a bottleneck.

- **Choose a correct ratio between young generations** (where objects are initially placed after instantiation) and the tenured generation (where old lived generations are moved).

    ○ For most applications, the correct ratio between the young generation and the tenured generation ranges between 1/3 and close to ½.

    ○ Keep this suggested configuration as reference for smaller environments and larger ones:

```
java -Xmx1024m -Xms1024m -XX:MaxNewSize=448m -
XX:NewSize=448m -XX:SurvivorRatio=6
java -Xmx2048m -Xms2048m -XX:MaxNewSize=896m -
XX:NewSize=896m -XX:SurvivorRatio=6
```

- Choose a Garbage collector algorithm which is consistent with your Service Level requirements.

- The serial collector (-XX:+UseSerialGC) performs garbage collector using a single thread which stops other JVM threads. This collector is fit for smaller applications, we don't advise using it for Enterprise applications

- The parallel collector (-XX:+UseParallelGC) performs minor collections in parallel and since J2SE 5.0 can perform major collections in parallel as well (-XX:+UseParallelOldGC). This collector is fit for multi-processor machines and applications requiring high throughput. It is also a suggested choices for applications which produce a fragmented Java heap, allocating large sized objects at different timelines

- The concurrent collector (-XX:+UseConcMarkSweepGC) performs most of its work concurrently using a single garbage collector thread that runs simultaneously with the application threads. It is fit for fast processor machines and applications with strict a service level agreement. It can be the best choice also for applications using a large set of long lived objects live HttpSessions.

In the next chapter we begin our exploration of the JBoss application server, starting at first with the basic configuration provided in the 4.X and 5.X releases, which is common to all applications. Then during the next chapters, we will explore the specific modules, which allow you to run Java EE applications.

Tuning the JBoss AS

3rd Circle of Hell: Gluttony. In this circle lie developers who over-consumpted database connections as a replacement for fixing connection leaks.

Tuning the application server is a complex activity which requires complete knowledge of the key server configuration files. JBoss application server has made a major change with release 5.0, moving from the JMX kernel to the newest POJO-based kernel. As a consequence, the configuration files and the memory requirements of the application server have changed as well.

- In the first part of this chapter, we will introduce the basic system requirements of JBoss AS 4.x and 5.x releases and how to create a customized, faster server configuration, using just the services required by your applications.

- In the next part, we will examine how the application server provides its basic services by means of resource pooling, which is a technique used to control the server resources and improve the performance of the applications using these resources.

- At the end, we will learn how the logging service influences the performance of your applications and how to choose a configuration which reduces to a minimum the overhead of logs notifications.

From release 4.x to 5.x, and on

The JBoss project was initially developed in 1999 as a middleware research product. At that time, the application server provided barely an EJB container but, thanks to the interest of a growing community, the project quickly expanded to incorporate a complete portfolio of products.

One of the most important milestones of the project was release 4.x which is still the most used in production environments: this release, built on top of the highly successful 3.x line, was the first production-ready Java EE 1.4 application server in the industry.

Some of the key features of this innovative release are: full support for Java Web Services and Service Oriented Architectures (SOA), full integration with the Hibernate persistence framework, and improved clustering and caching support.

At the end of 2008, a new major release of the application server hit the industry. The long awaited 5.0 release was finally born: based on the new **Microcontainer kernel** which replaced the earlier JMX implementation in most application server areas, release 5.x provides also the latest implementation of Java EE 1.5 features along with the integration of many other standalone projects.

However, all these new features come at a price. As a matter of fact release 5.0 and its minor releases, demand a greater amount of resources (basically memory and CPU), so it is generally considered a heavyweight release compared to 4.x.

The truth is that the 5.x release was designed to be a completely modular and extensible one so it's necessary to go beyond the basic configuration provided out of the box. Many developers experienced huge performance gains by selecting just a subset of services or by replacing the existing ones with custom services.

What about the future? release 5.x introduced a major change in the application server architecture, which is largely maintained also in the 6.x release. What we are expecting from the 6.x release is full integration with the newest Java EE 1.6 specifications, the complete integration of the POJO kernel and some important improvements in specific areas, like the Messaging system (HornetQ messaging system) and a new load balancing solution (`mod_cluster`).

Comparing server releases

At this point it could be useful to compare the requirements of different server versions. Release 4.x, based on the JMX kernel, has the advantage of being lighter compared to 5.x and 6.x. At startup, a default server configuration takes about 130 MB, committing half of this memory, and loading about 5,000 classes:

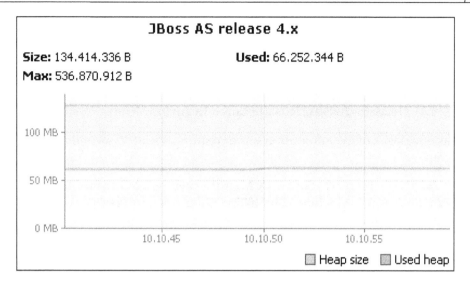

The new 5.x container effectively reproduces all the features of the 4.x JMX microkernel in the new POJO-based kernel. Compared with the older kernel, the new POJO kernel is based on the Microcontainer 2.0 project and offers a layered and easily extensible design (no references to JBoss classes) and much improved dependency injection and classloading.

What are the memory requirements of the new architecture? As you can see from the following image, at startup, the release 5.x of the application commits over double the amount of memory and loads about 10,000 classes:

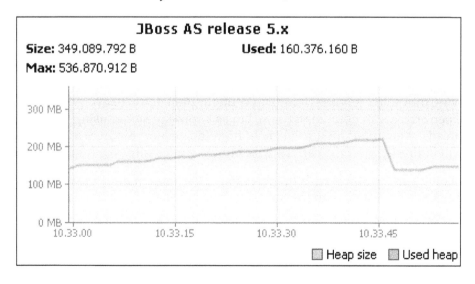

One of the major complaints of developers is the amount of time needed to startup release 5.x of the application server which accounts to one about 90 seconds on a typical developer's configuration:

12:01:58,138 INFO [ServerImpl] JBoss (Microcontainer) [5.1.0.GA (build: SVNTag=

JBoss_5_1_0_GA date=200905221053)] Started in 1m:32s:375ms

Whereas release 4.x of the application server requires about 30 seconds for starting up:

11:52:09,766 INFO [Server] JBoss (MX MicroKernel) [4.2.2.GA (build: SVNTag=JBoss_4_2_2_GA date=200710221139)] Started in 34s:484ms

This sensible difference is due to the different amount of classes loaded by the two containers and also to the extensive **custom meta data** scanning executed by JBoss AS 5.x (see this resouce for more information: `https://community.jboss.org/ wiki/JBoss5custommetadatafiles`).

In order to speed up your development and reduce hardware demands, you should consider creating a customized JBoss AS 5.x server configuration, removing all services that are not required by your application. This strategy requires a minimum of knowledge of JBoss AS's structure but it suits perfectly the nature of the application server, which allows deploying/undeploying services by means of simply adding and removing a file.

We will therefore dedicate the next section to learning how to provide a customized application server configuration.

Creating a custom application server configuration

Removing unwanted services from your configuration doesn't have a direct impact on the performance of your application, but as a consequence of using less memory and threads, your application will benefit from the greater resources available and thus will indirectly meet the performance targets more easily.

The following histogram reveals (in percentage) the amount of memory engaged by a single service, along with the time spent for starting it up and the number of classes loaded:

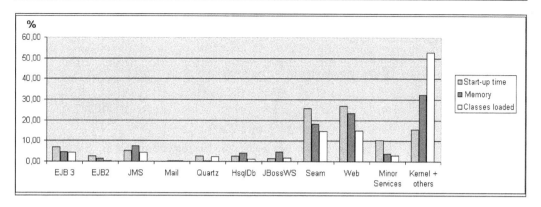

What draws your attention immediately is the relevance of **Seam** libraries which include the new **admin-console** application, accounting for about 18% of the total memory and a detrimental 25% in the time spent for starting it up.

The admin-console has been included by default in release 5.1 of the application server and it provides a better administration interface than the jmx-console. However, from the performance point of view, *you are strongly advised to remove this application from your server configuration.*

JBoss AS 6.0.0 includes an experimental new feature called support for **on-demand deployment** of web applications. The main intent of this feature is to speed the startup of the AS in development and test environments by deferring the deployment of the management console applications that ship with the AS.

Convenient slimming targets also include **Hypersonic Db**, which is an in-memory pure Java database. Even if Hypersonic Db is adequate for developing and testing applications, you should replace it in production with a solid alternative. Consider removing the **Mail Service** as well and the **Quartz Scheduler**, if you don't need to use a scheduler service.

Finally, the list of 'minor services' include a collection of services which are pretty useless for most applications like the JUDDI service, the Key Generator, BSH deployer, the XNIO-provider, SQL Exception Service, and JMX Remoting.

The Following is a table containing the checklist of services and how to remove them, borrowed from JBoss AS wiki:

Service	Files / directories to be removed
EJB3 services	`deploy/ejb3-connectors-jboss-beans.xml`
	`deploy/ejb3-container-jboss-beans.xml`
	`deploy/ejb3-interceptors-aop.xml`
	`deploy/ejb3-timerservice-jboss-beans.xml`
	`deploy/profileservice-secured.jar`
	`deployers/jboss-ejb3-endpoint-deployer.jar`
EJB 2 services	`deploy/ejb2-container-jboss-beans.xml`
	`deploy/ejb2-timer-service.xml`
JUDDI	`deploy/juddi-service.sar`
Key Generator	`deploy/uuid-key-generator.sar`
JMS	`deploy/messaging`
	`deploy/jms-ra.rar`
	`deployers/messaging-definitions-jboss-beans.xml`
Mail Service	`deploy/mail-service.xml`
	`deploy/mail-ra.rar`
Scheduling	`deploy/schedule-manager-service.xml`
	`deploy/scheduler-service.xml`
	`deploy/quartz-ra.rar`
Hypersonic DB	`deploy/hsqldb-ds.xml`
Jboss WS	`deploy/jbossws.sar`
	`deployers/jbossws.deployer`
Seam	`deploy/admin-console.war`
	`deployers/seam.deployer`
	`deployers/webbeans.deployer`
Minor services	`deployers/bsh.deployer`
	`deploy/hdscanner-jboss-beans.xml`
	`deployers/xnio.deployer`
	`deploy/jmx-remoting.sar`
	`deploy/profileservice-secured.jar deploy/` `sqlexception-service.xml`

Reference: `http://community.jboss.org/wiki/JBoss5xTuningSlimming`.

 Please note that the juddi service ships just with the "standard" server configuration.

JBoss AS pools

Most services provided by the application server are granted by means of the pooling of resources. Keeping these resources in a pool avoids the burden of re-creating costly resources like database connections and can be used as well to limit the amount of requests to be processed by the application server. As a matter of fact, allowing an indiscriminate number of requests to access your resources can be quite dangerous and can expose your system to potential threats.

JBoss AS defines a large list of pools, which, depending on the nature of your application, can become a potential bottleneck if you don't configure them appropriately.

The following table introduces the list of pools, adding the relevant configuration information for it. You need to replace "<server>" with your server configuration, for example JBOSS_HOME/server/default is the path of the default configuration.

Pool	Used for	Configuration
System thread pool	For JNDI naming	`<server>/conf/jboss-service.xml`
JDBC connection pool	When making JDBC connections	`<server>/deploy/xxx-ds.xml`
HTTP thread pool	When handling HTTP requests	`<server>/deploy/jboss-web.sar/server.xml`
AJP thread pool	When handling HTTP requests through `mod_jk`	`<server>/deploy/jboss-web.sar/server.xml`
WorkManager thread pool	In conjunction with JMS, as JBoss Messaging uses JCA inflow as the integration into EAP	`<server>/deploy/jca-jboss-beans.xml`
JBoss Messaging thread pool (for remote clients)	Pools the TCP sockets	`<server>/deploy/messaging/remoting-bisocket-service.xml`
EJB 3 (same JVM)	Will use the same thread pool that invoked the EJB. For example, local HTTP clients will use the HTTP thread pool to invoke the EJB	-
EJB (remote clients)	When making remote EJB calls	`<server>/deployers/ejb3.deployer/META-INF/ejb3-deployers-jboss-beans.xml`

In this chapter, we will cover the **System thread pool,** which is used for accessing resources through **Java Naming and Directory Interface (JNDI)**, and the **Java Database Connectivity (JDBC) connection pool** which handles database connections.

The **JBoss Messaging pools** and **EJB pools** are described in *Chapter 5, Tuning the Middleware Services*, that is devoted to middleware services tuning.

The **HTTP pool** and **AJP pool** on the other hand, are covered in *Chapter 8, Tomcat Web Server Tuning*, along with the web container-tuning configuration.

The System thread pool

The System thread pool is used by JBoss AS to control the requests which are accessing the application server resources through the JNDI tree. The Java Naming and Directory Interface is a Java API that allows Java software clients to discover and look up data and objects using a name.

This pool is defined in the `<server>/conf/jboss-service.xml` file. Here's the core section of it:

```
<mbean code="org.jboss.util.threadpool.BasicThreadPool"
    name="jboss.system:service=ThreadPool">
    <attribute name="Name">JBoss System Threads</attribute>
    <attribute name="ThreadGroupName">System Threads</attribute>
    <attribute name="KeepAliveTime">60000</attribute>
    <attribute name="MaximumPoolSize">10</attribute>
    <attribute name="MaximumQueueSize">1000</attribute>
    <attribute name="BlockingMode">run</attribute>    </mbean>
```

And this is the meaning of these parameters:

- `MinimumPoolSize`: The minimum number of threads to keep active. By default 0.
- `MaximumPoolSize`: The maximum number of threads which can be active (default 100).
- `KeepAliveTime`: How long to keep threads alive when there is nothing to do. Time is expressed in milli-seconds (default 60000 = 1 minute).
- `MaximumQueueSize`: The maximum number of requests that are waiting to be executed (default 1024).
- When all your threads are busy and the waiting Queue has also reached the MaximumQueueSize, then the last parameter (`BlockingMode`) comes into play.

Setting `BlockingMode` to `abort` will determine a RuntimeException when a new request attempts to enter the busy thread queue. On the contrary, the default `run` will give priority to the calling thread, which will be able to execute the task. Setting the parameter to `wait` will force the calling thread to wait until the thread queue has room, while the option `discard` will simply discard the calling thread:

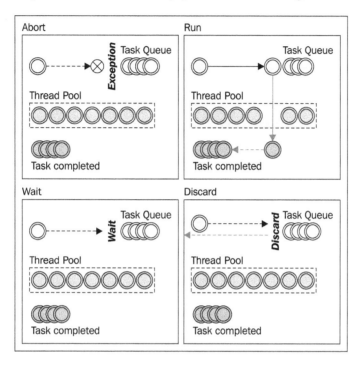

Actually, there is a last option "discardOldest" which works exactly as "discard", except that it ultimately performs a scan of the thread pool to see if a thread is about to complete before discarding the request.

JNDI lookups are *relatively expensive*, so caching an object that requires a lookup in client code or application code avoids incurring this performance hit more than once.

From Java EE 1.5 onwards, you can also use **dependency injection** to perform a single lookup to add the resources to your classes. For example, the following annotation:

```
@EJB MySession session;
```

is translated by the application server into:

```
MySession x = (MySession)
        new InitialContext().lookup(«java:comp/env/Class_
ID»);
Field f = MyClass.class.getDeclaredField(«session»);
f.set(this, x);
```

Notice that when using EJB 3.0's dependency injection there's a *slight overhead* because, behind the scenes, the application server uses **reflection** to set the EJB variable field in your class.

Finding out if the System thread pool is a bottleneck

The default settings for the System thread pool are generally good for most applications so we will not take long with this topic.

However, in the unfortunate event that you have to optimize an application which does not cache JNDI entries, the System thread pool can become an additional bottleneck for your application.

Discovering this threat is not complicated and can be done with a simple configuration hack. In practice, you should set the MaximumQueueSize to 0, which means that the application server will not accept any new task when the System thread pool is full:

```
<attribute name="MaximumQueueSize">0</attribute>
```

Now load test your application and check for any CommunicationException in your client console. You may find the following error trace thrown by the org.jnp.interfaces.NamingContext class:

```
Caused by: javax.naming.CommunicationException: Failed to
connect to server localhost:1099 [Root exception is javax.
naming.ServiceUnavailableException: Failed to connect to server
localhost:1099 [Root exception is java.net.ConnectException:
Connection refused: connect]]
```

```
    at org.jnp.interfaces.NamingContext.getServer(NamingContext.java:311)
    at org.jnp.interfaces.NamingContext.checkRef(NamingContext.java:1698)
```

Then it's time to upgrade your System thread pool configuration, increasing the
`MaximumPoolSize` attribute.

JDBC connection pool

A connection pool is a cache of database connections maintained by the application
server so that they can be reused when the database receives future requests for data.

Connection pools can dramatically enhance the performance of executing commands
against a database as opening and maintaining a database connection for each user is
a quite costly operation.

Configuring a connection pool with JBoss AS can be done by means of a simple
`-ds.xml` file which needs to be dropped in the `deploy` folder of the application
server.

```
<datasources>
   <local-tx-datasource>
      <jndi-name>MySQLDS</jndi-name>
      <connection-url>jdbc:mysql://localhost:3306/spring</connection-
       url>
      <driver-class>com.mysql.jdbc.Driver</driver-class>
      <user-name>spring_test</user-name>
      <password>spring_test13</password>

      <min-pool-size>1</min-pool-size>
      <max-pool-size>15</max-pool-size>

      <idle-timeout-minutes>10</idle-timeout-minutes>
      <blocking-timeout-millis>30000</blocking-timeout-millis>
   </local-tx-datasource>
</datasources>
```

The basic pool parameters are the `min-pool-size` attribute, which is used to
determine the minimum connections to store in a pool.

The `max-pool-size` element corresponds to the maximum limit of connections
allowed in a pool.

The actual amount of connections stored in a connection pool is a variable attribute,
in our example, *connections that are idle for over 10 minutes will be automatically
destroyed*, and the poll will be resized up to the `min-pool-size` attribute.

Since JBoss AS 5, there's an additional attribute, which can be used to bypass the `min-pool-size` limit, where you have idle connections. The attribute is `use-strict-min` — which therefore allows connections below the `min-pool-size` to be closed.

If you attempt to acquire a new connection from the pool when all resources are checked out, the application server will wait for a maximum time (in milliseconds) specified by the `blocking-timeout-millis`. If no resources can be acquired by that time, the following exception will be raised:

```
ERROR [STDERR] Caused by: javax.resource.ResourceException: No
ManagedConnections available within configured blocking timeout (
30000 [ms] )
ERROR [STDERR]      at org.jboss.resource.connectionmanager.Internal
ManagedConnectionPool.getConnection(InternalManagedConnectionPool.
java:305)
```

Calculating the optimal min-pool-size and max-pool-size

In order to calculate the optimal pool size it's important to know how many connections your application requires. The pool attributes can be monitored using the JMX-console, which contains a reference to the connection pool in the `jboss.jca` domain and an MBean definition in `name=<DataSourceName>,service=ManagedConnectionPool`.

For example, the DefaultDS can be configured by means of the MBean `name=DefaultDS,service=ManagedConnectionPool`.

`ConnectionCount` is the number of connections established with the database. These connections are *not necessarily in use* and after the idle timeout minute, they are candidates to be destroyed (provided that the application has not reached a `min-pool-size`).

If you want to know the actual amount of connections in use, you have to check the `InUseConnectionCount` attribute.

The most important attribute for calculating the optimal pool size is the `Max Connections In Use Count`, which can be obtained by invoking the `listStatistics` method of the managed pool.

The following is a sample output from the action:

```
Sub Pool Statistics:
 Sub Pool Count:1
-----------------------------------------------------------------
 Track By Transaction:true
 Available Connections Count:100
 Max Connections In Use Count:15
 Connections Destroyed Count:0
 Connections In Use Count:4
 Total Block Time:0
 Average Block Time For Sub Pool:0
 Maximum Wait Time For Sub Pool:0
 Total Timed Out Connections:0
-----------------------------------------------------------------
```

 If your Max Connections In Use Count equals to the max-pool-size, then your application is likely to have a bottleneck in your datasource configuration. The Block Time statistics should indicate exactly how much time has been spent waiting for a new connection.

To correctly size a connection pool for your application, you should create load test scripts and set the max-pool-size to a consistent value (let's say you expect a load of 100 concurrent users, then you could set this value to about 150).

Then, when the test is completed, check for the Max Connection In Use Count and set the max-pool-size to a relatively larger attribute (let's say 20% more).

If you want to avoid the overhead of pool resizing, you can set the min-pool-size *to the same value as* max-pool-size. You should as well add the following element to your DataSoruce configuration so that JBoss AS attempts to prefill the pool size at deployment time; otherwise the first user accessing the pool will pay the pool build-up cost:

```
<prefill />
```

The major limitation to this sort of eager initialization is that database connections are a *shared resource*, which should not be monopolized by a single application that never sets them free back to the database.

Also remember that setting the pool size attributes doesn't mean that you will *actually* be able to use that number of connections. Every RDMS has got a limited number of cursors, which are available for executing SQL statements. For example, Oracle DB has the OPEN_CURSOR parameter, which triggers the message *"ORA-01000: maximum open cursors"* exceeded if you try to reclaim new connections beyond this limit.

Using Prepared Statements efficiently

When a database receives a statement, the database engine first parses the SQL string and looks for syntax errors. Once the statement is parsed, the database needs to figure out the most efficient plan to execute the statement. This can be computationally quite expensive. Once the query plan is created, the database engine can execute it.

Ideally, if we send the same statement to the database twice, then we'd like the database to reuse the access plan for the first statement. This uses less CPU than if it regenerated the plan a second time. In Java, you can obtain a good performance boost by using Prepared Statements and, instead of concatenating the parameters as a string, by using markers:

```
PreparedStatement ps = conn.prepareStatement("select a,b from t where
c = ?");
```

This allows the database to reuse the access plans for the statement and makes the program execute more efficiently inside the database. This basically lets your application run faster or makes more CPU available to users of the database.

Prepared Statements can be cached by the application server itself when it's necessary to issue the same statements across different requests. Enabling the Prepared Statements cache is quite simple; all you have to do is insert the following fragment, with the desired cache size in your datasource file:

```
<prepared-statement-cache-size>32</prepared-statement-cache-size>
```

This attribute indicates the number of Prepared Statements per connection to be kept open and reused in subsequent requests.

In practice, JBoss AS keeps a list of Prepared Statements for each database connection in the pool. When an application prepares a new Statement on a connection, the application server checks if that statement was previously used. If it was, the PreparedStatement object will be recovered from the cache and this will be returned to the application. If not, the call is passed to the JDBC driver and the query/PreparedStatement object is added in that connections cache.

The cache used by Prepared Statements is an LRU cache (Least Recently Used). This means that statements are moved at the bottom of the cache until newer statements replace them.

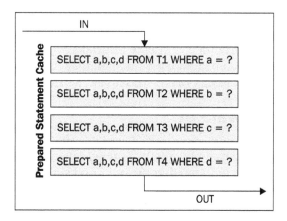

If you don't add this attribute, the default is 0 (zero), meaning no cache.

The performance benefit provided by the Prepared Statement cache is very application-specific, varying from 10% up to 30% for an application using a mix of different statements, Prepared Statements, and Callable Statements.

In the following benchmark we have tried to reproduce a similar scenario, scoring a consistent 20% gain for an application using a correctly sized Prepared Statement cache:

Label	# Samples	Average	Median	90% Line	Min	Max	Error %	Throughput	KB/sec
HTTP Request	5000	12	6	13	4	1527	0,00%	64,6/sec	17,1
TOTAL	5000	12	6	13	4	1527	0,00%	64,6/sec	17,1

Prepared Statement Cache OFF

Label	# Samples	Average	Median	90% Line	Min	Max	Error %	Throughput	KB/sec
HTTP Reque...	5000	8	3	6	2	2061	0,00%	78,3/sec	18,1
TOTAL	5000	8	3	6	2	2061	0,00%	78,3/sec	18,1

Prepared Statement cache ON

So, you might wonder, how do we set the optimal cache size? The rigorous approach is to check how many *unique Statements are sent to the DB*. If you haven't planned to include SQL logging in your application, then you can consider using some third-party projects like P6Spy, which intercepts calls issued to the database driver, and logs the statement along with useful timing statistics.

On the author's blog you can find a complete tutorial about tracing SQL statements with P6Spy and JBoss AS: `http://www.mastertheboss.com/jboss-server/259-how-to-trace-jdbc-statements-with-jboss-as.html`.

Two things to be aware of:

1. Prepared statements are *cached per connection*. The more connections you have, the more Prepared Statements you get (even when they are the same query). So use them with parsimony and don't simply guess how many are needed by your application.

2. When the connection pool shrinks because the idle timeout for a connection expires, Statements are *removed from the pool of cached Prepared Statements*. This can cause an overhead, which outweighs the benefit of caching statements.

One good compromise that I have tried on a few projects is to create two DataSources for your application, a larger one (let's say with up to 30 connections) with no Prepared Statement cache, and a smaller one with a Prepared Statement cache activated and `min-pool-size` equal to `max-pool-size`, in order to avoid any pool shrink. Here's a sample DataSource, which can be used as a template:

```
<datasources>
    <local-tx-datasource>
        <jndi-name>CachedMySQLDS</jndi-name>
        <connection-url>jdbc:mysql://localhost:3306/spring</connection-url>
        <driver-class>com.mysql.jdbc.Driver</driver-class>
        <user-name>user</user-name>
        <password>password</password>
        <min-pool-size>10</min-pool-size>
        <max-pool-size>10</max-pool-size>
        <prepared-statement-cache-size>10</prepared-statement-cache-size>
    </local-tx-datasource>
</datasources>
```

Detecting connection leaks

One of the first things you learn about Java Enterprise classes is that every time you have ended with your connection, you should close it (along with the Statements and ResultSet) in a `finally` block; this way you'll avoid running into a connection leak if the method has raised an exception:

```
Connection connection = null;
PreparedStatement stmt = null;
ResultSet rs = null;

try {
Connection connection = getConnection();
PreparedStatement stmt =   connection.prepareStatement("Select a from
b where c = 1";
ResultSet rs = stmt.executeQuery();

. . . .

}
catch (Exception exc) {

. . .

}
finally {

   try {

       if (rs != null) rs.close();
       if (stmt != null) stmt.close();
       if (connection != null) connection.close();

   }
   catch (SQLException exc) {

       . . .

   }
}
```

Connection leaks, like memory leaks, are not a direct cause of a performance loss but an inefficient use of system resources, which is often solved by allocating extra resources. Unfortunately system resources are not infinite so, if you need to allocate extra memory to cope with your leaks, there will be less resources available for your application.

Luckily, detecting connection leaks is quite easy and can be done by means of the `CachedConnectionManager` MBean which is defined in the `<server>/deploy/jca-jboss-beans.xml` file.

```
<mbean code="org.jboss.resource.connectionmanager.
CachedConnectionManager"
        name="jboss.jca:service=CachedConnectionManager">
    <depends optional-attribute-name="TransactionManagerServiceName">j
boss:service=TransactionManager</depends>
    <attribute name="SpecCompliant">false</attribute>
    <attribute name="Debug">true</attribute>
</mbean>
```

By setting the `Debug` attribute to `true`, the unclosed connections will be monitored by JBoss AS, which will issue this message on the console if you missed closing a connection:

```
17:41:24,520 INFO  [CachedConnectionManager] Closing a connection for
you.  Please close them yourself: org.jboss.resource.adapter.jdbc.
WrappedConnection@773a1
java.lang.Throwable: STACKTRACE
    at org.jboss.resource.connectionmanager.CachedConnectionManager.
register
Connection(CachedConnectionManager.java:290)
    at org.jboss.resource.connectionmanager.BaseConnectionManager2.
allocateC
onnection(BaseConnectionManager2.java:417)
    at org.jboss.resource.connectionmanager.BaseConnectionManager2$Con
nectio
nManagerProxy.allocateConnection(BaseConnectionManager2.java:842)
    at org.jboss.resource.adapter.jdbc.WrapperDataSource.
getConnection(Wrapp
erDataSource.java:88)
    at org.apache.jsp.connectionLeak_jsp._jspService(connectionLeak_
jsp.java:77)
    at org.apache.jasper.runtime.HttpJspBase.service(HttpJspBase.
java:70)
```

Please note that the class just below the method `WrapperDataSource.getConnection` in the Stacktrace: that's where you forgot to close the connection. (Precisely, in the `jspService` method of `connectionLeak.jsp` line 77).

If you need the count of unclosed connections along with their Stacktrace, you can then use the `listInUseConnections()` method from the `CachedConnectionManager` MBean which can be invoked from the JMX-console.

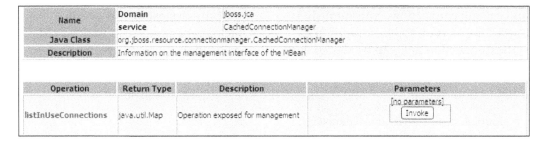

Name	Domain	jboss.jca
	service	CachedConnectionManager
Java Class	org.jboss.resource.connectionmanager.CachedConnectionManager	
Description	Information on the management interface of the MBean	

Operation	Return Type	Description		Parameters
listInUseConnections	java.util.Map	Operation exposed for management		[no parameters] Invoke

Closing connections is fundamental for keeping your application server healthy; however, Statements and ResultSets, that are instantiated during the connection need to be closed in the same way.

By adding the following fragment to your `-ds.xml`, the application server takes care of closing Statements and ResultSet if you miss it:

```
<track-statements>true</track-statements>
```

Use these helper statements only in the development stage!

Checking that your database interfaces are not causing any leak is extremely useful, however you need to know that rolling your applications in production with these flags activated is detrimental for the application performance. The same stands for `<new-connection-sql>` that executes a SQL statement every time a new connection is created or `<check-valid-connection-sql>` that checks if the connection from the pool is valid or it has gone stale.

Be sure to leaf off all of these statements when you are going for production if you don't want to pay a performance penalty.

Should you reuse connections or acquire new ones from the pool?

One of the most common misconceptions among Java developers is that acquiring and closing connections continuously from the pool stresses excessively your application server, so it's not rare to see classes like `DatabaseManager` which hold static Connection fields to be shared across the application.

If you are curious to know how much it costs (in terms of milliseconds) to acquire a connection from the pool and release it, the following code will show you:

```
double time1 = System.nanoTime();

Connection connection = datasource.getConnection();
connection.close();

double time2 = System.nanoTime();

System.out.println("Time to grab a connection " +(time2-
time1)/1000000);
[STDOUT]  0.218463
```

This test, executed on a Pentium 4 Dual Core 2.80 Ghz, reveals an unexpected low `0.2` milliseconds cost to check-in / check-out a connection from the server pool.

Of course this doesn't mean you need to abuse the connection pool when it's not necessary, for example, it's always good to reuse the same connection and statements if you are performing a set of database operation within the same thread.

However sharing your connection instance across several business methods is not a good idea as it can easily confuse who is using these classes and it can easily end up with connection leaks. So keep your code simple and tidy and don't be afraid to open and close your connections in every business method.

Logging for performance

In JBoss AS log4j is used as framework for logging. If you are not familiar with the log4j package and would like to use it in your applications, you can read more about it at the Jakarta website (http://jakarta.apache.org/log4j/).

Logging is controlled from a central `conf/jboss-log4j.xml` file. This file defines a set of appenders specifying the log files, what categories of messages should go there, the message format, and the level of filtering. By default, JBoss AS produces output to two appenders: the Console and a log File (located in `<server>/log/server.log`).

There are six basic log levels used: **TRACE, DEBUG, INFO, WARN, ERROR**, and **FATAL**. The logging threshold on the console is INFO, that means that you will see informational messages, warning messages, and error messages on the console but not general debug and trace messages. In contrast, there is no threshold set for the server.log file, so all generated logging messages will be logged there.

Choosing the best logging strategy

Logging information is an indispensable activity both in development and in production. However you should choose carefully what information is needed for debugging (development phase) and what information is needed for routine maintenance (production phase). Decide carefully about where to log information and about the formatting of the log messages so that the information can be processed and analyzed in the future by other applications.

Avoid logging unnecessary information. This will convolute the logging trace and affects badly the performance of your application. As a matter of fact, if you don't define any specific category for your classes, *they will inherit the default logging level of JBoss AS, which is set to INFO*. You should, as a general rule, stick to a higher level of logging for your classes, like WARN, for example.

If you don't want to modify the default logging level on the log4j file, you can pass the -Djboss.server.log.threshold parameter while starting the server. For example:

```
./run.sh -Djboss.server.log.threshold=WARN
```

In the following sections, we will uncover what are the best practices for logging your data with the minimum overhead for your application performance.

Which is the fastest appender?

As we said, JBoss AS defines two appenders for logging its activities: the Console appender and the File appender. The Console appender prints log information on the application server console. The File appender writes a log file which rotates every day or when it reaches a fixed size.

One of the biggest mistakes you could make is to roll your application in production with the server logs running on the console terminal. As a matter of fact, printing text to screen involves a lot of work for the OS in drawing the letters, scrolling, and a large amount of Java-native transitions which happen on every line break or flush.

Furthermore, on Windows OS, writing to the console is a blocking unbuffered operation, so writing lots of data to the console slows down (or blocks) your application.

The following Jmeter aggregate report documents the different throughput for a Servlet logging an 80 characters long text, on a test repeated 1000 times. The first test was executed against the Console appender, and the second with the File appender:

Label	# Samples	Average	Median	90% Line	Min	Max	Error %	Throughput	KB/sec
HTTP Request	1000	9	8	12	5	127	0,00%	100,2/sec	,0
TOTAL	1000	9	8	12	5	127	0,00%	100,2/sec	,0

Console Appender

Label	# Samples	Average	Median	90% Line	Min	Max	Error %	Throughput	KB/sec
HTTP Request	1000	3	3	4	2	74	0,00%	218,1/sec	,0
TOTAL	1000	3	3	4	2	74	0,00%	218,1/sec	,0

Default File Appender settings

As you can see, the throughput is more than double when the File appender is used. So as a golden rule, *disable Console logging in production and use only the File appender for better logging performance.*

You can further tune your File appender by setting the `ImmediateFlush` attribute to false:

```
<param name="ImmediateFlush" value="false" />
```

By default, the File appender performs a flush operation after writing each event, ensuring that the message is immediately written to disk. Setting the `ImmediateFlush` option to false can drastically reduce I/O activity since the Output-StreamWriter will buffer logs in memory before writing them to disk.

The performance gain is particularly important for shorter messages where throughput gains are in the range of 100% or even more. For longer messages it can account for somewhat less, and range between 40% and 60%.

This is the same test executed with the option `ImmediateFlush` set to false:

Label	# Samples	Average	Median	90% Line	Min	Max	Error %	Throughput	KB/sec
HTTP Request	1000	3	3	3	2	49	0,00%	277,5/sec	,0
TOTAL	1000	3	3	3	2	49	0,00%	277,5/sec	,0

File Appender ImmediateFlush = false

Another performance gain can be achieved by enabling the `BufferedIO` option. If set to `true`, the File will be kept open and the resulting Writer wrapped around a BufferedWriter. This leads to an increase in performance by an additional 10% to 40% compared to only disk I/O buffering (`ImmediateFlush=false`). The following image shows evidence of it, with a new throughput record for our Servlet:

Label	# Samples	Average	Median	90% Line	Min	Max	Error %	Throughput	KB/sec
HTTP Request	1000	3	3	3	2	97	0,00%	304,0/sec	,0
TOTAL	1000	3	3	3	2	97	0,00%	304,0/sec	,0
File Appender with ImmediateFlush = false and BufferIO = true									

Performance of `BufferedIO` anyway varies somewhat depending on the host machine, and can be significantly higher on systems which are heavily I/O loaded.

Should I use the AsyncAppender to improve my log throughput?

The AsyncAppender can be used to log events asynchronously.

Behind the scenes, this appender uses a *bounded queue* to store events. Every time a log is emitted, the `AsyncAppender.append()` method immediately returns after placing events in the bounded queue. An internal thread called the **Dispatcher** thread serves the events accumulated in the bounded queue

The AsyncAppender is included (but commented by default) in JBoss's log4j configuration. When you include it in your configuration, *you should take care that the appender references any other appender*. As a matter of fact, the AsyncAppender is a *composite* appender, which attaches to other appenders to produce asynchronous logging events. Here's an example of how to configure asynchronous logging for your File appender:

```
<appender name="ASYNC" class="org.apache.log4j.AsyncAppender">

<errorHandlerclass="org.jboss.logging.util.OnlyOnceErrorHandler"/>
  <appender-ref ref="FILE"/>
</appender>
```

Many developers wrongly believe that AsyncAppender is the fastest appender. This is true only in certain circumstances. The AsyncAppender does not improve logging throughput. On the contrary, a non-negligible number of CPU cycles is spent managing the bounded queue and synchronizing the dispatcher thread with various client threads.

Thus logging each event will take a little longer to complete, appending those events will hopefully take place at times where other threads are idle either waiting for new input to process or blocked on I/O intensive operations. In short, if you are running I/O bound applications, then you will benefit from asynchronous logging. On the contrary, CPU bound applications will not.

The following image documents how our optimized File appender throughput is reduced significantly when used in conjunction with AsyncAppender:

Label	# Samples	Average	Median	90% Line	Min	Max	Error %	Throughput	KB/sec
HTTP Request	1000	5	3	9	0	65	0,00%	191,4/sec	,0
TOTAL	1000	5	3	9	0	65	0,00%	191,4/sec	,0
Async Logging with File Appender Immediate = false and BufferIO = true									

You can try to increase the default **BufferSize** option (which is 128) so that you can raise the maximum number of logging events that can be buffered in the internal queue.

However, as we said, AsyncAppender does not always increase performance. Do not include it blindly in your code, but just after a benchmark. If you don't want to experiment too much with your configuration, our advice is to stay with the plain File appender, which is a safe bet.

Which layout should I choose for my logs?

The JBoss AS log configuration by default includes the **PatternLayout** for formatting log messages. PatternLayout provides a flexible layout configurable, which is encoded by means of a pattern string.

For example, the File appender uses the following layout pattern:

```
<param name="ConversionPattern" value="%d %-5p [%c] %m%n"/>
```

This means that the current format date is first printed (`%d`), then the priority of the logging event should be left justified to a width of five characters (`%-5p`). The `%c` string is used to output the category of the logging event. Finally the `%m` identifier outputs the application-supplied message with the carriage return (`%n`).

You should choose carefully the identifiers which are fed to the layout pattern. For example, the default File appender pattern formats the date (`%d`) using the ISO8601 standard, thus relying on the pattern string of the `java.text.SimpleDateFormat`. Although part of the standard JDK, the performance of `SimpleDateFormat` is quite poor.

For better results it is recommended to use the log4j date formatters. These can be specified using one of these strings: ABSOLUTE, DATE.

For example, with a few characters changes:

```
<param name="ConversionPattern" value="%d{ABSOLUTE} %-5p [%c] %m%n"/>
```

You can get an astonishing 10% performance boost, as shown by the following picture:

Label	# Samples	Average	Median	90% Line	Min	Max	Error %	Throughput	KB/sec
HTTP Request	1000	2	3	3	2	38	0,00%	336,6/sec	,0
TOTAL	1000	2	3	3	2	38	0,00%	336,6/sec	,0

File Appender with ImmediateFlush = false and BufferIO = true and optimized Layout

Besides the date pattern, other conversion characters that can badly influence your performance are as follows:

- C: Generates the caller class information. Slow.
- l: Used to output the line number from where the logging request was issued. Slow.
- M: Used to output the method name where the logging request was issued. Very slow.
- F: Used to output the file name where the logging request was issued. Very slow.

Is it enough to increase the log threshold to get rid of log charge?

The short answer is: it depends. When logging is turned off entirely or for a level below the threshold, the cost of a log request consists of a method invocation plus an integer comparison. On the same test hardware (Pentium 4 Dual Core 2.80 Ghz) this cost is typically in the 5 to 50 nanosecond range.

However, any logging instruction might involve the "hidden" cost of parameter construction. For example, for some logger writing:

```
logger.debug("Entry number: " +i+" is "+entry[i]);
```

This incurs in the cost of constructing the message parameter, that is, converting both integer i and entry[i] to a string, and concatenating intermediate strings, *regardless* of whether the message will be logged or not.

The cost of parameter construction can be quite high and depends on the size of the parameters involved. *So, as a rule of thumb, avoid using parameter construction within the logging request.*

If you want to get rid of any logging penalty, you should wrap the call to the logger, for example:

```
if (DEBUG) {
   logger.debug("Entry number: " +i+" is "+entry[i]);
}
```

You could conveniently set the DEBUG variable to false in production. Some compilers will not even add the logger call to the class's byte code, because it is guaranteed never to occur.

How does logging hierarchy influence performance?

When deciding your logging strategy, consider that in log4j the loggers are organized in a parent-child relationship. For example, a logger named com is the parent logger of the child logger com.sample.

In the logger hierarchy, the child logger inherits the properties and the logger components from its immediate parent. In short, this means that all the logging events captured by the child logger com.sample will be processed by the child logger itself and also by its parent logger com.

In log4j, by setting the additivity of the logger to false, you can circumvent ancestor loggers, thus improving the performance significantly.

This can be done by configuring the attribute additivity on the logger:

```
<logger name="com.sample" additivity="false" >
   <level value="INFO" />
   <appender-ref ref="CONSOLE"/>
   <appender-ref ref="FILE"/>
</logger>
```

Or programmatically with the method: logger.setAdditivity(false);

So, by setting the additivity to false for the logger com.sample, it will not be necessary for the logger to traverse the unused com logger but it will be directly linked to the root category, thereby increasing the performance significantly.

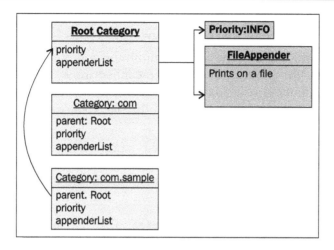

Summary

In this chapter, we have covered the basic structure of the application server and some of the core services like the thread pool, the connection pool, and the logging system. The basic rules of thumb we have learnt can be resumed as follows:

- The new release 5.x of the application server is the state-of-art as it concerns modular and extensible services. The system requirements for this release are higher than with 4.x. In order to get the most from this release you can *conveniently remove the services not used by your applications.*

- You can cut down by nearly 50% the application server basic requirements by removing the `admin_console`, the scheduler service, EJB2 support, the Hypersonic DB, and a set of minor services.

- JBoss AS generally dispatches its services by means of a pool of resources.

- The System thread pool is used to serve JNDI clients and can be configured by means of `<server>/conf/jboss-service.xml`. The default settings are usually good for most applications.

- The connection pool is used to cache database connections in order to avoid the burden of opening and closing new connections.

  - In order to find the optimal minimum and maximum pool size you should check the `Max Connections In Use Count` attribute of your Managed Connection Pool after a consistent benchmark. Allow 15-20% additional resources to keep a safety margin.

  - The PreparedStatement cache is a performance booster as it allows sharing Statements across requests. An excessive sized cache can anyway exhaust the amount of available db cursors.

  - Detect database leaks in the development stage by means of the `CachedConnectionManager` Mbean and `<track-statements>` element in your DataSource configuration.

- The JBoss AS default logging framework is log4j. Choose carefully the amount of information which needs to be logged. Limit your logging just to warning and error messages in production.

  - Appending your logs on a *File* usually has the best throughput. Setting the parameter `ImmediateFlush = false` and `BufferedIO = true` generally results in much better performance.

  - *Asynchronous appender* does not always provide the best performance, especially for CPU bound applications. You can try it for applications with high I/O demands.

  - Choose carefully the *layout of your logs*. Stay away from `c`, `l`, `M`, and `F` character conversions. Replace the default date (`%d`) with the log4j pattern (`%d{ABSOLUTE}`).

  - *Wrap your logging statements* with a conditional statement if the message is built with string manipulation arguments.

  - Always set the `additivity` *to* `false` in your loggers if you don't need to inherit any attribute from parent loggers, besides the root logger.

5
Tuning the Middleware Services

4th Circle of Hell: Avarice and Prodigality: Those who hoarded possession of the EJB container or squandered resources, forgetting to invoke remove on Stateful Beans.

Tuning the middleware services is a key step to ensure a positive experience for customers running Java EE applications. JBoss AS 5.x integrates all the Java EE 1.5 features and, while this book is being written, release 6 of the application server has gone through the fifth milestone, including most of the new exciting features of Java EE 1.6.

This chapter will cover the following topics:

- In the first part of this chapter, we will cover **Enterprise JavaBeans** (**EJB**), which are a fundamental server side component of Java EE. We will discuss the performance of their main subtypes (Stateless Beans and Stateful Beans) and which factors can enhance or decrease their throughput.

- In the next part, we will learn about **Java Messaging Service** (**JMS**), which has been implemented by means of different providers in releases 5.x and 6.x of the application server. This section includes a sample tuning session of an application, which needs to improve the JMS throughput, using the new JBoss AS 6 provider (HornetQ).

The prerequisite of this chapter is that the reader has already got some experience of the topics we are going to cover as we will introduce them with a very short recap.

Introduction to Enterprise Java Beans

Enterprise Java Bean technology hit the industry in 1999 and was quickly adopted by large companies. Unfortunately, problems were quick to appear and the reputation of EJBs began to suffer as a result. Some developers felt that the APIs of the EJB standard were far more complex than those developers were used to. An abundance of checked exceptions, required interfaces, and the implementation of the bean class as an abstract class were all unusual and counter-intuitive for many programmers.

This lead to a widespread perception that EJBs introduced complexity without delivering real benefits.

As a consequence, a counter-movement has grown up at grass-root level among programmers. The main products of this movement were the so-called 'lightweight' (that is, in comparison to EJB) technologies of Hibernate (for persistence and object-relational mapping) and Spring framework (which provided an alternate and far less verbose way to encode business logic). Despite lacking the support of big business, these technologies grew in popularity and were adopted more and more by businesses who had become disillusioned with EJBs.

The only alternative to save EJB technology was a deep change from the earlier, complex EJB specifications and a decisive step towards simpler paradigms delivered by frameworks like Spring and Hibernate.

Accordingly, the EJB 3.0 specification (JSR 220) was a radical departure from its predecessors, following this new paradigm. It shows a clear influence from Spring in its use of POJOs, and its support for dependency injection to simplify configuration and integration of heterogeneous systems. Gavin King, the creator of Hibernate, participated in the EJB 3.0 process and is an outspoken advocate of the technology. Many features, originally in Hibernate, were incorporated in the Java Persistence API such as the replacement for Entity Beans in EJB 3.0. The EJB 3.0 specification relies heavily on the use of annotations, a feature added to the Java language with its 5.0 release, to enable a much less verbose coding style.

In practical terms, EJB 3.0 is a completely new API, bearing little resemblance to the previous EJB specifications. In particular, the former distinction into three main types (Session Bean, Entity Bean, and Message Driven Bean) has been narrowed to just two main types:

- Session Beans: The basic business objects. They can be either "Stateful" or "Stateless" and can be invoked using the RMI-IIOP protocol.

- Message Driven Beans: (also known as MDBs) It supports asynchronous execution, but using a messaging paradigm.

The former **Entity Bean** component has been replaced by **Entities**, which is governed by the JPA specification. Entities and data persistence will be discussed in detail in *Chapter 6, Tuning the Persistence Layer*.

In the next section, we will discuss Session Beans, while Message Driven Beans are covered in the last section which is about JBoss Messaging System.

Session Beans

The EJB specification defines two types of Session Beans:

Stateless Session Beans (SLSB) are business objects that do not have a state associated with them; they are typically used for on-off operations like fetching a list of elements from a legacy system.

Instances of stateless session beans are pooled. When a client accesses a SLSB, the EJB container checks if there are any available instances in the pool. If any, the instance is returned to the client and *will be used exclusively from the client until its thread is completed.*

If no instances are available, the container creates a new one which will be returned to the client. As for any middleware service, the number of clients that can be served is not unlimited so the EJB container can control the amount of instances to be created.

In JBoss AS 5.x and 6.x the stateless session bean pool is configured in the file, `<server>/deploy/ejb3-interceptors-aop.xml`. The following is the part of the configuration related to the pool:

```
    <domain name="Stateless Bean" extends="Intercepted Bean"
  inheritBindings="true">
        . . . .
      <annotation expr="class(*) AND !class(@org.jboss.ejb3.
annotation.Pool)">
        @org.jboss.ejb3.annotation.Pool (value="ThreadlocalPool",
maxSize=30, timeout=10000)
      </annotation>
    </domain>
```

The preceding XML fragment translated in human terms, means that if you have not defined any pool annotation for your EJB (`!class(@org.jboss.ejb3. annotation.Pool`), then the default configuration will be used, which includes the `ThreadlocalPool` strategy, allowing a maximum size of 30 instances in the pool. If no instances are available, the EJB container will keep waiting for the `timeout` specified (in milliseconds) after which the request will be cancelled. We will discuss pool strategies in the next section of this chapter.

Stateful Session Beans (SFSB) are business objects having a state that is, they keep track of which calling client they are dealing with throughout a session and thus access to the bean instance is *strictly limited to only one client at a time*.

A typical scenario for a SFSB is a web store checkout process, which might be handled by a stateful session bean that would use its state to keep track of items the customer is purchasing.

Stateful session beans remain in the EJB container until they are explicitly removed, either by the client, or by the container when they timeout. Meanwhile, the EJB container might need to passivate inactive stateful session beans to disk. This requires overhead and constitutes a performance hit to the application. If the passivated stateful bean is subsequently required by the application, the container activates it by restoring it from disk.

By explicitly removing SFSBs when finished, applications will decrease the need for passivation and minimize container overhead and improve performance. Also, by explicitly removing SFSBs, you do not need to rely on timeout values.

The configuration for stateful beans is a bit more complex as it's split into two parts:

- Non-clustered cache configuration: used for single node applications.
- Clustered cache configuration: used for applications, deployed in a cluster of JBoss instances.

Here's the core section of it:

```
    <domain name="Stateful Bean" extends="Base Stateful Bean"
inheritBindings="true">
        <!-- NON Clustered cache configuration -->
.....
            @org.jboss.ejb3.annotation.CacheConfig (maxSize=100000,
idleTimeoutSeconds=300, removalTimeoutSeconds=0)
        </annotation>
        <!-- Clustered cache configuration -->
.....
```

```
         @org.jboss.ejb3.annotation.CacheConfig (name="sfsb-cache",
    maxSize=100000, idleTimeoutSeconds=300, removalTimeoutSeconds=0)
         </annotation>
      </domain>
```

The `maxSize` parameter is the maximum number of stateful beans allowed in the cache.

`idleTimeoutSeconds` defines the maximum length of time in seconds a stateful session EJB should remain in cache. After this time has elapsed, JBoss removes the bean instance from the cache and starts to passivate it.

`removalTimeoutSeconds` defines how long (in seconds) the bean remains active before it is completely removed. The default 0 represents infinity, so by default SFSB are not removed from the container.

How to configure the optimal size for stateless pool?

As stated earlier, stateless bean instances are held in a pool whose configuration is contained in `ejb3-interceptors-aop.xml`. The optimal pool configuration is based on two factors:

1. The maximum and minimum pool size.
2. The locking strategy used by the pool to ensure thread safety of instances.

Finding out the optimal pool size, can be determined with a benchmark which simulates the production load. Once that you have completed your benchmark, you need to monitor the highest peak of request to your EJB.

The information we need is stored in the MBean dedicated to your deployment unit: as a matter of fact, every time you deploy a component like an EJB, an MBean is added in the `jboss.j2ee` domain. This MBean contains the required statistics for the component.

Supposing you have deployed your EJB in a `jar` archive named `ejb3.jar`, which is a part of the `Application.ear` archive, you will find in the `jboss.j2ee` domain the following MBean entry in your JMX console:

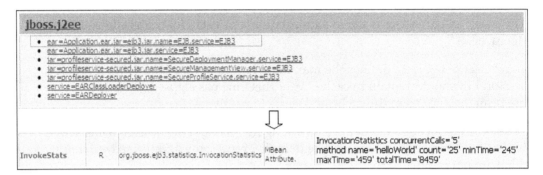

By clicking on the MBean, you can access to the EJB statistics which are contained in the `InvokeStats` attribute.

From the preceding statistics, you understand that your EJB has serviced requests with `helloWorld` method scoring a minimum response time of 245 ms. and a maximum response time of 459 ms. The total time spent calling this method was about 8.4 seconds for 25 total requests. (five of these are running concurrently).

The `concurrentCalls` attribute is a live value captured from the application server: in order to determine what was the peak of concurrentCalls that have been dispatched to your EJB, you need to poll the MBeans during the benchmark. One of the simplest ways to purse this task is by means of the **twiddle** command line utility located in the `JBOSS_HOME/bin` of your distribution.

The twiddle shell can be conveniently inserted in any batch script, which keeps polling at fixed intervals. Here's how to access to this information from a Windows platform:

```
twiddle -s localhost get "jboss.j2ee:ear=Application.ear,jar=ejb3.jar,nam
e=StatelessEJB,service=EJB3" InvokeStats
```

What you need to adapt in your script is just the host name where JBoss AS is running (`-s` option) and, of course, the full MBean name.

The Linux/Unix equivalent is:

```
twiddle.sh -s localhost get "jboss.j2ee:ear=Application.ear,jar=ejb3.jar,
name=StatelessEJB,service=EJB3" InvokeStats
```

So, once you have captured *the highest peak of concurrent requests*, you can calculate the `maxSize` size adding a safety margin, which can vary from 10% to 20% depending on the nature of the application.

Moving to the initial pool size, we have to report that, although the `MinimumSize` element appears in the `conf/standardjboss.xml` file, the EJB container does not honor this parameter. So at present *there is no way to set up an initial pool size* for stateless beans. If you really need to initialize some EJB at startup (supposing you have a costly startup for your EJB) you can opt for any startup strategy such as a Startup Servlet or an MBean service.

The other strategic element, which can be configured in your pool, is the locking strategy used. The default value uses ThreadLocal variables to avoid synchronization issues.

SLSBs can be however configured to use an alternative pooling mechanism named **StrictMaxPool** that will only allow a fixed number of concurrent requests to run at one time. If there are more requests running than the pool's strict size, those requests will block until an instance becomes available.

Here's the key configuration, which needs to be changed:

```
<annotation expr="!class(@org.jboss.annotation.ejb.PoolClass)">
        @org.jboss.annotation.ejb.PoolClass (value=org.jboss.ejb3.
StrictMaxPool.class, maxSize=5, timeout=10000)
  </annotation>
```

You can also opt for a granular configuration by setting a different locking strategy at EJBs level. See this wiki for information: `http://www.jboss.org/ejb3/docs/reference/build/reference/en/html/session-bean-config.html`.

A sample benchmark reveals that, in some circumstances, the `ThreadlocalPool` outperforms the `StrictMaxPool` implementation by about 20%.

Label	# Samples	Average	Median	90% Line	Min	Max	Error %	Throughput	KB/sec
HTTP Requ...	150000	945	387	2762	148	11679	0,00%	95,0/sec	28,0
TOTAL	150000	945	387	2762	148	11679	0,00%	95,0/sec	28,0
Stateless Bean benchmark - ThreadlocalPool policy									
Label	# Samples	Average	Median	90% Line	Min	Max	Error %	Throughput	KB/sec
HTTP Requ...	150000	1208	1237	1494	150	2279	0,00%	77,3/sec	22,8
TOTAL	150000	1208	1237	1494	150	2279	0,00%	77,3/sec	22,8
Stateless Bean benchmark - StrictMaxPool policy									

The difference tends to be higher when the EJBs are carrying out heavy-duty tasks, which are locking the instance to the client. In such scenarios, the `StrictMaxPool` policy will be particularly restrictive and should thus be avoided.

On the other hand, consider that the `Threadlocal Pool` implementation tends to make the pool as large as the thread pool that services the EJB. This can be counterproductive in a scenario where you have resources which are starving. For example, you might need to have an exact control of your EJBs if they are strictly dependant on an external resource like a JMS queue. That's why the default policy for MDBs, which are in the pool, is the `StrictMaxPool`.

How to configure the optimal size of stateful cache?

As we introduced earlier, JBoss EJB container uses a cache of bean instances to improve the performance of stateful session beans. The cache stores active EJB instances in memory so that they are immediately available for client requests. The cache contains EJBs that are currently in use by a client and instances that were recently in use. Stateful session beans in cache are bound to a particular client.

Finding out the optimal size for stateful cache follows the same pattern we have learnt with SLSBs, just you need to watch for different attributes.

Again open your JMX console and find out your EJB 3 unit through the `jboss.j2ee` domain. There you will find a few attributes that will interest you:

Attribute Name	Access	Type		Description	Attribute Value
CacheSize	R	int		MBean Attribute.	300
PassivatedCount	R	int		MBean Attribute.	0
CreateCount	R	int		MBean Attribute.	300
InvokeStats	R	org.jboss.ejb3.statistics.InvocationStatistics		MBean Attribute.	InvocationStatistics concurrentCalls='180' method name='doSomething' count='120' minTime='250' maxTime='672' totalTime='754898'
CurrentSize	R	int		MBean Attribute.	300
RemoveCount	R	int		MBean Attribute.	180
MaxSize	R	int		MBean Attribute.	100000

The **CacheSize** is the current size of the stateful cache. If the amount of this cache approaches the **MaxSize** attribute, then you should consider raising the maximum element of SFSBs in the cache (refer to the earlier section for information about the configuration of the stateful cache).

Here's how you can poll this attribute from the twiddle command line utility (Windows users):

```
twiddle -s localhost get "jboss.j2ee:ear=Application.ear,jar=ejb3.jar,nam
e=StatefulEJB,service=EJB3" CacheSize
```

This is the equivalent shell for Unix readers:

```
twiddle.sh -s localhost get "jboss.j2ee:ear=Application.ear,jar=ejb3.jar,
name=StatefulEJB,service=EJB3" CacheSize
```

Finally, you should pay attention to the RemoveCount attribute, which dictates the amount of SFSBs, which have been removed after use. In a well-written application, the growth of this attribute should follow the same trend of CreateCount that is basically a counter of the SFSBs created. If that's not your case or worst than all, you have a RemoveCount set to 0, then it's time to inform your developers there's a time bomb in your code.

Comparing SLSBs and SFSBs performance

In the last years, many dread legends have grown up about the performance of stateful session beans. You probably have heard vague warnings about their poor scalability or their low throughput.

If you think it over, the main difference between SLSB and SFSB is that stateful beans need to keep the fields contained in the EJB class in memory (unless they are passivated) so, inevitably they will demand more memory to the application server.

However, a well designed application, which reduces both the size of the session and its time span (by carefully issuing a remove on the bean as soon as its activities are terminated) should have no issues at all when using SFSB.

The following is a test executed on a JBoss 5.1.0 platform hosted on a 4 dual Xeon machine with 8 GB of RAM. We have set up a benchmark with 200 concurrent users, each performing a set of operations (select, insert, update) as part of a simulated web session. The following is the heap and CPU graph for the *stateless bean* usage:

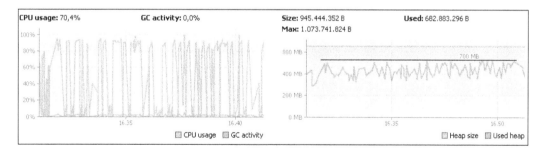

In the stateful bean benchmark, we are storing intermediate states in the EJB session as fields. The following is the VisualVM graph for the *stateful bean* counterpart:

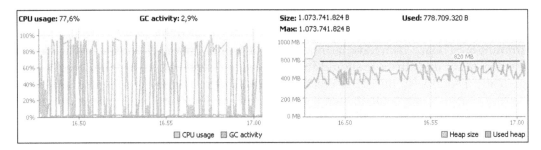

As you can see, both kinds of session beans managed to complete the benchmark with a maximum of 1GB of RAM. SFSBs sit on a higher memory threshold than their SLSBs counterpart, however the memory trend is not different from the stateless session bean one.

If you carefully examine the graph, you'll see that the most evident difference between the two components is a *higher CPU usage and GC activity* for the SFSB. That's natural because the EJB container needs to perform CPU-intensive operations like marshalling/unmarshalling fields of the beans.

And what about the throughput? The following graph shows the JMeter aggregate report for both tests executed. As you can see, the difference is less than you would expect (around 10%):

Label	# Samples	Average	Median	90% Line	Min	Max	Error %	Throughput	KB/sec
HTTP Requ...	150000	640	604	993	202	2041	0,00%	221,1/sec	8,8
TOTAL	150000	640	604	993	202	2041	0,00%	221,1/sec	8,8
Stateless Bean benchmark - 200 users									
Label	# Samples	Average	Median	90% Line	Min	Max	Error %	Throughput	KB/sec
HTTP Requ...	150000	671	634	1043	202	2273	0,00%	211,1/sec	8,4
TOTAL	150000	671	634	1043	202	2273	0,00%	211,1/sec	8,4
Stateful Bean benchmark - 200 users									

When things get wilder

The preceding benchmark reflects an optimal scenario where you have short-lived sessions with few items stored as fields. In such a situation it's common that you will see little difference in throughput between the two kinds of session beans.

Adding some nasty things to this benchmark would reveal a different scenario. Supposing that your EJB client issues the remove() method on the session bean after a longer (random) amount of time and that our session data is inflated with a 50 KB String, the memory requirements of the applications would change drastically, leading to an OutOfMemory Exception with the current configuration:

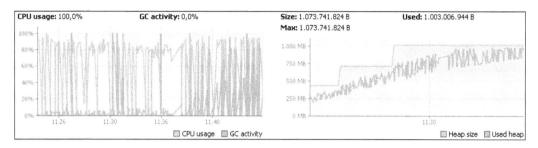

While this second approach simulates some evident architectural mistakes, most of the applications sit somehow between these two scenarios. Ultimately the requirements (and the performance) of your SFSBs can conceptually be thought of as a product of Session time and Session size (that is, session time x session size). Carefully design your architecture to reduce both these factors as much as possible and verify with a load test if your application meets the expected requirements.

Are you using over 1024 concurrent users?

Some operating systems, such as Linux limit the number of file descriptors that any process may open. The default limit is 1024 per process. Java Virtual Machine opens many files in order to read in the classes required to run an application. A file descriptor is also used for each socket that is opened. This can prevent a larger number of concurrent clients.

On Linux systems you can increase the number of allowable open file handles in the file, `/etc/security/limits.conf`. For example:

```
serveruser      soft    nofile  20000
serveruser      hard    nofile  20000
```

This would allow up to 20000 file handles to be open by the server user.

Is it possible that Stateful Beans are faster then Stateless Beans?

There are some non-official benchmarks which show that, in some scenarios, the SFSB can outperform SLSB. If you think it over, the application server tries to optimize the usage of SLSB instances and first searches for free beans in the pool, afterwards either waits until an "in-use" instance is returned to the pool, or creates a new one. There is no such optimization for SFSB, so the application server simply routes all requests to the same instance, which is sometimes faster than the SLSB approach.

One thing you could try, provided you have plenty of memory available on your application server, is disabling stateful session bean passivation. This will avoid the cost of marshalling/unmarshalling objects that have been idle for a while, thus introducing a tradeoff between memory and performance.

You have got several options to disable passivation: **the simplest is to set** *a removal timeout smaller (but greater than zero) then the idle timeout* **in the file** `deploy/ejb3-interceptors-aop.xml`.

You can also disable passivation at EJB level by changing the stateful cache strategy to the `NoPassivationCache` strategy. This requires simply to add the annotation `@Cache(org.jboss.ejb3.cache.NoPassivationCache.class)` at class level.

The following is the aftermath of our new benchmark with *passivation disabled*:

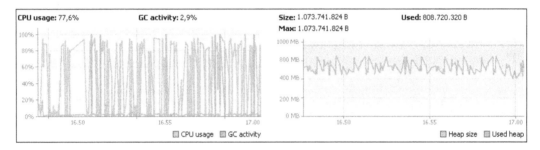

And the corresponding JMeter aggregate report:

Label	# Samples	Average	Median	90% Line	Min	Max	Error %	Throughput	KB/sec
HTTP Requ...	150000	641	514	1003	200	2253	0,00%	216,3/sec	8,4
TOTAL	150000	641	514	1003	200	2253	0,00%	216,3/sec	8,4
Stateful Benchmark - 200 users - no Passivation									

Three things have basically changed:

1. The amount of memory demanded by the application has grown by about 5-7%. Consider that, however, in this benchmark the EJB session lasted about one minute. Longer sessions could lead to an OutOfMemory Exception with this configuration (1 GB RAM).

2. The Garbage collector activity has increased as well, as we are getting closer to the maximum memory available.

3. The overall throughput has increased since the lifecycle for the SFSB is now much simpler without passivation.

Definitively, this benchmark shows that it is possible, under some circumstances, that well designed SFSBs can have the same rough performance as that of SLSBs (or even outperform them), however without an increase in the application server memory, this improvement will be partly lost in additional garbage collector cycles.

Session Beans and Transactions

One of the most evident differences between an EJB and a simple RMI service is that EJB are transactional components. Simply put, a transaction is a grouping of work that represents a single unit or task.

If you are using **Container Managed Transaction** (the default), the container will automatically start a transaction for you because the default transaction attribute is required. This guarantees that the work performed by the method is within a global transaction context.

However transaction management is an expensive affair and you need to verify if your EJB methods really need a transaction. For example, a method, which simply returns a list of objects to the client, usually does not need to be enlisted in a transaction.

For this reason, it's considered a tuning best practice to **remove unneeded transactions from your EJB**. Unfortunately, this is often underestimated by developers who find if easier to define a generic transaction policy for all methods:

```
<container-transaction>
    <method>
        <ejb-name>PayrollEJB</ejb-name>
        <method-name>*</method-name>
    </method>
    <trans-attribute>Required</trans-attribute>
</container-transaction>
```

Using EJB 3 annotations, you have no excuse for your negligence, you can explicitly disable transactions by setting the transaction type to NOT_SUPPORTED with a simple annotation, as follows:

```
@TransactionAttribute(TransactionAttributeType.NOT_SUPPORTED)
public List<PayRoll> findAll() {
    …
}
```

JBoss Transaction patch

One potential performance bottleneck of the **JBoss Transaction service** is the `TransactionImple.isAlive` check. A patch has been released by JBoss team, which can be applied on top of the application server. See `https://jira.jboss.org/browse/JBTM-757` for more information.

Customizing JBoss EJB container policies

The preceding tip is valid across any application server. You can, however, gain an additional boost in performance by customizing the JBoss EJB container. As a matter of fact the EJB container is tightly integrated with the **Aspect Oriented Programming (AOP)** framework. Aspects allow developers to more easily modularize the code base, providing a cleaner separation from application logic and system code.

If you take a look in the `ejb3-interceptors-aop.xml` configuration file, you will notice that every domain contains a list of **Interceptors**, which are invoked on the EJB instance. For example, consider the following key section from the stateless bean domain:

```
<domain name="Stateless Bean" extends="Intercepted Bean"
inheritBindings="true">
. . . . . . .
    <bind pointcut="execution(public * *->*(..))">
        <interceptor-ref name="org.jboss.aspects.
tx.TxPropagationInterceptor"/>
        <interceptor-ref name="org.jboss.ejb3.
tx.CMTTxInterceptorFactory"/>
        <interceptor-ref name="org.jboss.ejb3.stateless.
StatelessInstanceInterceptor"/>
        <interceptor-ref name="org.jboss.ejb3.
tx.BMTTxInterceptorFactory"/>
        <interceptor-ref name="org.jboss.ejb3.
AllowedOperationsInterceptor"/>
        <interceptor-ref name="org.jboss.ejb3.entity.
TransactionScopedEntityManagerInterceptor"/>
        <stack-ref name="EJBInterceptors"/>
    </bind>
. . . . . . .
</domain>
```

Interceptors extend the `org.jboss.ejb3.aop.AbstractInterceptor` class and are invoked separately on the bean instance. Supposing you are not using Transactions in your EJBs, you might consider customizing the EJB container by commenting out the interceptors which are in charge of propagating the Transactional Context.

By issuing another benchmark on your stateless beans, this reveals an interesting 10% boost in the throughput of your applications:

Label	# Samples	Average	Median	90% Line	Min	Max	Error %	Throughput	KB/sec
HTTP Requ..	150000	630	604	953	200	1953	0,00%	235,3/sec	8,8
TOTAL	150000	630	604	953	200	1953	0,00%	235,3/sec	8,8
No tx Stateless Bean benchmark - 200 users									

Customizing the single deployment unit

In the previous example, we applied changes at EJB container level. However, this is a brute force change as it applies the new Interceptor stack on all your EJBs. You can opt for a softer solution that adds your customized domain in a `*-aop.xml` file along with your deployment unit.

Here's an example, which could be used for non Transactional EJBs:

```xml
<?xml version="1.0" encoding="UTF-8"?>
<aop xmlns="urn:jboss:aop-beans:1.0">
    <domain name="Non Tx Stateless Bean" extends="Intercepted Bean"
inheritBindings="false">
        <bind pointcut="execution(public * *->*(..))">
            <interceptor-ref name="org.jboss.ejb3.stateless.
StatelessInstanceInterceptor"/>
            <interceptor-ref name="org.jboss.ejb3.
AllowedOperationsInterceptor"/>
            <stack-ref name="EJBInterceptors"/>
        </bind>
    </domain>
</aop>
```

Notice the `inheritBindings=false` which means that this configuration overrides the default settings, otherwise the customized domain will inherit from the base bean configuration.

Introduction to the Java Messaging system

The **Java Message Service (JMS)** API is part of the Java EE specification and describes how to design components that create, send, receive, and read messages. JMS introduces a distributed communication that is loosely coupled, reliable, and asynchronous.

A JMS application is composed of the following parts:

- A JMS provider is a messaging system that implements the JMS interfaces and provides administrative and control features. The current release of JBoss AS (5.1.0) uses JBoss Messaging system as a default provider. This provider has been replaced by the HornetQ Messaging system in release 6.0 of the application server..

- Messages are the objects that communicate information between JMS clients.

- Administered objects are preconfigured JMS objects created by an administrator for the use of clients. There are two kinds of administered objects:

  ○ Connection factories: A connection factory is the object a client uses to create a connection with a provider. Every connection factory encapsulates a set of connection configuration parameters that has been defined by an administrator.

  ○ Destinations: A destination is the object a client uses to specify the target of messages it produces and the source of messages it consumes. There can be two kinds of destinations: Queues and Topics. A queue is a staging area that contains messages that have been sent to a single consumer and are waiting to be read. A JMS queue guarantees that each message is processed only once. A topic, on the other hand, is a distribution mechanism for publishing messages that are delivered to multiple subscribers.

- JMS clients are the programs or components, written in the Java programming language, that produce and consume messages.

A special case of a JMS consumer is the **Message Driven Bean (MDB)**, which is an Enterprise Java Bean that acts as a message listener for a particular queue or topic. In several aspects, MDBs resemble stateless session beans. In particular:

- MDB instances retain no data or conversational state for a specific client.

- All instances of a MDB are equivalent, allowing the EJB container to assign a message to any message-driven bean instance. The container can pool these instances to allow streams of messages to be processed concurrently.

For this reason, you can configure the MDB pool using the same tactics we have described for the stateless pool (refer to the section named, *How to configure the optimal size for stateless pool*). However, top performance gains for MDBs are not achieved by the pool settings but by means of optimal configuration of administered objects (connection factories and destinations).

Entering the JBoss Messaging system

Before discussing optimal JMS settings, we need to understand how the JBoss messaging system fits into the overall application server architecture. The following image will let you understand the concept better:

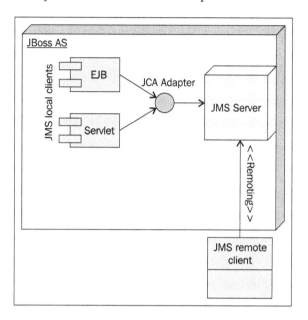

As you can see, JBoss Messaging uses Java Connector's pool as an inflow for messages which are sent by local clients (in the same JVM). The configuration of the Java Connector Architecture (JCA) pool can be found in the file `<server>/deploy/jca-jboss-beans.xml`, which is based on the `WorkManager` pool:

```
<bean name="WorkManagerThreadPool" class="org.jboss.util.threadpool.
BasicThreadPool">
. . . . . .
    <property name="maximumQueueSize">1024</property>
    <property name="maximumPoolSize">100</property>
    <property name="keepAliveTime">60000</property>
</bean>
```

In short, this is the meaning of the preceding parameters:

- `maximumQueueSize`: Specifies the maximum amount of work admitted in the queue.
- `maximumPoolSize`: Specifies the maximum number of active threads.
- `keepAliveTime`: Describes how long to keep threads alive after their last work (default one minute).

The configuration of the JCA thread pool is generally good for most applications so we will not spend much time on it. Similarly, you can configure JMS remote clients by means of the `<server>\deploy\messaging\remoting-bisocket-service.xml` file. Remote clients use the **Remoting** framework for connecting to the application server by means of a variety of protocols like HTTP or SSL. This can be particularly useful for situations like firewall restrictions where common JMS ports are blocked.

The most relevant parameter, as far as performance is concerned, is `JBM_clientMaxPoolSize` which specifies how many connections are stored in the client pool. This basically limits how many connections/sessions a client can open at a time.

```
<mbean code="org.jboss.remoting.transport.Connector"
       name="jboss.messaging:service=Connector,transport=bisocket"
       display-name="Bisocket Transport Connector">
    <attribute name="Configuration">
      <config>
        <invoker transport="bisocket">
              . . . . .
            <attribute name="JBM_clientMaxPoolSize"
isParam="true">200</attribute>
              . . . . .
      </config>
    </attribute>
  </mbean>
```

The next section will discuss tuning the JBoss JMS provider, which is the area where you can achieve the most relevant performance gains.

Tuning JBoss JMS provider

The JBoss message provider has changed frequently with recent major releases of the application server. Former 3.x and 4.x releases were based on the **JBossMq** messaging system. The current release (5.x) of JBoss AS uses the **JBoss Messaging** framework, while upcoming releases are geared towards the new **HornetQ** messaging provider.

As this book is definitely forward-looking, we will complete this chapter with a sample case based on the newer (HornetQ) messaging provider.

Tuning JBoss Messaging (JBoss AS 5.x)

The JBoss Messaging provider ships by default with release 5.x of the application server. The configuration is distributed in the folder `<server>/deploy/messaging`, between the following files:

File	Usage
`connection-factories-service.xml`	Connection factory configuration file.
`destinations-service.xml`	Default Messaging destinations.
`hsqldb-persistence-service.xml`	Default `hsql` persistence configuration file.
`jms-ds.xml`	The JMS provider loader.
`legacy-service.xml`	Messaging Destinations deployment descriptor.
`messaging-jboss-beans.xml`	Messaging user-security policy definition.
`messaging-service.xml`	ServerPeer MBean configuration.
`remoting-bisocket-service.xml`	Standard bisocket-based Remoting service deployment descriptor.

As far as tuning is concerned, we are mainly interested in the Connection factory configuration file and the JMS destinations configuration file.

How do you tune the JBoss Messaging Connection factory?

A Connection factory encapsulates the JMS connections parameters and is bound in the JNDI naming service. The configuration file for Connection factories is located in the file `deploy\messaging\connection-factories-service.xml`.

The default non-clusterable configuration contains a bare-bones definition of the factory:

```
    <mbean code="org.jboss.jms.server.connectionfactory.
ConnectionFactory"
      name="jboss.messaging.connectionfactory:service=ConnectionFacto
ry"
      xmbean-dd="xmdesc/ConnectionFactory-xmbean.xml">
      <depends optional-attribute-name="ServerPeer">jboss.
messaging:service=ServerPeer</depends>
      <depends optional-attribute-name="Connector">jboss.messaging:ser
vice=Connector,transport=bisocket</depends>
      <depends>jboss.messaging:service=PostOffice</depends>
      <attribute name="JNDIBindings">
        <bindings>
          <binding>/ConnectionFactory</binding>
```

```
            <binding>/XAConnectionFactory</binding>
            <binding>java:/ConnectionFactory</binding>
            <binding>java:/XAConnectionFactory</binding>
        </bindings>
    </attribute>
</mbean>
```

In order to tune your factory you can introduce the following attributes (default values are given for each attribute):

```
<attribute name="PrefetchSize">150</attribute>
<attribute name="DupsOKBatchSize">2000</attribute>
<attribute name="SlowConsumers">false</attribute>
```

- `PrefetchSize` is an optional attribute that determines how many messages client side message consumers will buffer locally. Pre-fetching messages prevents the client from having to go to the server each time a message is consumed to say it is ready to receive another message. *This greatly increases throughput*. The default value for `PrefetchSize` is `150`. Larger values give better throughput but require more memory.

- The setting `DupsOKBatchSize` works with the `DUPS_OK_ACKNOWLEDGE` JMS acknowledge mode. This means that message consumers might occasionally issue multiple acknowledgments of the messages. By setting this parameter the JMS provider determines how many acknowledgments it will buffer locally before sending. Again here there's a *tradeoff between performance (larger value) and memory (smaller value)*.

- The attribute `SlowConsumers` can be used if some of your consumers are slow at consuming messages. By setting this property to `true` you make sure the connection will not buffer any messages. This can be used to distribute the load of messages equally, preventing faster consumers from "capturing" all messages. However consider that this will disable client messaging buffering, for performance, always set this to `false`.

How do you tune JBoss Messaging destinations?

Creating a new messaging destination is just a matter of dropping a `-service.xml` file either in the `<server>/deploy` folder or in `<server>/deploy/messaging`.

```
<mbean code="org.jboss.jms.server.destination.QueueService"
    name="jboss.messaging.destination:service=Queue,name=sampleQue
ue"
    xmbean-dd="xmdesc/Queue-xmbean.xml">
  <depends optional-attribute-name=»ServerPeer»>jboss.
messaging:service=ServerPeer</depends>
  </mbean>
```

You can fine tune your destination configuration by adding the following attributes (default values are used as attribute values):

```
<attribute name="FullSize">75000</attribute>
<attribute name="PageSize">2000</attribute>
<attribute name="DownCacheSize">2000</attribute>
```

- `FullSize` — this is the maximum number of messages held by the queue or topic subscriptions in memory at any one time. When the amount of messages to be delivered exceeds the `FullSize` value, the messages are moved to a temporary destination named "DownCache".

  This parameter has a direct impact on the performance of your JMS application, however bear in mind that by increasing the default value the memory requirements of your application will increase accordingly. The following image shows the JVM memory graph of two different benchmarks: the first with the default `FullSize` and the second with a custom value:

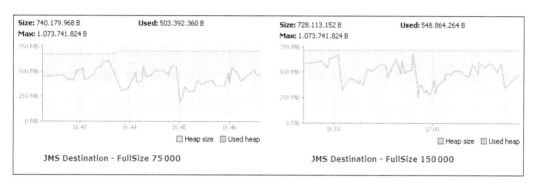

- `DownCacheSize` — as anticipated, this setting determines the max number of messages that the DownCache will hold before they are flushed to storage. This enables the write to occur as a single operation, thus aiding performance.

- `PageSize` — when loading messages from the queue or subscription, this is the maximum number of messages to pre-load in one single operation. Also, this element is crucial for the performance of heavy-duty JMS applications. Discovering the optimal `PageSize` requires some trials; you can try increasing it, until you hit a plateau, which means you have reached the optimal page size. For example, running a benchmark of 100.000 messages, each one with a payload of 1 KB, you will see that a `PageSize` of 5000 messages is the optimal value, using a typical developer configuration.

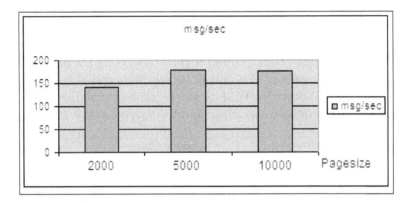

Tuning HornetQ (JBoss AS 6.x)

HornetQ is the new high performance messaging provider for the JBoss AS 6.x release. Its core has been designed as a simple set of Plain Old Java Objects (POJOs) without any dependencies on any other JBoss classes which is why it can be used stand-alone, embedded in your applications, or integrated with the application server.

The main configuration file is located in the folder, `<server>/deploy/hornetq/hornetq-configuration.xml`.

The two key elements, which can influence your application's performance, are the **journal** and **transport** configuration. The journal handles the persistence of messages and transactions using a high performance algorithm implemented by the HornetQ team.

The transport configuration is based on **Netty**, which is an asynchronous event-driven network application framework.

How to configure HornetQ journal for optimal performance?

In order to tune HornetQ's journal you have to check its configuration in the file `hornetq-configuration.xml`.

This is the part of the configuration related to the journal:

```
<journal-directory>
  ${jboss.server.data.dir}/hornetq/journal
</journal-directory>

<journal-min-files>10</journal-min-files>
```

- `journal-directory` is the filesystem directory where the journal is written. Put the journal on its own physical volume. If the disk is shared with other processes for example, transaction co-ordinator, database or other journals which are also reading and writing from it, then this may greatly reduce performance since the disk head may be skipping all over the place between the different files.

- `journal-min-files` reflects the minimum number of journal files to be created. If you see new files being created on the journal data directory too often, i.e. lots of data is being persisted, you need to increase the minimal number of files, this way the journal would reuse more files instead of creating new data files

> HornetQ transparently supports huge queues containing millions of messages while the server is running with limited memory with the paging feature.
>
> In such a situation, it's not possible to store all of the queues in memory at any one time, so HornetQ transparently pages messages into and out of memory as they are needed, thus
>
> allowing massive queues with a low memory footprint.
>
> HornetQ will start paging messages to disk, when the size of all messages in memory for an address exceeds a configured maximum size.
>
> Paging directory is configured by default in the following directory:
>
> `<paging-directory>${jboss.server.data.dir}/hornetq/paging</paging-directory>`

Other parameters which are not specified in the default configuration are:

- `journal-file-size`: The journal file size should be aligned to the capacity of a cylinder on the disk. The default value 10 MB should be enough on most systems.

- `journal-type`: This parameter lets you choose the I/O libraries which are used to append data to the journal. Valid values are NIO or ASYNCIO.

  Choosing NIO selects the Java NIO journal. Choosing ASYNCIO selects the Linux asynchronous IO journal. If you choose ASYNCIO but are not running Linux, or you do not have libaio installed, then HornetQ will detect this and automatically fall back to using NIO.

  The Java NIO journal gives great performance, but if you are running HornetQ using Linux Kernel 2.6 or later, we highly recommend using the ASYNCIO journal for the best persistence performance especially under high concurrency.

- `journal-aio-flush-on-sync`: HornetQ, by default, is optimized by the case where you have many producers and thus it combines multiple writes in a single OS operation. So, setting this option to false will give you a performance boost, making your system scale much better. However if you have few producers, it might be worth setting this property to true, which means that your system will flush every sync with an OS call.

Do you need message security and persistence?

If you don't need message persistence, you might greatly increase the performance of your JMS applications by setting `persistence-enabled` to `false` in `hornetq-configuration.xml`.

You may get as well a small performance boost by disabling security by setting the `security-enabled` parameter to `false`.

How do you configure HornetQ transport for optimal performance?

HornetQ transport is based on Netty's framework, which greatly simplifies and streamlines network programming such as TCP and UDP socket server.

The basic configuration comes with a preconfigured connector/acceptor pair (netty-throughput) in `hornetq-configuration.xml` and JMS Connection factory (`ThroughputConnectionFactory`) which can be used to give the very best throughput, especially for small messages

Acceptors are used on the server to define which connections can be made to the HornetQ server, while **connectors** are used by a client to define how it connects to a server. The most relevant parameters for transport configuration are TCP buffer sizes and the `TCP_NODELAY` property.

TCP buffer sizes. These properties can be used to change the TCP send and receive buffer sizes. If you have a fast network and fast machines, you may get a performance boost by increasing this buffer which defaults to 32768 bytes (32 KB).

Here's how to set the TCP send and receive buffer to 64 KB:

```
<param key="hornetq.remoting.netty.tcpsendbuffersize" value="65536"
type="Integer"/>
 <param key="hornetq.remoting.netty.tcpreceivebuffersize"
value="65536" type="Integer"/>
```

However, note that *TCP buffer sizes should be tuned according to the bandwidth and latency of your network.* You can estimate your optimal TCP buffer size with the following formula:

```
buffer_size = bandwidth * RTT
```

Where bandwidth is measured in bytes per second and network round trip time (RTT) is in seconds. RTT can be easily measured using the ping utility.

If you are interested in low-level network details, here's how you calculate this parameter:

Bandwidth can be calculated with O/S tools, for example Solaris/Linux users can issue the `iperf` command:

```
iperf -s
------------------------------------------------------------
---
Server listening on TCP port 5001
TCP window size: 60.0 KB (default)
------------------------------------------------------------
---
[  4] local 172.31.178.168 port 5001 connected with
172.16.7.4 port 2357
[ ID] Interval        Transfer      Bandwidth
[  4]  0.0-10.1 sec   6.5 MBytes   45 Mbit/sec
```

And here's the **RTT**, roughly calculated with the ping utility:

```
ping proxyserver (204.228.150.3) 56(84) bytes of data.
64 bytes from proxyserver (204.228.150.3): icmp_seq=1
ttl=63 time=0.30 ms
```

So by multiplying the two factors, with a little math, we estimate an optimal 165KB TCP buffer size:

```
45 Mbit/sec * 0.30 ms  = 45e6 * 30e-3  = 1,350,000
bits / 8 / 1024 = 165 KB
```

Another important parameter, well known by network administrators, is TCP_ NODELAY, which can be set with the parameter:

```
<param key="hornetq.remoting.netty.tcpnodelay" value="true" />
```

This parameter relates to Nagle's algorithm, which is a low-level algorithm that tries to minimize the number of TCP packets on the network, by trying to fill a TCP packet before sending it. TCP packets have a 40-byte header, so if you try to send a single byte you incur a lot of overhead as you are sending 41 bytes to represent 1 byte of information. (This situation often occurs in Telnet sessions, where most key presses generate a single byte of data that is transmitted immediately.)

For Enterprise applications, however, the TCP segment includes a larger data section. So enabling the Nagle's algorithm would delay transmission, increasing bandwidth at the expense of latency. For this reason you should always set the TCP_NODELAY property to true.

Before writing packets to the transport, HornetQ can be configured to batch up writes for a maximum of batch-delay milliseconds. This can increase overall throughput for very small messages. It does so at the expense of an increase in average latency for message transfer. If not specified, the default value for batch-delay property is 0 ms

Basic JMS tuning

Tuning the JMS provider is essential to reach the maximum performance of your message-based applications. However, a poorly written JMS application will never reach a decent throughput if you don't pay attention to some basic rules.

The first important rule is to reduce as much as possible the size of the message, which is being sent. A JMS message is basically composed of a header, a set of properties and the body of the message.

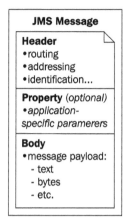

So at first you should get rid of the properties which you don't need and inflate the message. For example, use the `setDisableMessageID` method on the `MessageProducer` class to disable message ids if you don't need them. This decreases the size of the message and also avoids the overhead of creating a unique ID.

Also invoking `setDisableMessageTimeStamp` method on the `MessageProducer` class disables message timestamps and contributes to making the message smaller.

On the contrary, you should use `setTimeToLive`, which controls the amount of time (in milliseconds) after which the message expires. By default, the message never expires, so setting the optimal message age, will reduce memory overhead, thus improving performance.

As far as the message body is concerned, you should avoid using messages with a large data section. Verbose formats such as XML take up a lot of space on the wire and performance will suffer as result. Consider using `ByteMessages` if you need to transfer XML messages to ensure that the message is transmitted efficiently, avoiding unnecessary data conversion.

Also you should be careful with the `ObjectMessage` type. `ObjectMessage` is convenient but it comes at a cost: the body of an `ObjectMessage` uses Java serialization to serialize it to bytes. The Java serialized form of even small objects is very verbose so takes up a lot of space on the wire, also Java serialization is slow compared to custom marshalling techniques. Only use `ObjectMessage` if you really can't use one of the other message types, for example if you really don't know the type of the payload until runtime.

Another element which influences the performances of your messages is the acknowledge mode:

- CLIENT_ACKNOWLEDGE mode is the least feasible option since the JMS server cannot send subsequent messages till it receives an acknowledgement from the client.

- AUTO_ACKNOWLEDGE mode follows the policy of delivering the message once-and-only once but this incurs an overhead on the server to maintain this policy and requires an acknowledgement to be sent from the server for each message received on the client.

- DUPS_OK_ACKNOWLEDGE mode has a different policy of sending the message more than once thereby reducing the overhead on the server but might impose an overhead on the network traffic by sending the message more than once.

From a performance point of view, usually DUPS_OK_ACKNOWLEDGE gives better performance than AUTO_ACKNOWLEDGE. You might consider this as an alternative to create a transacted session and batch up many acknowledgements with one acknowledge/commit.

Another thing you should always consider is re-using your JMS resources such as connections, sessions, consumers, and producers. Creating JMS resources is expensive and should be absolutely avoided for every message to be sent or consumed.

You should re-use temporary queues across many requests. As a matter of fact, when you are issuing a message using a temporary queue request-response pattern, the message is sent to the target and a reply-to header is set with the address of a local temporary queue. Instead of creating a new temporary queue you should just send back the response to the address specified in the reply-to.

An example use case with HornetQ

You have been hired by Acme Ltd to improve the performance of a Stock Trading application, which uses a JMS system for querying stock values, and to issue orders. The company has recently migrated to the HornetQ messaging system and has a performance goal of delivering 3 K (3000) messages per second. The average size of JMS messages is 1 KB.

The specifications of the system are to persist JMS messages for stock orders but not for stock quotation queries (which account for 80% of the traffic) where it can be acceptable for messages to be lost, in case of a system crash.

The system architecture is described as follows:

- JBoss 6.0.0 M5 with HornetQ 2.1.1 installed
- Linux System Fedora running on Xeon 4 Dual Core 32 Mb

The Acme project team has installed HornetQ with default values and, after a system warm-up, has launched a first batch of orders:

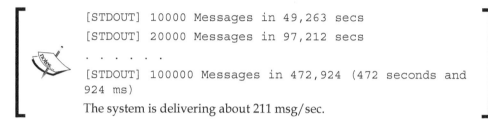

```
[STDOUT] 10000 Messages in 49,263 secs
[STDOUT] 20000 Messages in 97,212 secs
. . . . . .
[STDOUT] 100000 Messages in 472,924 (472 seconds and
924 ms)
```
The system is delivering about 211 msg/sec.

We are far away from the performance expectations; however don't despair, there's much room for improvement.

The first drastic remedy to your system will be to differentiate message persistence depending on the type of operation. Since most JMS messages are stock queries, you can send them as non-persistent messages. On the other hand, JMS messages bearing orders will be persisted.

```
if (isStockQuery) {
    sender.send(queue,message,javax.jms.DeliveryMode.NON_PERSISTENT
,1,0);
}
else {
  // Default persistent mode
    sender.send(message);
}
```

Here's the new benchmark output:

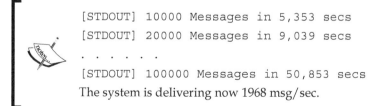

```
[STDOUT] 10000 Messages in 5,353 secs
[STDOUT] 20000 Messages in 9,039 secs
. . . . . .
[STDOUT] 100000 Messages in 50,853 secs
```
The system is delivering now 1968 msg/sec.

We have made a huge leap towards our target. The next change in the list, is installing libaio on our Linux system so that the journal can actually use the default ASYNCIO mode:

```
$ sudo yum install libaio
```

That's the new benchmark, using ASYNCIO:

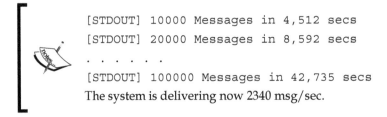

```
[STDOUT] 10000 Messages in 4,512 secs
[STDOUT] 20000 Messages in 8,592 secs
. . . . . .
[STDOUT] 100000 Messages in 42,735 secs
```
The system is delivering now 2340 msg/sec.

We are getting closer to our goal. The next optimization we will try is to set the `tcpnodelay` parameter to `true` which means disabling Nagle's algorithm. As a matter of fact this algorithm could yield some benefits for very small packets (in the range of a few bytes, think about a telnet session), however a typical JMS message is much bigger and bypassing this algorithm gives a definite performance boost.

```
<param key="hornetq.remoting.netty.tcpnodelay" value="true" />
```

Here's the new benchmark:

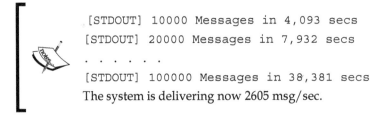

```
[STDOUT] 10000 Messages in 4,093 secs
[STDOUT] 20000 Messages in 7,932 secs
. . . . . .
[STDOUT] 100000 Messages in 38,381 secs
```
The system is delivering now 2605 msg/sec.

The next optimization we will include is tuning `tcpsend/receivebuffersize`. By multiplying network bandwidth X latency we have estimated the optimal network TCP buffer to 256 KB. So we will change the configuration accordingly:

```
<param key="hornetq.remoting.netty.tcpsendbuffersize" value="262144" />
<param key="hornetq.remoting.netty.tcpreceivebuffersize" value="262144" />
```

Running a new benchmark does not reveal any improvement in the message throughput:

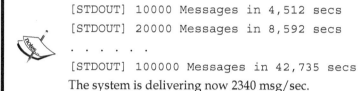

```
[STDOUT]  10000 Messages in 4,512 secs
[STDOUT]  20000 Messages in 8,592 secs
. . . . . .
[STDOUT]  100000 Messages in 42,735 secs
```
The system is delivering now 2340 msg/sec.

What might be the cause of it is that the operating system is not ready to use a TCP buffer size of 256 KB. By default, most Linux operating systems are tuned for low latency with a general purpose network environment.

As we have got plenty of memory on this machine, we will set the max OS send buffer size (wmem) and receive buffer size (rmem) to 12 MB for queues on all protocols. In other words, we will increase the amount of memory that is allocated for each TCP socket when it is opened or created while transferring files.

```
$ echo 'net.core.wmem_max=12582912' >> /etc/sysctl.conf
$ echo 'net.core.rmem_max=12582912' >> /etc/sysctl.conf
```

You also need to set minimum size, initial size, and maximum size in bytes:

```
$ echo 'net.ipv4.tcp_rmem= 10240 87380 12582912' >> /etc/sysctl.conf
$ echo 'net.ipv4.tcp_wmem= 10240 87380 12582912' >> /etc/sysctl.conf
```

Note: on Solaris you can use the ndd shell command to set the send(xmit) and receive(recv) buffer size. For example, the following command sets both buffers to 75.000 bytes.

```
ndd -set /dev/tcp tcp_xmit_hiwat 75000
ndd -set /dev/tcp tcp_recv_hiwat 75000
```

The new benchmark, with modified system kernel settings, shows a much-improved throughput:

```
[STDOUT]  10000 Messages in 3,524 secs
[STDOUT]  20000 Messages in 6,947 secs
. . . . . .
[STDOUT]  100000 Messages in 32,937 secs
```
We have reached 3.036 msg/sec, meeting the desired target.

It can be theoretically possible to obtain some additional improvements by reducing the size of JMS Messages (for example by removing properties which are not required). Also the journal logging can be further optimized by putting its log files on different physical volume from the paging directory. If you are frequently writing in these two locations on the same physical volume, the hard disk head has got the tough job to skip continuously between the two directories. The same rule can be applied for the transaction logs, in case you're using XA transactions in the AS.

Summary

In this chapter, we have covered two core middleware services: EJB and JMS service.

With proper tuning, you can greatly improve the performance of your stateless and stateful session beans.

The two elements you can use to fine tune performance of stateless beans (SLSB) are pool size and locking strategy.

- The optimal maximum size can be determined by inspecting the value of `concurrentCalls` attributes from the component statistics.

- Locking strategy can be chosen between `ThreadLocalPool` (default) and `StrictMaxPool`. The default `ThreaLocalPool` strategy delivers better throughput because it uses Thread local variables instead of synchronization. `StrictMaxPool` can be used to acquire an exact control over the maximum number of concurrent EJB instances.

- Stateful session beans (SFSBs) have higher CPU and memory requirements depending on the size of non-transient Objects contained in them and on the time span of the Session. If you keep them short, the performance of SFSBs can be assimilated to that of stateless session beans.

- Additional SFSB performance can be gained by disabling passivation, at the expense of higher memory consumption. So you should increase the JVM threshold to avoid garbage collector stealing this benefit.

- Extreme tuning resource is to modify the EJB container interceptor's stack by removing unnecessary AOP classes. Transaction interceptors are a potential candidate.

JBoss JMS is served by different providers in the releases 5.X and 6.X.

- The JBoss AS 5.x provider is JBoss Messaging Service. You can fine tune its ConnectionFactory by setting these two attributes:
  - `PrefetchSize`: indicates how many messages client side message consumers will buffer locally. The default value for `PrefetchSize` is 150. Larger values give better throughput but require more memory.
  - You should ensure that the attribute `SlowConsumers` is set to `false` otherwise this will disable client messaging buffering, which badly degrade your performance.
- The single destination should consider tuning the following parameters:
  - `PageSize`: indicates the maximum number of messages to pre-load in one single operation.
  - `FullSize`: this is the maximum number of messages held by the queue or topic subscriptions in memory at any one time. If you have a very high ratio of messages to be delivered, you should further increase the default value which is 75.000. Increase as well `DownCacheSize` to flush messages on the storage sparingly.
- The JBoss AS 6.x default JMS provider is HornetQ, which can be used also embedded in your application or as standalone JMS server. You can tune HornetQ in two major areas: the journal (where messages are persisted) and the tuning transport, which uses Netty libraries.
  - If you are frequently writing to the journal it's important to keep logging files in separate hard disk volumes to improve hard disk transfer rates. You are strongly advised to use Linux `ASYNCIO` libraries if your operating system supports it.
  - HornetQ transport tuning requires the setting of an appropriate TCP send/receive buffer size. You should modify these properties according to your operating system settings.
- Set the property `disabletcpdelay` to `true` to disable Nagle's algorithm and improve performance.
- Follow JMS best practices, which include reducing the size of the messages, re-using your JMS resources (connections, sessions, consumers ,and producers) and consider if you really need message persistence, which is the most expensive factor of a JMS session.

6

Tuning the Persistence Layer

5th Circle of Hell: Wrath and Sullenness: Here lay unfortunate developers blaming the application server for poor performance while neglecting to use a Connection Pool.

Data persistence is a key ingredient of any enterprise application and it has been a part of the JDK API since its very first release. Most readers certainly agree that data persistence is the most common cause of bottleneck in your applications. Unfortunately, isolating the root of the problem is not a straightforward affair and requires investigating in many areas: from the SQL code, to the interfaces used to issue SQL statements. Other potential areas that might affect your data persistence are the database configuration and finally, the underlying network and database hardware.

For this reason, we have divided this chapter into three main sections in order to cover all factors which can drag the performance of your data persistence:

- The first section introduces some principles of good database design. If your database design doesn't conform to some commonly agreed rules, chances are high that you will find it hard to achieve the performance needed for a successful application.

- The next section illustrates how to improve the performance of the Java Database Connectivity (JDBC) API, which allows connecting to a legacy database by means of drivers released by database vendors.

- The last section covers the core concepts about Java Persistence API and the Hibernate framework, which is used by JBoss AS as a persistence engine.

Designing a good database

Before you begin the development of your application, both logical and physical database design must be right there. Once the application has been implemented, it's simply too late to fix an inaccurate database design, leaving no other choice than buying a larger amount of fast, expensive hardware to cope with the problem.

Designing a database structure is usually the task of a database administrator. However, it's not rare in today's tight-budget world that the software architect takes care to design the database schemas as well. That's why you should be aware of a few basic concepts like database normalization, database partitioning, and good column indexing.

Reducing the space needed by your database

One of the most basic optimizations is to design your tables to take as little space on the disk as possible. This makes disk reads faster and uses less memory for query processing.

In order to reduce the amount of space used by your tables, you should first choose, for your columns, the smallest data type possible. As a matter of fact, the smaller your data types, the more indexes (and data) can fit into a block of memory, the faster your queries will be.

Secondly, you should carefully choose between a **normalized** database and a **de-normalized** database.

Database normalization eliminates redundant data, which usually makes updates faster since there is less data to change. However, a normalized schema causes joins for queries, which makes queries slower. The following image shows database normalization versus database de-normalization:

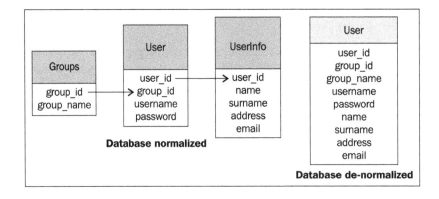

On the other hand, a de-normalized database replicates most of the information in one or several tables, thus speeding up data retrieval but reducing the performance of updates.

The DBA point of view

The primary objective of normalization is data integrity. So if you are choosing to de-normalize your database, be aware that having multiple copies of the same data can easily get out of sync due to programmer or system errors.

Applications involving many transactions, also known as **Online Transaction Processing**, generally perform better with a normalized schema, which guarantees fast updates/inserts.

As a matter of fact, most of the applications involving extremely large amounts of transactions are slowed down by *row locks*, which are necessary to guarantee the integrity of transactions. On the other hand, reporting types of application (**Online Analytical Processing**) performing massive amounts of selects are generally faster with a de-normalized schema.

Your first goal in the design process should be to normalize your data. Next, you can test your design with realistic data and transactions. At this point, if you see that de-normalization will help, then by all means you can apply it. But don't assume that you need to de-normalize data until you can prove (through testing) that it's the right thing to do.

With JPA O/R mapping you can use the **@Embedded** annotation for de-normalized columns to specify a persistent field whose @Embeddable type can be stored as an intrinsic part of the owning entity and share the identity of the entity.

Partitioning the database

If you are designing a database that potentially could be very large, holding millions or billions of rows, you should consider the option of partitioning your database tables. You can partition your database in two ways:

- **Horizontal partitioning** divides what would typically be a single table into multiple tables, creating many smaller tables instead of a single, large table. The advantage of this is that it is generally much faster to query a single small table than a single large table.

The next image shows an example of how you could split your `Sales` table in different sub-tables depending on the region which sales are related to:

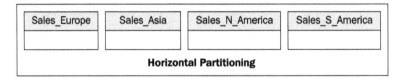

Horizontal Partitioning

Also, you could split tables on a time basis, for example, you might partition the table into separate sub-tables for each year of transactions.

- **Vertical Partitioning** distributes a table with many columns into multiple tables with fewer columns, so that only certain columns are included in a particular dataset, with each partition including all rows.

> Although partitioning is considered a dangerous premature optimization for small to medium scale projects, if you are dealing with huge sets of data, it is often a prudent choice. Adapting your application to a different partitioning logic can lead to major architectural changes; this can be far more expensive in time and money.

For example, a table that contains a number of very wide BLOB columns that aren't referenced often, can be split into two tables with the most-referenced columns in one table and the seldom-referenced text or BLOB columns in another. Here's an example of vertical partitioning:

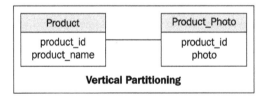

Vertical Partitioning

By removing the large data columns from the table, you get a faster query response time for the more frequently accessed `Product` data. Wide tables can slow down queries, so you should always ensure that all columns defined in a table are actually needed.

Using JPA/Hibernate mapping, you can easily map the above case with a lazy one-to-many relationship between the `Product` table and the `ProductPhoto` table. The `ProductPhoto` contains a less frequently accessed BLOB data type, which can be lazy loaded, that is queried just when the client requests the specific fields of the relationship.

Using indexes

Effective indexes are one of the best ways to improve performance of a database schema. Just like the reader searching for a word in a book, an index helps when you are looking for a specific record or set of records with a WHERE clause.

Since index entries are stored in sorted order, indexes also help when processing ORDER BY clauses. Without an index, the database has to load the records and sort them during execution.

Though indexes are indispensable for fast queries, they can have some drawbacks as well, in particular when the time comes to modify records. As a matter of fact, any time a query modifies the data in a table the indexes on the data must change too. Try to use a maximum of four or five indexes on one table, not more. If you have a read-only table, then the number of indexes may be safely increased.

There are a number of guidelines to building the most effective indexes for your application which are valid for every database, in particular:

- **Index on appropriate columns**: In order to achieve the maximum benefit from an index, you should choose to index the most common column, that is, in your WHERE clauses for queries against this table.

- **Keep indexes small**: Short indexes are faster to process in terms of I/O and are faster to compare. An index on an integer field provides optimal results.

- **Choose distinct keys**: If the fields bearing the index have small or no duplicate values, it is highly selective and provides the best performance results.

- **Structure the composite index correctly**: If you create a composite (multicolumn) index, the order of the columns in the keys are very important. Put the most unique data element, the element that has the biggest variety of values, first in the index. The index will find the correct page faster.

Not many Hibernate/JPA users know that you can define indexes in the table configuration of Hibernate. For example, if you need to define an index named `index1` on the columns `column1` and `column2` you should use this simple annotation:

```
@Table(appliesTo="tableName", indexes = { @
Index(name="index1", columnNames={"column1",
"column2"} ) } )
```

Tuning JDBC

Java Database Connectivity API was the first interface used by Java programmers to connect to database systems. Even if many new database persistence methods for Java programmers have been developed recently (for example, Entity, JDO, Hibernate, and many others), most database access code running in today's systems is written as plain JDBC.

The reason for the popularity of JDBC, besides the obvious fact that it was the first API released, is that it does not require any special knowledge to get started with it. Just feed the native SQL to your JDBC interfaces and collect the result.

JDBC tuning follows the same pattern as any tuning process, that is, you should at first measure the performance of your application in production and then evaluate possible corrections. However, it's worth to know some basic tuning techniques, which are available from the outset without sacrificing good design and coding practices.

These basic principles, which are described in the following sections, can also be used as a foundation for frameworks built on top of JDBC, for example, Hibernate. More precisely you should:

- Introduce a database Connection Pool that reuses your connections
- Make use of proper JDBC features, such as fetch size and batch size
- Use `Prepared` statements in your application and configure a `Prepared` statement cache at application server level

Using a Connection Pool

The first basic rule you need to follow when programming JDBC is to use a Connection Pool when accessing a database. Establishing database connections, depending upon the platform, can take from a few milliseconds up to one second. This can be a meaningful amount of time for many applications, if done frequently. As depicted in the following image, the Connection Pool is located in the path of a JDBC connection:

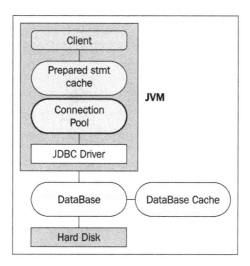

A Connection Pool allows the reuse of physical connections and minimizes expensive operations in the creation and closure of sessions. Also, maintaining many idle connections is expensive for a database management system, and the pool can optimize the usage of idle connections (or disconnect, if there are no requests).

From the programmer's point of view, what the application server provides you is a Connection object implemented by JBoss AS as org.jboss.resource.adapter.jdbc.WrappedConnection.

For example, if you are interested in retrieving the underlying implementation of an OracleConnection from the Connection Pool of JBoss AS perform the following commands:

```
Connection conn = myJBossDatasource.getConnection();
WrappedConnection wrappedConn = (WrappedConnection)conn;
Connection underlyingConn = wrappedConn.getUnderlyingConnection();
OracleConnection oracleConn = (OracleConnection)underlyingConn;
```

You might be wondering what the advantage of retrieving the underlying Connection implementation is. One good reason is if you need to access some custom properties, which are not available through the base Connection interface. For example, if you are using an Oracle thin driver and you need to debug your **Prepared Statement Cache Size**, you can use the `getStatementCacheSize()` method of the `OracleConnection` object:

```
System.out.println("Stmt Cache size is " +  oracleConn.
getStatementCacheSize());
```

For more details about configuring the Connection Pool, you can refer to *Chapter 4, Tuning the JBoss AS*, where we have dissected all the performance details about it.

Setting the proper fetch size

The fetch size is the number of rows physically retrieved from the database at one time by the JDBC driver as you scroll through a `ResultSet` with the `next()` method.

If you set the query fetch size to 100, when you retrieve the first row, the JDBC driver retrieves at once the first 100 rows (or all of them if fewer than 100 rows satisfy the query). When you retrieve the second row, the JDBC driver merely returns the row from local memory — it doesn't have to retrieve that row from the database. This feature improves performance by reducing the number of calls (which are frequently network transmissions) to the database.

To set the query fetch size, use the `setFetchSize()` method on the `Statement` (or `PreparedStatement` or `CallableStatement`) before execution.

The optimal fetch size is not always obvious. Usually, a fetch size of one half or one quarter of the total expected result size is optimal.

As a general rule, setting the query fetch size is mostly effective for a large `ResultSet`. If you set the fetch size much larger than the number of rows retrieved, it's likely that you'll get a performance decrease, not an increase.

Setting a higher default fetch size on JBoss AS

If you plan to set increase the default Row Prefetch for all your statements, then you can do it by means of the **defaultRowPrefetch** Connection property. If you acquire the Connection from JBoss AS Datasource, then you need to add the following property to your – ds.xml file:

```
<connection-property name="defaultFetchSize">50</
connection-property>
```

The following micro-benchmark shows the different timing when retrieving a set of 500 records using a fetch size of 10 (default), 250, and 1000 records respectively. As you can see, using a fetch size around ¼ and ½ of the expected list of records usually produces the best results, while using an exaggeratedly high value is counter productive both from the performance view and from the memory usage.

Label	# Samples	Average	Median	90% Line	Min	Max	Error %	Throughput	KB/sec
HTTP Request	500	1047	902	1333	292	6905	0,00%	7,7/sec	2,1
TOTAL	500	1047	902	1333	292	6905	0,00%	7,7/sec	2,1

Default fetch size

Label	# Samples	Average	Median	90% Line	Min	Max	Error %	Throughput	KB/sec
HTTP Request	500	657	492	1266	108	5208	0,00%	9,0/sec	2,4
TOTAL	500	657	492	1266	108	5208	0,00%	9,0/sec	2,4

Fetch size 250 records

Label	# Samples	Average	Median	90% Line	Min	Max	Error %	Throughput	KB/sec
HTTP Request	500	1042	826	2292	106	4561	0,00%	6,5/sec	1,7
TOTAL	500	1042	826	2292	106	4561	0,00%	6,5/sec	1,7

Fetch size 1000 records

Caution! The memory used by row fetching does not depend only on the number of rows!

The cost of maintaining the local cache of fetched rows depends on the sum of many factors: The number of columns, the defined size of each column, and the fetch size. For example, if using an Oracle database, for each column assume 2 bytes per char in the defined size for character types, 4 KB for LOBs and RAWs, and 22 bytes for everything else. Sum the sizes of the columns, and then multiply by the fetch size.

As you can imagine, the cost of row fetching can be much higher for certain data types like blob, image, and so on. You are advised to use smaller fetch sizes for these types while you can try bigger numbers for other simpler column types.

Use batch updates for bulk insert/updates

In situations where you want to issue several inserts or updates in the same unit of work, update batching lets you to group those statements together and transmit them to the database as one set of instructions. Like setting the query fetch size, update batching works by reducing the number of network transmissions between the application and the database.

For example, consider a website for online sales. When customers create orders, they often order multiple items. Usually when the order is recorded, the items on the order are recorded at the same time. Update batching allows the multiple inserts for the order to be transmitted to the database at once.

Update batching is supported for SQL issued via `PreparedStatement`, `CallableStatement`, and `Statement` objects. As with manipulating the query fetch size, the amount of performance improvement with batching statements varies between database vendors. Also, the network speed plays an important role in determining the real benefit of bulk updates.

Here's a benchmark comparing a bulk insert of 250 records with and without batch updates. As you can see, the throughput is almost 20 times higher when switching to batch updates.

Label	# Samples	Average	Median	90% Line	Min	Max	Error %	Throughput	KB/sec
HTTP Request	500	430	386	601	307	972	0,00%	2,3/sec	,6
TOTAL	500	430	386	601	307	972	0,00%	2,3/sec	,6

250 inserts - no batching

Label	# Samples	Average	Median	90% Line	Min	Max	Error %	Throughput	KB/sec
HTTP Request	500	26	18	48	12	132	0,00%	37,9/sec	10,1
TOTAL	500	26	18	48	12	132	0,00%	37,9/sec	10,1

250 inserts - with batching

Use Prepared Statements instead of Statements

As explained in *Chapter 4, Tuning the JBoss AS*, a Prepared Statement greatly enhances the performance of your queries because it avoids the burden of parsing the SQL statement over and over again. Using Prepared Statements brings the additional advantage of safely binding values to SQL parameters. So, for example, the quote characters in the given search are escaped and are no longer treated as control characters but as a part of the search string value.

 Prepared Statements are also helpful in preventing **SQL injection**, which happens when user input is either incorrectly filtered for string literal escape characters or user input is not strongly typed and thereby unexpectedly executed.

Besides using Prepared Statements in your application code, you can configure JBoss AS to use a **PreparedStatement cache** to store a set of Statements across different requests using an LRU cache. As you can see from the next image, the Prepared Statement cache sits between the Client and the Connection pool:

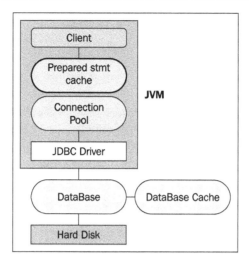

This can greatly improve the performance of queries which are executed often in your application. We will not re-hash the same concepts just exposed earlier so refer to *Chapter 4, Tuning the JBoss AS*, to learn more about the Prepared Statement cache.

Tuning JDBC networking

A JDBC connection is, behind the scenes, a socket connection to the legacy systems. So you can apply the same low-level network tuning which is generally used for socket-data transmission.

For example, it is useful to set the TCP send and receive buffer to a higher value than the default (32 KB), if your system allows it:

```
<connection-property name="tcpSndBuf">65534</connection-property>
<connection-property name="tcpRcvBuf">65534</connection-property>
<connection-property name="tcpNoDelay">true</connection-property>
```

Please note that not all JDBC drivers honor the same connection properties, while some of them might provide additional properties which are particularly suited to the underlying database. So use these properties with caution, if you really need to fix some network issues with your relational database.

Tuning Hibernate and JPA

Programming with JDBC API is quite simple as it is merely a thin layer over the database programming interfaces. However there are some downsides, which you need to consider:

- First, using native SQL language in your code exposes your application to a tight coupling with the database where your code has been initially developed. Even if the SQL dialects are similar, each database performs differently depending on the structure of the query, necessitating vendor-specific tuning in most cases.
- Second, when you are using plain JDBC, you need to bridge the gap between the relational model and the object model by creating a layer of intermediate objects or collections which host the data fetched from the DB. This is an unnecessary effort because ORM tools, such as Hibernate, can do it for you out of the box.
- Finally, by using an intermediate layer which sits between your code and the database it's possible to add additional services like caching which, if properly used, can greatly improved the performance of your applications.

JBoss AS has taken on the open-source project **Hibernate** that ships out of the box along with the application server libraries. Meanwhile, since the release of 1.5 of Java EE, a new specification has been added, namely the **Java Persistence API** (JPA), which allows designing your persistence layer using a Java-standard specification.

These two technologies are *similar* from one point of view since they are both fit for bridging the gap between the Java world and the legacy systems. However, they are *semantically* different because JPA is a standard Java EE specification while Hibernate is an Object Relational Mapping framework which can be used as a JPA implementation or as a standalone technology. Suggesting which strategy delivers the best application design is out of the scope of this book; rather we will show which are the best strategies to improve data persistence using both approaches. Since JBoss AS uses Hibernate as JPA Provider, we can easily provide a unified section of best practices which can be applied to both Hibernate and JPA.

Optimizing object retrieval

Efficient data loading is the most important factor when we aim at improving the performance of Hibernate and JPA.

Since every SQL statement issued to a database bears a cost, your goal is to minimize the number of statements and to simplify them so that querying can be as efficient as possible. You do this by applying the best fetching strategy for each collection or association.

Supposing you have the following scenario: You have a list of customers, who are buying items from your website. This kind of relation is generally expressed as a one-to-many relationship where you have for every customer (one) a set of items (many):

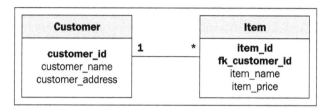

By default, Hibernate uses lazy data fetching, which means that you issue a query like this:

```
Query q = entityManager.createQuery("from Customer c where c.name =
'John Smith'");
```

Here, only the fields from `Customer` are initially loaded. If you then request the ordered items through the `customer.getItems()` method, this would also fill the collection of items ordered with another database hit.

In most cases, this approach is the best solution because it avoids fetching data that might not be requested at that time. However, this solution has a potential pitfall, which can be perceived by setting the property **hibernate.show_sql** to true:

```
<property name="hibernate.show_sql" value="true"/>
```

This is the log emitted by Hibernate when you request the customer's items:

```
//Query 1
select customer0_.ID as ID1_, customer0_.COUNTRY as COUNTRY1_,
customer0_.NAME as NAME1_ from customer customer0_ where
customer0_.NAME=? Limit ?
// Query 2
select items0_.CUSTOMER_ID as CUSTOMER5_1_, items0_.ID as ID1_,
items0_.ID as ID0_0_, items0_.CUSTOMER_ID as CUSTOMER5_0_0_,
items0_.PRICE as PRICE0_0_, items0_.PRODUCT as PRODUCT0_0_,
items0_.QUANTITY  as QUANTITY0_0_ from item items0_ where items0_.
CUSTOMER_ID=?
```

In spite of the fact that Hibernate uses a complex set of aliases to reference the underlying fields, it's evident that for every customer requested, there will be an additional query on the `Item` table to fetch the ordered items.

This problem is also known as the **n+1 problem** and tends to become a serious bottleneck as the number of parent objects retrieved increases. (Think about issuing a full table scan on the Customer table and accessing the ordered items).

It's about time to measure this scenario with some numbers: Let's assume we are performing a full table scan of the table Customer, containing 10000 records, each one accounting for 100 items ordered. The following JMeter benchmark accounts for our use case, which we will try to optimize in the next sections:

Label	# Samples	Average	Median	90% Line	Min	Max	Error %	Throughput	KB/sec
HTTP Reque...	500	948	556	1915	409	9732	0,00%	3,9/sec	,1
TOTAL	500	948	556	1915	409	9732	0,00%	3,9/sec	,1

Query: from Customer

In order to speed up data retrieval, we will analyze some possible solutions that include limiting the data fetched with paging, using a different fetch strategy or retrieving the data in bulk batches.

Ultimately, we will stress the importance of using Named Queries to improve the performance of Hibernate/JPA queries, which are executed repeatedly.

Limiting the amount of data fetched with pages

The first optimization will be to limit the amount of data retrieved from the database using the methods setFirstResults()/maxResults() of the class Query:

```
Query q = entityManager.createQuery("from Customer c");

q.setFirstResult(page*100).setMaxResults(100);
```

Now, we are fetching only 100 records (setMaxResults), starting from the page counter(setFirstResults). The new benchmark, using this smaller set of customers, follows here:

Label	# Samples	Average	Median	90% Line	Min	Max	Error %	Throughput	KB/sec
HTTP Reque...	500	98	83	97	81	2208	0,00%	13,2/sec	,2
TOTAL	500	98	83	97	81	2208	0,00%	13,2/sec	,2

Query: from Customer - max 100 records

As you can see, the throughput is multiplied by almost 4 times. Although the initial problem (caused by n+1 data extraction) has just been bypassed (but not solved), for many kinds of applications this approach can be just enough to meet the service-level agreements.

Additionally, data paging can be a convenient solution for applications, which are presenting data in pages, like most web applications do. Just be aware that you need to hit the database each time you navigate through pages.

Fetching parent and child items with a single query

Lazy loading is an excellent fetching strategy. However, if you need to access the fields of the association with a single query you can use a fetch join strategy. What is a fetch join? The Hibernate core documentation explains that *"a fetch join allows associations or collections of values to be initialized along with their parent objects, using a single select"*.

In practice, the joined fetched entities (in our example the items bought by a customer) must be a part of an association that is referenced by an entity returned from the query.

Let's see how our query changes using a join fetch:

```
Query q = entityManager.createQuery("from Customer c left outer join
fetch  c.items order by c.id");
```

By executing this statement, we'll see that Hibernate now loads both an Item and its Customer in a single SQL statement:

```
select customer0_.ID as ID25_0_, items1_.ID as ID24_1_, customer0_.
COUNTRY as COUNTRY25_0_, customer0_.NAME as NAME25_0_, items1_.
CUSTOMER_ID as CUSTOMER5_24_1_, items1_.PRICE as PRICE24_1_, items1_.
PRODUCT as PRODUCT24_1_, items1_.QUANTITY as QUANTITY24_1_, items1_.
CUSTOMER_ID as CUSTOMER5_0__, items1_.ID as ID0__ from customer
customer0_ left outer  join item items1_ on customer0_.ID=items1_.
CUSTOMER_ID order by customer0_.ID

. . . . . . . .// Other customers
```

And this is the corresponding benchmark which fetches the whole set of 5000 customers, each one bearing 100 items ordered.

Label	# Samples	Average	Median	90% Line	Min	Max	Error %	Throughput	KB/sec
HTTP Reque...	500	106	90	109	80	3303	0,00%	13,5/sec	,3
TOTAL	500	106	90	109	80	3303	0,00%	13,5/sec	,3
Query: from Customer c left outer join fetch c.items									

So, by using a fetch join strategy we have reached a higher throughput even compared to data paging which loads a limited set of data. At this point the reader might ask, *why not use together, paging with a fetch join strategy?* The next section covers this point.

Combining join fetches and paging

Before answering this question, a small preamble is necessary: paging features are not implemented internally by Hibernate or JDBC but using the database native functions that limit the number of records fetched by the query. For this reason, every DB will use its *own proprietary syntax*; for example, Oracle uses ROWNUM while MySQL uses LIMIT and OFFSET, and so on.

This leads to an important aspect to consider: If we query using a join, the logical table created by the database does not necessarily correspond to the collections of objects we are dealing with. As a matter of fact, the outcome of the join might duplicate customers in the logical tables but the database doesn't care about that since it's working with tables and not with objects.

In order to deal with this problem, Hibernate does not issue a statement with a native SQL instruction (such as LIMIT or ROWNUM). Instead, it fetches all of the records and performs the paging in memory, as indicated by the logs:

WARNING: firstResult/maxResults specified with collection fetch; applying in memory!

Running a new benchmark using a join fetch and paging reveals a reduction in throughput that is now lower than a simple join fetch without paging.

Label	# Samples	Average	Median	90% Line	Min	Max	Error %	Throughput	KB/sec
HTTP Reque…	500	131	100	107	79	1618	0,00%	12,3/sec	,2
TOTAL	500	131	100	107	79	1618	0,00%	12,3/sec	,2

Query: from Customer c left outer join fetch c.items - max 100 records

So, as a rule of thumb, either use join fetches or paging to reduce the time spent in retrieving data but don't use them together as the result might be a reduction in performance.

Speeding up your Hibernate queries with batches

Let's recap quickly our initial use case, using the default lazy loading strategy. If our session/entity manager has 5000 customers attached to it then, by default, for each first access to one of the customers' item collection, Hibernate will issue an SQL statement to fill that collection. At the end, 5000 statements will be executed to fetch the customers and their 100 collections.

Batch fetching is an optimization of the lazy select fetching strategy which can be used to define how many identical associations to populate in a single database query. You can apply it using the **@BatchSize** annotation at class level:

```
@BatchSize(size = 50)
```

or by means of the class's XML configuration file:

```
<class name="Item" batch-size="50">...</class>
```

When iterating through 5000 customers, Hibernate will load the items for the first 50, then for the next 50, and so on.

Here's a benchmark on our set of customers using a batch size of 50.

Label	# Samples	Average	Median	90% Line	Min	Max	Error %	Throughput	KB/sec
HTTP Requ...	500	246	172	361	133	6686	0,00%	10,1/sec	,2
TOTAL	500	246	172	361	133	6686	0,00%	10,1/sec	,2

Query: from Customer - Batch size 100

The throughput is still smaller than what you can achieve with the join fetch strategy. However, it carries the advantage that data can be lazy loaded; for this reason, when the referenced collections are seldom loaded, batch fetching can turn out to be the best data retrieval option.

As a side note, you can also define a default batch size for your Session Factory with the following property, which sets a default of 5.

```
<property name="default_batch_fetch_size">5</property>
```

Using named queries to speed up your queries

Until now, we have used queries defined in the single EJB methods requesting data. If you don't want to spread your queries across your methods, you can use **named queries** to declare them at class level and recall them wherever you need them:

```
@NamedQueries(
{
  @NamedQuery(
    name = "listCustomers",
    query = "FROM Customer c WHERE c.name = :name"
  )
})

public class Customer implements Serializable    {

}
```

The advantage, in terms of performance, is that the persistence provider will *precompile* HQL/JP QL named queries to SQL as part of the deployment or initialization phase of an application. This avoids the overhead of continuously parsing HQL/JP QL and generating SQL.

Even with a cache for converted queries, dynamic query definition will always be less efficient than using named queries.

A raw benchmark reveals that named query can outperform the standard query by about 10 percent:

Label	# Samples	Average	Median	90% Line	Min	Max	Error %	Throughput	KB/sec
HTTP Requ...	500	263	251	251	250	2922	0,00%	9,0/sec	2,3
TOTAL	500	263	251	251	250	2922	0,00%	9,0/sec	2,3

Query benchmark

Label	# Samples	Average	Median	90% Line	Min	Max	Error %	Throughput	KB/sec
HTTP Requ...	500	237	228	229	228	2746	0,00%	9,8/sec	2,5
TOTAL	500	237	228	229	228	2746	0,00%	9,8/sec	2,5

Named Query benchmark

Named queries also enforce the best practice of using query parameters. Query parameters help to keep the number of distinct SQL strings parsed by the database to a minimum. Because databases typically keep a cache of SQL statements on hand for frequently accessed queries, this is an essential part of ensuring peak database performance.

Improving the performance of bulk SQL statements

We have learnt how to improve the performance of a large set of queries. However, what about inserts or updates? Performing a large set of SQL statements (such as `insert`, `update`, or `delete`) can become a serious threat to your application's performance.

Generally updates and deletes should be performed, whenever possible, as HQL or even single SQL statements. For example, if you had to modify all columns of the `Person` table, you should possibly issue a statement, which is close to the database engine:

```
update Person p set p.name='xxx' where p.surname='yyy'
```

Inserts can be a little trickier as it's not possible to group them with a single SQL statement. So, unless you plan to use a stored procedure instead, your choice is restricted to plain JDBC updates (discussed earlier) or creating objects in a loop.

In the latter option, if you want to avoid the burden of synchronizing your classes with the DB for every insert, you should set a fetch size, like we did earlier for selects, and flush manually your insert when the batch reaches the desired size.

For example, here's how to perform a bulk insert of 1000 persons, by flushing every 50 records:

```
Session session =HibernateUtil.getSessionFactory().openSession();

session.beginTransaction();

for (int index = 0; index <1000;index++) {

    Person person = new Person();
    book.setCountry("Usa");
    book.setCity("NY");
    person.setName("Inhabitant n." + index);

    session.save(person);
    // Flush every 50 records
    if (index % 50== 0) {
        session.flush();
        session.clear();
    }
}
session.getTransaction().commit();
session.close();
```

Consider that the larger the batch of statements, the better performance you will achieve but you will accordingly use a greater amount of memory to be stored in the session. It's just one more trade-off between memory and performance.

Evaluating using caches to speed up your queries

A major justification for using object/relational persistence layer against direct JDBC is its potential for caching. Although, we will repeat it again, nothing beats a good database design and good fetching strategies. There is no doubt that for some kinds of applications, caching can have a serious impact on performance.

We will introduce the Hibernate caching system and show how to enable and use the first and second level Hibernate cache. This information and these rules can be applied to caching in general and are valid for more than just Hibernate applications.

Hibernate caches

A cache is a representation of the current database state either in memory or on the disk of the application server machine. Hibernate uses different types of caches, which are used for different purposes. Let us first have a look at these cache types:

- The first cache type is the **session cache** (also known as first level cache). The session cache caches object within the current session.

- The second cache type is the **second level cache**. This cache works at the SessionFactory level and is responsible for caching objects across sessions.

The following image shows where Hibernate caches are located in the path of a JDBC connection:

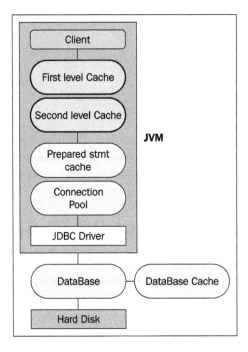

Additionally, Hibernate classifies the **query cache**, which is responsible for caching queries and their results, and the **timestamp cache**, which is used to decide whether a cached query is stale.

The first-level cache

The first-level cache ensures that when the application requests the same persistent object twice in a particular session, it gets back the same (identical) Java instance. This, sometimes, helps avoid unnecessary database traffic. More important, it ensures that changes made in a particular unit of work are always immediately visible to all other code executed inside that unit of work.

You don't have to do anything special to enable the session cache. It's, by default, on and cannot be disabled. As a matter of fact, Hibernate first tries to retrieve the object within the session. If this fails, the object will be loaded from the database. The object's retrieval and storage is handled by the `PersistenceContext` object, which is kept within the Hibernate session.

Whenever you pass an object to `save()`, `update()`, or `saveOrUpdate()`, and whenever you retrieve an object using `load()`, `find()`, `list()`, `iterate()`, or `filter()`, that object is added to the session cache. When `flush()` is subsequently called, the state of that object will be synchronized with the database.

Here's an example of first-level cache usage:

```
Session session = getSessionFactory().openSession();
Transaction tx = session.beginTransaction();

// Database hit
Customer person1 = (Customer) session.load(Customer.class, 1L);

// Loaded from the cache
Customer person2 = (Customer) session.load(Customer.class, 1L);

System.out.println(person2.getFirstName());
tx.commit();
session.close();
```

If you don't want this synchronization to occur, or if you're processing a huge number of objects and need to manage memory efficiently, you can use the `evict()` method of the session to remove the object and its collections from the first-level cache. To completely evict all objects from the session cache, call `Session.clear()`.

The second-level cache

The key characteristic of the second-level cache is that it is used across sessions, which also differentiates it from the session cache, which only, as the name says, has session scope.

The first thing to realize about the second-level cache is that Hibernate cache does not store instances of an entity. Instead, Hibernate uses something called **dehydrated state**. A dehydrated state can be thought of as a deserialized object, just like an array of strings, integers, and so on, and the ID of the entity is the pointer to the dehydrated entity.

Conceptually, you can think of it as a map, which contains the ID as key and an array as value. Or something like the following for a cache region:

```
{ id -> { attribute1, attribute2, attribute3 } }
{ 1 -> { "name", 100, null } }
{ 2 -> { "another name", 30, 4 } }
```

If the entity holds a collection of other entities then the other Entity also needs to be cached. In this case, it could look something like the following:

```
{ id -> { attribute1, attribute2, attribute3, Set{item1..n} } }
{ 1 -> { "name", 20, null , {1,2,5} } }
{ 2 -> { "another name", 30, 4 {4,8}} }
```

This is important for two reasons: at first, Hibernate doesn't need to hassle client code that can erroneously manipulate the cache objects and, most important, the relationships and associations do not become 'stale', and are easy to keep up to date as they are simply identifiers.

Configuring the second-level cache on JBoss AS

Hibernate provides a pluggable system to define cache providers using the property **hibernate.cache.provider_class**; by default, **Ehcache** is used as the caching provider which is good for transactional single-node applications.

When we are dealing with a clustered solution, however, we need a provider which is able to keep synchronized the set of data across the cluster. JBoss AS 5.x and 6.x ship with **JBoss Cache** framework which is a fully transactional, replicated, clustered cache also based on the **JGroups** multicast library.

JBoss Cache supports replication or invalidation, synchronous or asynchronous communication, and optimistic and pessimistic locking. We will look more in detail at the JBoss Cache framework in the next chapter, which is about clustering; now, we will continue discussing the features of the second-level cache.

In order to configure the second-level cache, you need to change the Hibernate configuration file (or the application's `persistence.xml` file if you are using JPA) and enable some specific properties.

Supposing you are using the second-level cache within a JPA application, you should update your `persistence.xml` file (located in the `META-INF` folder of your application) as follows:

```
<persistence version="1.0" xmlns="http://java.sun.com/xml/ns/
persistence" xmlns:xsi="http://www.w3.org/2001/XMLSchema-instance"
xsi:schemaLocation="http://java.sun.com/xml/ns/persistence http://
java.sun.com/xml/ns/persistence/persistence_1_0.xsd">
   <persistence-unit name="AppStore" transaction-type="JTA">
   <provider>org.hibernate.ejb.HibernatePersistence</provider>
     <jta-data-source>java:/MySqlDS</jta-data-source>
     <properties>
        <property name="hibernate.dialect" value="org.hibernate.dialect.
MySQLDialect"/>
        <property name="hibernate.cache.use_second_level_cache"
value="true"/>

        <property  name="hibernate.cache.region.factory_class"
 value="org.hibernate.cache.jbc2.
JndiMultiplexedJBossCacheRegionFactory"/>
        <property name="hibernate.cache.region.jbc2.cachefactory"
value="java:CacheManager"/>
        <property name="hibernate.cache.region.jbc2.cfg.entity"
value="mvcc-entity"/>
        <property name="hibernate.cache.region.jbc2.cfg.collection"
value="mvcc-entity"/>
     </properties>
   </persistence-unit>
</persistence>
```

The key property, which activates the second-level cache, is `hibernate.cache.use_second_level_cache`, which needs to be set to `true`.

In the next property (`hibernate.cache.region.factory_class`), we are telling Hibernate to use JBoss Cache as its second-level cache implementation

The next parameter (`hibernate.cache.region.jbc2.cachefactory`) is specific of JBoss Cache implementation; it specifies the JNDI name under which the `CacheManager` to use is bound. There is no default value, thus the user must specify the property.

The `hibernate.cache.region.jbc2.cfg.collection` property is, as well, specific to JBoss Cache and details the name of the configuration that should be used for collection caches.

Once you have activated the second-level cache, it's time to tell JBoss Cache which entities we are going to cache. Suppose we want to test caching the `Customer` object:

```
@Entity
@Cache(usage = CacheConcurrencyStrategy.TRANSACTIONAL, region =
"customers")
public class Customer implements Serializable    {
}
```

The **CacheConcurrencyStrategy** defines how to stores items in the cache and how to retrieve them later. JBoss Cache allows two different strategies:

- **Transactional**, used in the above example, guarantees full transactional isolation up to repeatable read, if required. You can use this strategy for read-mostly data where it's critical to prevent stale data in concurrent transactions, in the rare case of an update.

- **Read-only**, a concurrency strategy suitable for data which never changes.

> Choosing the right `CacheConcurrencyStrategy` plays a vital role in the performance of your cache. As a matter of fact if your data is just a reference, that is it never changes, you should always use the read-only strategy so that the cache provider does not need to synchronize the state of the object with the value stored in the cache.

The query cache

Entity cache requires that you access your database rows by means of its primary key. Sometimes this strategy cannot be applied and you need a more flexible way to collect your data, like caching the result of a query:

```
List blogs = session.createQuery("from Person p where p.name = :name
and p.surname = :surname");
```

The HQL statement that comprised the query can be cached as well (including any parameter values) along with the primary keys of all entities that comprise the result set.

In order to use the query cache, you need to follow a simple two-step procedure:

- At first, declare in your configuration (`persistence.xml` or `hibernate.cfg.xml`) that you want to use the query cache (by default, it's disabled):

```
<property name="hibernate.cache.use_query_cache" value="true"/>
```

- Then you need to specify which queries will be stored in the cache. Much the same way as with entities, you can apply at class-level, an annotation for this purpose:

```
@NamedQueries(
{
  @NamedQuery(
    name = "findCustomersByName",
    query = "FROM Customer c WHERE c.name = :name",
    hints = { @QueryHint(name = "org.hibernate.cacheable", value =
"true") }
    )
})
```

In the example that we just saw, we have added in the NamedQuery definition, a QueryHint annotation; this tells our caching provider to store the result of a query on the Customer table, filtered by name in the query cache.

You might wonder how your caching provider understands if the data stored in the query cache is synchronized with the content of the database. The answer is in the timestamp cache, which is actually used to decide if a cached query result set is stale. Hibernate looks in the timestamp cache for the timestamp of the most recent insert, update, or delete made to the queried table. If it's later than the timestamp of the cached query results, then the cached results are discarded and a new query is issued.

> As a consequence, not all queries will benefit from caching. For example, if a search screen has many different search criteria, then it's unlikely that the user will choose the same criterion twice. In this case, the cached query results won't be utilized, and we'd be better off not enabling caching for that query.

Entity cache versus query cache

Although entity cache and query cache are used for the same purpose, that is reducing the amount of database hits, the semantics of the two kinds of caching are significantly different.

Entity caching takes advantage of the fact that a database row (that reflects an entity's state) can be locked, with cache updates applied with that lock in place. This is extremely useful to ensure cache consistency across the cluster.

There is no clear database analog to a query result set that can be efficiently locked to ensure consistency in the cache. As a result, the fail-fast semantics used with the put operation of entity caching are not available; instead, query caching has semantics akin to an entity insert, including costly synchronous cluster updates and the JBoss Cache two-phase commit protocol.

To make things worse, Hibernate must aggressively invalidate query results from the cache any time any instance of one of the entity classes involved in the query's WHERE clause changes. As stated before, this is done by means of the timestamp cache, which checks the latest timestamp for every operation executed on a query.

As a consequence of these semantics, you need to use query cache with caution and mainly for data which is **read only or seldom updated**. Always monitor your application performance with cache disabled first and then with cache enabled. If you don't see any substantial benefit from caching your queries then you better stay away from query cache, which will otherwise consume system resources.

In the following screenshots we are trying to enforce these statements with an example:

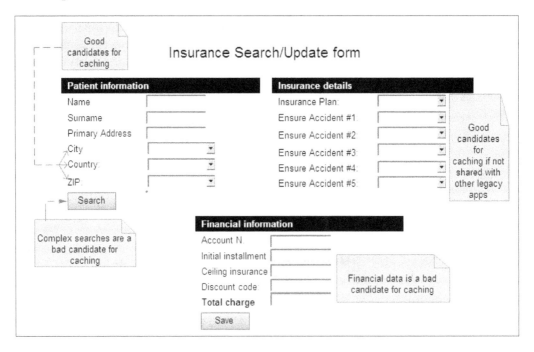

Here is a search and update form for an insurance company. As you can see on the left-hand side, it's not advisable to store the result of a complex set of searches in the query cache. On the other hand, items like **Country**, **City**, or **Zip** code are excellent candidates for caching as they reflect static data.

Functional information, such as insurance plans or department areas, can be as well candidates for caching, provided that no other legacy applications operate on those elements.

Finally, financial data, which is the result of highly-selective queries and is updated often, should be rarely considered as worth caching.

Optimizing data synchronization

The core concept of any ORM framework is that your classes reflect the state of the database at the current time. This means that you need to synchronize your JVM data with the database at certain times. By default, Hibernate and JPA use `FlushMode.AUTO`, which results in a synchronization before every HQL, SQL, or criteria query.

This guarantees that your classes' data will always reflect the content of the database but it is detrimental for performance since DML like UPDATE, INSERT, and DELETE operations execute in addition to a SELECT for the query.

For example, consider the following EJB method, which performs a set of transactions to finalize an order:

```
public Long customerTransaction(Long customerId, Long itemId){
    Item item = em.find(Item.class, itemId);
    Customer customer = em.find(Customer.class,customerId);
    item.setCustomer(customer);
    customer.addOrder(item);

    Query q1 = em.createNamedQuery("findCustomer");
    q.setParameter("Id", customerId);
    Customer customer = (Customer)q.getSingleResult();
    // Update Customer
    addCustomerOrder(item);

    Query q2 = em.createNamedQuery("findItems");
    q2.setParameter("Id", itemId);
    Item item = (Item)q2.getSingleResult();
    // Update Item
    reduceStock(item);
```

```
Query q3 = em.createNamedQuery("findCustomerBalance");
q3.setParameter("Id", customerId);
Long balance = (Long)q3.getSingleResult();
return balance;
}
```

Since here we are performing a chain of query-update-query-update-query-commit, this results in flushing the current data to the DB at least three times.

Hibernate/JPA offers the `FlushMode.COMMIT`, which decouples transaction demarcation from the synchronization. By using manual flushing, you can delay the execution of inserts and updates which are sent in bulk with the `flush()`.

So, in the previous example, that would turn to a single flush, triggered by the commit of the session.

Caution!

By turning to `FlushMode.COMMIT`, you have to expect that queries may return stale data or data that conflicts with the state of data in your current session. Managing your own transactional space can be tricky and leads to bugs in your code so use this flush mode with caution.

To test the effect of using `FlushMode` on performance, we have created a benchmark for the sample EJB transaction with the two `FlushMode` values of COMMIT and AUTO. The performance obtained with a `FlushMode` of COMMIT was about 10 percent higher than the one obtained with the default `FlushMode` (AUTO):

Label	# Samples	Average	Median	90% Line	Min	Max	Error %	Throughput	KB/sec
HTTP Requ...	500	322	314	323	301	2933	0,00%	8,1/sec	2,1
TOTAL	500	322	314	323	301	2933	0,00%	8,1/sec	2,1

Benchmark FlushMode.COMMIT

Label	# Samples	Average	Median	90% Line	Min	Max	Error %	Throughput	KB/sec
HTTP Requ...	500	376	363	373	351	5955	0,00%	7,3/sec	2,0
TOTAL	500	376	363	373	351	5955	0,00%	7,3/sec	2,0

Benchmark FlushMode.AUTO

A sample use case

In this chapter, we have covered several advanced concepts about caches. By now, you should be aware that you can greatly improve the performance of your application by caching read-only or read-mostly data. However, the cache can turn to a potential waste of memory and even a bottleneck when it's not used appropriately.

The following use case aims to show the rationale behind the choice of using or not using caches in your application.

Consider an application, which is a part of a *Provisioning System* managing network resources, which are planned to be allocated. In order to give to the end user a complete view of the network, the main panel displays the available resources in a tree, as displayed in the following image:

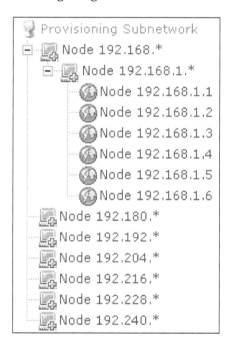

Since the network includes potentially hundreds of thousands resources, inner leaves are lazy loaded, when the user navigates across the tree.

The performance of the frontend GUI is however poor, since browsing through the nodes takes an average of 1.8 seconds. By using Eclipse Profiling tools, we have identified the methods, which are at the root of the bottleneck:

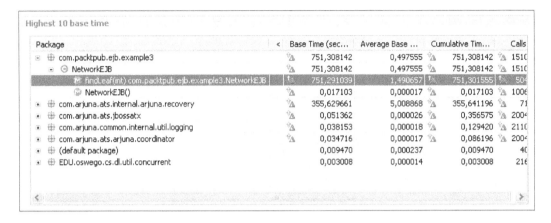

Highest 10 base time

Package	<	Base Time (sec...	Average Base ...	Cumulative Tim...	Calls
⊟ ⊕ com.packtpub.ejb.example3		751,308142	0,497555	751,308142	1510
⊟ ⊙ NetworkEJB		751,308142	0,497555	751,308142	1510
findLeaf(int) com.packtpub.ejb.example3.NetworkEJB		751,291039	1,490657	751,301555	504
⊙ NetworkEJB()		0,017103	0,000017	0,017103	1006
⊕ com.arjuna.ats.internal.arjuna.recovery		355,629661	5,008868	355,641196	71
⊕ com.arjuna.ats.jbossatx		0,051362	0,000026	0,356575	2004
⊕ com.arjuna.common.internal.util.logging		0,038153	0,000018	0,129420	2110
⊕ com.arjuna.ats.arjuna.coordinator		0,034716	0,000017	0,086196	2004
⊕ (default package)		0,009470	0,000237	0,009470	40
⊕ EDU.oswego.cs.dl.util.concurrent		0,003008	0,000014	0,003008	216

As you can see, the method `loadLeaf()` takes an average of 1.49 seconds to complete. So, it's responsible for over 80 percent of the time to update the GUI.

We have further analyzed the actual queries sent to the database by using a monitoring tool like P6Spy (discussed in Chapter 4, *Tuning the JBoss AS*) and we have discovered that about 50 percent of the actual queries use a combination of 500 possible parameters in the `loadLeaf()` method.

Besides browsing the tree, the end user additionally performs one update operation every four actions.

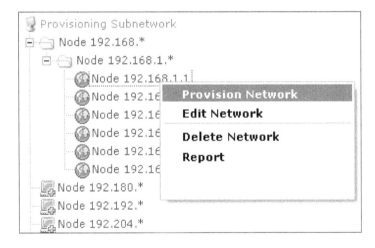

We take this into account, since it might potentially invalidate the content of some references held in the query cache.

Based on this data, we have launched a first benchmark without any cache optimization, which we will use as a starting point of comparison. The initial throughput stays around **30,5/min** with an average of 1.85 seconds to elaborate a response.

Label	# Samples	Average	Median	90% Line	Min	Max	Error %	Throughput	KB/sec
HTTP Requ...	100000	1852	1018	3565	1007	9646	0,00%	30,5/min	,1
TOTAL	100000	1852	1018	3565	1007	9646	0,00%	30,5/min	,1
No Cache Benchmark									

Starting from this state, we will try to introduce the second-level caching and see if it helps in speeding up the rendering of the GUI. Supposing you can retrieve the network resources with a find by primary key, we will tag the tree entities with the @Cache annotation and configure the `persistence.xml` to activate the second-level cache.

Here's the new benchmark, with entity caching enabled:

Label	# Samples	Average	Median	90% Line	Min	Max	Error %	Throughput	KB/sec
HTTP Requ...	100000	636	1001	1103	4	2288	0,00%	1,6/sec	,4
TOTAL	100000	636	1001	1103	4	2288	0,00%	1,6/sec	,4
Entity Cache Benchmark - Hit ratio 50%									

As you can see, the throughput is over three times higher and the average time dipped to 0.6 seconds per response.

Entity caching, however, is not always a viable solution as sometimes the application requires a different strategy (apart from *finding with primary key*) to collect data. So, if your only possible choice is the query cache, we will configure the persistence provider to activate it and tag the `findLeaf` query as *cacheable*.

Here's the benchmark with query cache enabled:

Label	# Samples	Average	Median	90% Line	Min	Max	Error %	Throughput	KB/sec
HTTP Requ...	100000	1273	1042	2120	1002	2703	0,00%	47,1/min	,2
TOTAL	100000	1273	1042	2120	1002	2703	0,00%	47,1/min	,2
Query Cache Benchmark - Hit ratio 50%									

The application has still scored a 50 percent throughput gain by using caching. However, the performance gains are reduced due to the fact that the query cache discards the items in the cache and after that an update is performed on that row.

So, in definitive, this is a typical scenario where the second-level cache brings consistent benefits to your applications because we have:

- A prevalence of reads against updates
- Slow queries / slow network
- A high cache hit ratio

Should these conditions change, the usefulness of the second-level cache will be reduced or can be even detrimental for the performance of the application.

By repeating the benchmark with different cache hit ratios, we have noticed that query caching will be pretty useless at a cache hit ratio of 20 percent, while dropping at 10 percent or lower, it becomes even detrimental.

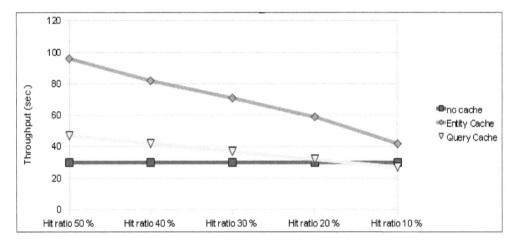

Entity caches, on the other hand, seem promising to increase the performance of your applications also with lower cache hit ratios. However, in such a scenario, the entity cache will keep storing data in the cache, which will be rarely used. The application memory budget will progressively be reached and, in the long run, the performance of the application will then be reduced.

As a proof of concept, we have compared the garbage collector statistics of a benchmark scoring a 50 percent cache hit ratio with the one running a cache hit ratio of 10 percent. Here's a snapshot taken from VisualVM garbage collector plugin:

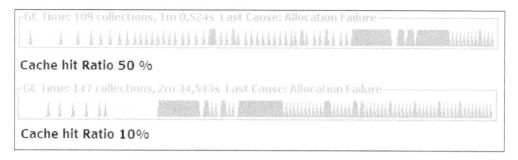

It's evident that caching with a low cache hit ratio will result in decreased performance due to de-optimization of the JVM garbage collector. In the end, low cache hit ratios forces memory fragmentation and expedites major and full garbage collections.

Summary

In this chapter, we have covered data persistence tuning from various points of view. In particular, we have started discussing database design techniques, then we have moved to plain JDBC programming, reaching the heart of the application server with JPA and Hibernate tuning. Summing up, the most important things learnt are resumed here:

- Good database design depends on the type of application you are running.
    - ° Applications using lots of transactions benefit from database normalization because there is less data to change and thus reduced lock contention.
    - ° On the other hand, Online Analytical Processing systems (like report applications) are generally faster with a denormalized schema because they can benefit from faster queries.
    - ° Database schemas holding huge amount of records can perform much better if the data is partitioned.
    - ° A solid database design also requires a correct use of indexes. Generally, you should apply indexes to fields used in the WHERE clause. Consider, however, that too many indexes will slow down database updates.

- JDBC programming is the foundation for understanding complex frameworks, which are built on the top of this API.

    ○ You should always acquire database connections from a Connection Pool which reuses connections each time they have terminated their job.

    ○ Setting the correct fetch size when browsing from a database cursor can improve your JDBC performance of about 10 percent. An optimal fetch size should be about ¼ up to ½ of the estimated query count.

    ○ You should always use batch updates to perform bulk insert/ updates. A bulk insert performed with batches is generally 20 times faster then with plain statements.

    ○ PreparedStatements should be used wherever a query is executed several times in an application.

- Hibernate and the JPA Specification are built on the top of JDBC programming allowing the bridging of the gap between the database layer and the Java objects.

    ○ Retrieving data with Hibernate and JPA requires applying the correct fetch strategy. By default, data is lazily loaded which avoids the cost of early loading relationships. This, however, carries the problem of additional queries executed to fetch the parent-child relationship, also known as *n+1 problem*.

    ○ Data Paging can be used by means of the `setFirstResults()`/ `maxResults()` methods of the class Query. This allows loading a smaller page of data with a consistent time saving.

    ○ Using Join fetches you can combine data extraction of parent-child relationship with a single SQL statement. In most cases, this optimization is the logical solution to the n+1 problem.

    ○ Batch fetching is an optimization of the lazy select fetching strategy, which can be used to define how many identical associations to populate in a single database query.

- Caching is one of the main benefits of Hibernate/JPA over JDBC programming. There are basically two types of caching:

    ○ The first-level cache allows caching objects within the current session.

    ○ The second-level cache is responsible for caching objects across sessions. This cache contains a subset of caches, namely the entity cache, the query cache, and the timestamp cache.

- You should cache data which is read only or seldom modified.

- Before applying any caching strategy at first monitor your system performance without cache. Then you can progressively try to introduce caches verifying if the performance has increased or not.

- Expect the most consistent performance gains with entity caching. Use query caching with caution as frequent updates might reduce (or negate completely) the benefit of this cache.

JBoss AS Cluster Tuning

6th Circle of Hell: Heresy. This circle houses administrators who accurately set up a cluster to use Buddy Replication. Without caring about steady sessions.

Clustering allows us to run applications on several parallel instances (also known as cluster nodes). The load is distributed across different servers, and even if any of the servers fails, the application is still accessible via other cluster nodes. Clustering is crucial for scalable Enterprise applications, as you can improve performance by simply adding more nodes to the cluster.

In this chapter, we will cover the basic building blocks of JBoss Clustering with the following schedule:

- A short introduction to JBoss Clustering platform
- In the next section we will cover the low level details of the JGroups library, which is used for all clustering-related communications between nodes
- In the third section we will discuss JBoss Cache, which provides distributed cache and state replication services for the JBoss cluster on top of the JGroups library

Introduction to JBoss clustering

Clustering plays an important role in Enterprise applications as it lets you split the load of your application across several nodes, granting robustness to your applications. As we discussed earlier, for optimal results it's better to limit the size of your JVM to a maximum of 2-2.5GB, otherwise the dynamics of the garbage collector will decrease your application's performance.

Combining relatively smaller Java heaps with a solid clustering configuration can lead to a better, scalable configuration plus significant hardware savings.

The only drawback to scaling out your applications is an increased complexity in the programming model, which needs to be correctly understood by aspiring architects.

JBoss AS comes out of the box with clustering support. There is no all-in-one library that deals with clustering but rather a set of libraries, which cover different kinds of aspects. The following picture shows how these libraries are arranged:

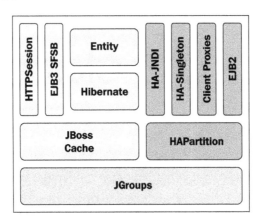

The backbone of JBoss Clustering is the **JGroups** library, which provides the communication between members of the cluster. Built upon JGroups we meet two building blocks, the **JBoss Cache** framework and the **HAPartition** service.

JBoss Cache handles the consistency of your application across the cluster by means of a replicated and transactional cache.

On the other hand, HAPartition is an abstraction built on top of a JGroups Channel that provides support for making and receiving RPC invocations from one or more cluster members. For example **HA-JNDI** (High Availability JNDI) or **HA Singleton** (High Availability Singleton) both use HAPartition to share a single Channel and multiplex RPC invocations over it, eliminating the configuration complexity and runtime overhead of having each service create its own Channel. (If you need more information about the HAPartition service you can consult the JBoss AS documentation http://community.jboss.org/wiki/jBossAS5ClusteringGuide.).

In the next section we will learn more about the JGroups library and how to configure it to reach the best performance for clustering communication.

Configuring JGroups transport

Clustering requires communication between nodes to synchronize the state of running applications or to notify changes in the cluster definition.

JGroups (`http://jgroups.org/manual/html/index.html`) is a reliable group communication toolkit written entirely in Java. It is based on IP multicast, but extends by providing reliability and group membership.

Member processes of a group can be located on the same host, within the same Local Area Network (LAN), or across a Wide Area Network (WAN). A member can be in turn part of multiple groups.

The following picture illustrates a detailed view of JGroups architecture:

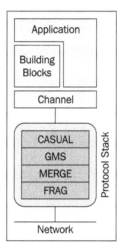

A JGroups process consists basically of three parts, namely the Channel, Building blocks, and the Protocol stack. The *Channel* is a simple socket-like interface used by application programmers to build reliable group communication applications. *Building blocks* are an abstraction interface layered on top of Channels, which can be used instead of Channels whenever a higher-level interface is required. Finally we have the *Protocol stack*, which implements the properties specified for a given channel.

> In theory, you could configure every service to bind to a different Channel. However this would require a complex thread infrastructure with too many thread context switches. For this reason, JBoss AS is configured by default to use *a single Channel* to multiplex all the traffic across the cluster.

The Protocol stack contains a number of layers in a bi-directional list. All messages sent and received over the channel have to pass through all protocols. Every layer may modify, reorder, pass or drop a message, or add a header to a message. A fragmentation layer might break up a message into several smaller messages, adding a header with an ID to each fragment, and re-assemble the fragments on the receiver's side.

The composition of the Protocol stack (that is, its layers) is determined by the creator of the channel: an XML file defines the layers to be used (and the parameters for each layer).

> Knowledge about the Protocol stack is not necessary when just using **Channels** in an application. However, when an application wishes to ignore the default properties for a Protocol stack, and configure their own stack, then knowledge about what the individual layers are supposed to do is needed.

In JBoss AS, the configuration of the Protocol stack is located in the file, `<server>\deploy\cluster\jgroups-channelfactory.sar\META-INF\jgroups-channelfactory-stacks.xml`.

The file is quite large to fit here, however, in a nutshell, it contains the following basic elements:

```
Protocol Stacks configuration

<UDP Transport configuration />

<protocol_stacks>

    <stack name="udp" />
    <stack name="udp-async" />
    <stack name="udp-sync" />

    <stack name="tcp" >
          <TCP Transport configuration />
    </stack>

    <stack name="tcp-sync" />

    <stack name="jbm-control" />
    <stack name="jbm-data" />

</protocol_stacks>
```

The first part of the file includes the **UDP** transport configuration. UDP is the default protocol for JGroups and uses multicast (or, if not available, multiple unicast messages) to send and receive messages.

 A multicast UDP socket can send and receive datagrams from multiple clients. The interesting and useful feature of multicast is that a client can contact multiple servers with a single packet, without knowing the specific IP address of any of the hosts.

Next to the UDP transport configuration, three protocol stacks are defined:

- udp: The default IP multicast based stack, with flow control
- udp-async: The protocol stack optimized for high-volume asynchronous RPCs
- udp-sync: The stack optimized for low-volume synchronous RPCs

Thereafter, the **TCP transport configuration** is defined. TCP stacks are typically used when IP multicasting cannot be used in a network (for example, because it is disabled) or because you want to create a network over a WAN (that's conceivably possible but sharing data across remote geographical sites is a scary option from the performance point of view).

You can opt for two TCP protocol stacks:

- `tcp`: Addresses the default TCP Protocol stack which is best suited to high-volume asynchronous calls.
- `tcp-async`: Addresses the TCP Protocol stack which can be used for low-volume synchronous calls.

If you need to switch to TCP stack, you can simply include the following in your command line args that you pass to JBoss:

`-Djboss.default.jgroups.stack=tcp`

Since you are not using multicast in your TCP communication, this requires configuring the addresses/ports of all the possible nodes in the cluster. You can do this by using the property `-Djgroups.tcpping.initial_hosts`. For example:

`-Djgroups.tcpping.initial_hosts=host1[7600],host2[7600]`

Ultimately, the configuration file contains two stacks which can be used for optimising JBoss Messaging Control Channel (`jbm-control`) and Data Channel (`jbm-data`).

How to optimize the UDP transport configuration

The default UDP transport configuration ships with a list of attributes, which can be tweaked once you know what they are for. A complete reference to the UDP transport configuration can be found on the JBoss clustering guide (`http://docs.jboss.org/jbossclustering/cluster_guide/5.1/html/jgroups.chapt.html`); for the purpose of our book we will point out which are the most interesting ones for fine-tuning your transport. Here's the core section of the UDP transport configuration:

The biggest performance hit can be achieved by properly tuning the attributes concerning `buffer size` (`ucast_recv_buf_size`, `ucast_send_buf_size`, `mcast_recv_buf_size`, and `mcast_send_buf_size`).

```
<UDP
  singleton_name="shared-udp"
  mcast_port="${jboss.jgroups.udp.mcast_port:45688}"
  mcast_addr="${jboss.partition.udpGroup:228.11.11.11}"
  tos="8"
  ucast_recv_buf_size="20000000"
  ucast_send_buf_size="640000"
  mcast_recv_buf_size="25000000"
  mcast_send_buf_size="640000"
  loopback="true"
  discard_incompatible_packets="true"
  enable_bundling="false"
  max_bundle_size="64000"
  max_bundle_timeout="30"
  . . . .
/>
```

As a matter of fact, in order to guarantee optimal performance and adequate reliability of UDP multicast, it is essential to size network buffers correctly. Using inappropriate network buffers the chances are that you will experience *a high frequency of UDP packets being dropped* in the network layers, which therefore need to be retransmitted.

The default values for JGroups' UDP transmission are 20MB and 64KB for unicast transmission and respectively 25MB and 64KB for multicast transmission. While these values sound appropriate for most cases, they can be insufficient for applications sending lots of cluster messages. Think about an application sending a thousand 1KB messages: with the default receive size, we will not be able to buffer all packets, thus increasing the chance of packet loss and costly retransmission.

Monitoring the intra-clustering traffic can be done through the `jboss.jgroups` domain Mbeans. For example, in order to monitor the amount of bytes sent and received with the UDP transmission protocol, just open your `jmx-console` and point at the `jboss.jgroups` domain. Then select your cluster partition. (Default the partition if you are running with default cluster settings). In the following snapshot (we are including only the relevant properties) we can see the amount of Messages sent/received along with their size (in bytes).

Name	Domain	jboss.jgroups
	cluster	DefaultPartition
	type	protocol
	protocol	UDP
Java Class	org.jgroups.jmx.protocols.UDP	
Description	Management Bean.	

Attribute Name	Access	Type	Description	Attribute Value
MessagesSent	R	long	MBean Attribute.	356
MessagesReceived	R	long	MBean Attribute.	471
BytesSent	R	long	MBean Attribute.	34718
BytesReceived	R	long	MBean Attribute.	45688

Besides increasing the JGroups' buffer size, another important aspect to consider is that most operating systems allow a maximum UDP buffer size, which is generally *lower* than JGroups' defaults. For completeness, we include here a list of default maximum UDP buffer size:

Operating System	Default Max UDP Buffer (in bytes)
Linux	131071
Windows	No known limit
Solaris	262144
FreeBSD, Darwin	262144
AIX	1048576

So, as a rule of thumb, you should always configure your operating system to take advantage of the JGroups' transport configuration. The following table shows the command required to increase the maximum buffer to 25 megabytes. You will need root privileges in order to modify these kernel parameters:

Operating System	Command
Linux	`sysctl -w net.core.rmem_max=26214400`
Solaris	`ndd -set /dev/udp udp_max_buf 26214400`
FreeBSD, Darwin	`sysctl -w kern.ipc.maxsockbuf=26214400`
AIX	`no -o sb_max=8388608` (AIX will only allow 1MB, 4MB, or 8MB)

Another option that is worth trying is `enable_bundling`, **which** specifies whether to enable message bundling. If true, the transport protocol would queue outgoing messages until `max_bundle_size` bytes have accumulated, or `max_bundle_time` milliseconds have elapsed, whichever occurs first.

The advantage of using this approach is that the transport protocol *would send bundled queued messages in one single larger message*. Message bundling can have significant performance benefits for channels using asynchronous high volume messages (for example, `JBoss Cache` components configured for `REPL_ASYNC`. JBoss Cache will be covered in the next section named Tuning JBoss Cache).

On the other hand, for applications based on a synchronous exchange of RCPs, the introduction of message bundling would introduce a considerable latency so it is not recommended in this case. (That's the case with JBoss Cache components configured as `REPL_SYNC`).

How to optimize the JGroups' Protocol stack

The Protocol stack contains a list of layers protocols, which need to be crossed by the message. A layer does not necessarily correspond to a transport protocol: for example a layer might take care to fragment the message or to assemble it. What's important to understand is that when a message is sent, it travels down in the stack, while when it's received it walks just the way back.

For example, in the next picture, the **FLUSH** protocol would be executed first, then the **STATE**, the **GMS**, and so on. Vice versa, when the message is received, it would meet the **PING** protocol first, them **MERGE2**, up to **FLUSH**.

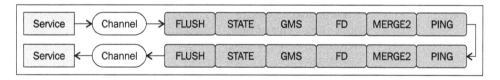

Following here, is the list of protocols triggered by the default UDP's Protocol stack.

```
<stack name="udp"
          description="Default: IP multicast based stack, with flow
control.">
      <config>
          <PING timeout="2000" num_initial_members="3"/>
          <MERGE2 max_interval="100000" min_interval="20000"/>
          <FD_SOCK/>
          <FD timeout="6000" max_tries="5" shun="true"/>
          <VERIFY_SUSPECT timeout="1500"/>
          <pbcast.NAKACK use_mcast_xmit="false" gc_lag="0"
              retransmit_timeout="300,600,1200,2400,4800"
              discard_delivered_msgs="true"/>
          <UNICAST timeout="300,600,1200,2400,3600"/>
          <pbcast.STABLE stability_delay="1000"
desired_avg_gossip="50000"
              max_bytes="400000"/>
          <pbcast.GMS print_local_addr="true" join_timeout="3000"
              shun="true"
              view_bundling="true"
              view_ack_collection_timeout="5000"/>
          <FC max_credits="2000000" min_threshold="0.10"
             ignore_synchronous_response="true"/>
          <FRAG2 frag_size="60000"/>
          <pbcast.STATE_TRANSFER/>
          <pbcast.FLUSH timeout="0"/>
      </config>
</stack>
```

The following table will shed some light on the above cryptic configuration:

Category	Usage	Protocols
Transport	Responsible for sending and receiving messages across the network	IDP, TCP, and TUNNEL
Discovery	Used to discover active nodes in the cluster and determine which is the coordinator	PING, MPING, TCPPING, and TCPGOSSIP
Failure Detection	Used to poll cluster nodes to detect node failures	FD, FD_SIMPLE, FD_PING, FD_ICMP, FD_SOCK, and VERIFY_SUSPECT

Category	Usage	Protocols
Reliable Delivery	Ensures that messages are actually delivered and delivered in the right order (FIFO) to the destination node	CAUSAL, NAKACK, pbcast. NAKACK, SMACK, UNICAST, and PBCAST
Group Membership	Used to notify the cluster when a node joins, leaves or crashes	pbcast.GMS, MERGE, MERGE2, and VIEW_SYNC
Flow Control	Used to adapt the data-sending rate to the data-receipt rate among nodes	FC
Fragmentation	Fragments messages larger than a certain size. Unfragments at the receiver's side	FRAG2
State transfer	Synchronizes the application state (serialized as a byte array) from an existing node with a newly joining node	pbcast.STATE_TRANSFER and pbcast.STREAMING_STATE_TRANSFER
Distributed garbage collection	Periodically deletes those that have been seen by all nodes from the memory in each node	pbcast.STABLE

While all the above protocols play a role in message exchanging, it's not necessary that you know the inner details of all of them for tuning your applications. So we will focus just on a few interesting ones.

The FC protocol, for example can be used to adapt the rate of messages sent with the rate of messages received. This has the advantage of creating an homogeneous rate of exchange, where no sender member overwhelms receiver nodes, thus preventing potential problems like filling up buffers causing packet loss. Here's an example of FC configuration:

```
<FC max_credits="2000000"
    min_threshold="0.10"
    ignore_synchronous_response="true"/>
```

The message rate adaptation is done with a simple credit system in which each time a sender sends a message a credit is subtracted (equal to the amount of bytes sent). Conversely, when a receiver collects a message, a credit is added.

- `max_credits` specifies the maximum number of credits (in bytes) and should obviously be smaller than the JVM heap size

- `min_threshold` specifies the value of `min_credits` as a percentage of the `max_credits` element

- `ignore_synchronous_response` specifies whether threads that have carried messages up to the application should be allowed to carry outgoing messages back down through FC without blocking for credits

The following image depicts a simple scenario where HostA is sending messages (and thus its `max_credits` is reduced) to HostB and HostC, which increase their `max_credits` accordingly.

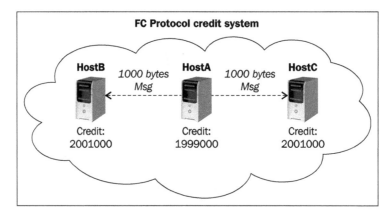

The FC protocol, while providing a control over the flow of messages, can be a bad choice for applications that are issuing synchronous group RPC calls. In this kind of applications, if you have fast senders issuing messages, but some slow receivers across the cluster, *the overall rate of calls will be slowed down*. For this reason, *remove FD from your protocol list if you are sending synchronous messages* or just switch to the udp-sync protocol stack.

Besides JGroups, some network interface cards (NICs) and switches perform **ethernet flow control** (IEEE 802.3x), which causes overhead to senders when packet loss occurs. In order to avoid a redundant flow control, you are advised to remove ethernet flow control. For managed switches, you can usually achieve this via a web or Telnet/SSH interface. For unmanaged switches, unfortunately the only chance is to hope that ethernet flow control is disabled, or to replace the switch.

If you are using NICs, you can disable ethernet flow control by means of a simple shell command, for example, on Linux with the `ethtool`:

```
/sbin/ethtool -A eth0 autoneg off tx on rx on
```

If you want simply to verify if ethernet flow control is off:

```
/sbin/ethtool -a eth0
```

One more thing you must be aware of is that, by using JGroups, cluster nodes must store all messages received for potential retransmission in case of a failure. However, if we store all messages forever, we will run out of memory. The distributed garbage collection service in JGroups periodically removes messages that have been seen by all nodes from the memory in each node. The distributed garbage collection service is configured in the `pbcast.STABLE` sub-element like so:

```
<pbcast.STABLE stability_delay="1000"
    desired_avg_gossip="5000"
    max_bytes="400000"/>
```

The configurable attributes are as follows:

- `desired_avg_gossip`: Specifies the interval (in milliseconds) between garbage collection runs. Setting this parameter to 0 disables this service.

- `max_bytes`: Specifies the maximum number of bytes to receive before triggering a garbage collection run. Setting this parameter to 0 disables this service.

You are advised to set a `max_bytes` value if you have a high-traffic cluster.

Tuning JBoss Cache

JBoss Cache provides the foundation for many clustered services, which need to synchronize application state information across the set of nodes.

The cache is organized as a tree, with a single root. Each node in the tree essentially contains a map, which acts as a store for key/value pairs. The only requirement placed on objects that are cached is that they implement `java.io.Serializable`.

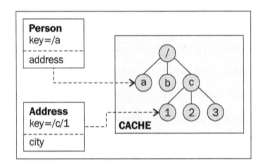

Actually EJB 3 Stateful Session Beans, HttpSessions, and Entity/Hibernate rely on JBoss Cache to replicate information across the cluster. We have discussed thoroughly data persistence in *Chapter 6, Tuning the Persistence Layer*, so we will focus in the next sections on SFSB and HttpSession cluster tuning.

The core configuration of JBoss Cache is contained in the JBoss Cache Service. In JBoss AS 5, the scattered cache deployments have been replaced with a new **CacheManager** service, deployed via the `<server>/deploy/cluster/jboss-cache-manager.sar/META-INF/jboss-cache-manager-jboss-beans.xml`.

The CacheManager acts as a factory for creating caches and as a registry for JBoss Cache instances. It is configured with a set of named JBoss Cache configurations. Here's a fragment of the standard SFSB cache configuration:

```
<entry><key>sfsb-cache</key>
    <value>
        <bean name="StandardSFSBCacheConfig"
class="org.jboss.cache.config.Configuration">
            <property
name="clusterName">${jboss.partition.name:DefaultPartition}-
SFSBCache</property>
            <property
name="multiplexerStack">${jboss.default.jgroups.stack:udp}</property>
            <property name="fetchInMemoryState">true</property>
            <property name="nodeLockingScheme">PESSIMISTIC</property>
            <property name="isolationLevel">REPEATABLE_READ</property>
```

```
            <property name="useLockStriping">false</property>
            <property name="cacheMode">REPL_SYNC</property>

  .  .  .  .  .
          </bean>
      </value>
  </entry>
```

Services that need a cache ask the CacheManager for the cache by name, which is specified by the `key` element; the cache manager creates the cache (if not already created) and returns it.

The simplest way to reference a custom cache is by means of the `org.jboss.ejb3.annotation.CacheConfig` annotation. For example, supposing you were to use a newly created Stateful Session Bean cache named `custom_sfsb_cache`:

```
@Stateful
@Clustered
@CacheConfig(name="custom_sfsb_cache")
public Class SFSBExample {
}
```

The CacheManager keeps a reference to each cache it has created, so all services that request the same cache configuration name will share the same cache. When a service is done with the cache, it releases it to the CacheManager. The CacheManager keeps track of how many services are using each cache, and will stop and destroy the cache when all services have released it.

Understanding JBoss Cache configuration

In order to tune your JBoss Cache, it's essential to learn some key properties. In particular we need to understand:

- How data can be transmitted between its members. This is controlled by the `cacheMode` property.
- How the cache handles concurrency on data between cluster nodes. This is handled by `nodeLockingScheme` and isolationLevel configuration attributes.

Configuring cacheMode

The `cacheMode` property determines how JBoss Cache keeps in sync data across all nodes. Actually it can be split in two important aspects: how to notify changes across the cluster and how other nodes accommodate these changes on the local data.

As far data notification is concerned, there are the following choices:

- **Synchronous** means the cache instance sends a notification message to other nodes and before returning waits for them to acknowledge that they have applied the same changes. Waiting for acknowledgement from all nodes *adds delay*. However, if a synchronous replication returns successfully, the caller knows for sure that all modifications have been applied to all cache instances.

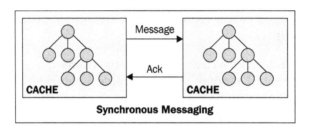

Synchronous Messaging

- **Asynchronous** means the cache instance sends a notification message and then immediately returns, without any acknowledgement that changes have been applied. The Asynchronous mode is most useful for cases like session replication (for example, Stateful Session Beans), where the cache sending data expects to be the only one that accesses the data. Asynchronous messaging adds a small potential risk that a fail over to another node may generate stale data, however, for many session-type applications this risk is acceptable given the major performance benefits gained.

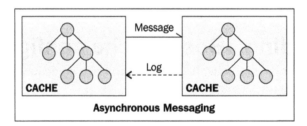

Asynchronous Messaging

- **Local** means the cache instance doesn't send a message at all. You should use this mode when you are running JBoss Cache as a single instance, so that it won't attempt to replicate anything. For example, JPA/Hibernate Query Cache uses a local cache to invalidate stale query result sets from the second level cache, so that JBoss Cache doesn't need to send messages around the cluster for a query result set cache.

As far as the second aspect is concerned (what should the other caches in the cluster do to reflect the change) you can distinguish between:

Replication: means that the cache replicates cached data across all cluster nodes. This means the sending node needs to include the changed state, increasing the cost of the message. Replication is necessary if the other nodes have no other way to obtain the state.

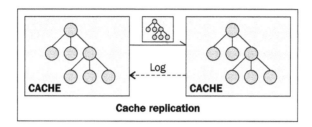

Cache replication

Invalidation means that you do not wish to replicate cached data but simply inform other caches in a cluster that data under specific addresses are now stale and should be evicted from memory. Invalidation reduces the cost of the cluster update messages, since only the cache key of the changed state needs to be transmitted, not the state itself.

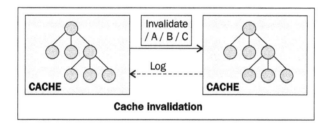

Cache invalidation

By combining these two aspects we have a combination of five valid values for the `cacheMode` configuration attribute:

CacheMode	Action	Used by
REPL_SYNC	Synchronous replication messages are sent	HAPartitionCache
REPL_ASYNC	Asynchronous replication messages are sent	EJB 3 SFSBs, HttpSession, Replicated QueryCache, TimestampCache
INVALIDATION_SYNC	Synchronous invalidation messages are sent	Entity and Collection Caches
INVALIDATION_ASYNC	Asynchronous invalidation messages are sent	None
LOCAL	No cluster messages are needed	Local Query cache

Should I use invalidation for session data?

No, you shouldn't. As a matter of fact, data invalidation it is an excellent option for a clustered JPA/Hibernate Entity cache, since the cached state can be re-read from the database in case of failure. If you use the invalidation option, with SFSBs or HttpSession, then you lose *failover capabilities*. If this matches with your project requirements, you could achieve better performance by simply turning off the cache.

Configuring cache concurrency

JBoss Cache is a thread-safe caching API, and uses its own efficient mechanisms of controlling concurrent access. Concurrency is configured via the `nodeLockingScheme` and `isolationLevel` configuration attributes.

There are three choices for `nodeLockingScheme`:

- **Pessimistic** locking involves threads/transactions acquiring locks on nodes before reading or writing. Which is acquired depends on the `isolationLevel` but in most cases a non-exclusive lock is acquired for a read and an exclusive lock is acquired for a write. Pessimistic locking requires a considerable overhead and allows lesser concurrency, since *reader threads must block until a write has completed* and released its exclusive lock (potentially a long time if the write is part of a transaction). The drawbacks include the potential for deadlocks, which are ultimately solved by a `TimeoutException`.

- **Optimistic** locking seeks to improve upon the concurrency available with Pessimistic by creating a workspace for each request/transaction that accesses the cache. All data is versioned; on completion of non-transactional requests or commits of transactions the version of data in the workspace is compared to the main cache, and an exception is raised if there are inconsistencies. This eliminates the cost of reader locks but, because of the cost associated with the parallel workspace, *it carries a high memory overhead and low scalability*.

- **MVCC** is the new locking schema that has been introduced in JBoss Cache 3.x (and packed with JBoss AS 5.x). In a nutshell, MVCC reduces the cost of slow, and synchronization-heavy schemas with a *multi-versioned* concurrency control, which is a locking scheme commonly used by modern database implementations to control concurrent access to shared data.

The most important features of MVCC are:

1. Readers don't acquire any locks.
2. Only one additional version is maintained for shared state, for a single writer.
3. All writes happen sequentially, to provide fail-fast semantics.

How does MVCC can achieve this?

For each reader thread, the MVCC's interceptors wraps state in a lightweight container object, which is placed in the thread's InvocationContext (or TransactionContext if running in a transaction). All subsequent operations on the state are carried out on the container object using Java references, which allow repeatable read semantics even if the actual state changes simultaneously.

Writer threads, on the other hand, *need to acquire a lock* before any writing can start. Currently, **lock striping** is used to improve the memory performance of the cache, and the size of the shared lock pool can be tuned using the concurrencyLevel attribute of the locking element.

After acquiring an exclusive lock on a cache Full Qualified Name, the writer thread then wraps the state to be modified in a container as well, just like with reader threads, and then copies this state for writing. When copying, a reference to the original version is still maintained in the container (for rollbacks). Changes are then made to the copy and the copy is finally written to the data structure when the write completes.

Should I use MVCC with session data too?

While MVCC is the default and recommended choice for JPA/Hibernate Entity caching, as far as Session caching is concerned, Pessimistic is still the default concurrency control. Why? As a matter of fact, *accessing the same cached data by concurrent threads it's not the case with a user's session*. This is strictly enforced in the case of SFSB, whose instances are not accessible concurrently. So don't bother trying to change this property for session data.

Configuring the isolationLevel

The isolationLevel attribute has two possible values, READ_COMMITTED and REPEATABLE_READ which correspond in semantics to database-style isolation levels. Previous versions of JBoss Cache supported all database isolation levels, and if an unsupported isolation level is configured, it is either upgraded or downgraded to the closest supported level.

REPEATABLE_READ is the default isolation level, to maintain compatibility with previous versions of JBoss Cache. READ_COMMITTED, while providing a slightly weaker isolation, has a significant performance benefit over REPEATABLE_READ.

Tuning session replication

As we have learnt, the user session needs replication in order to achieve a consistent state of your applications across the cluster. Replication can be a costly affair, especially if the amount of data held in session is significant. There are however some available strategies, which can mitigate a lot the cost of data replication and thus improve the performance of your cluster:

- Override isModified method: By including an isModified method in your SFSBs, you can achieve fine-grained control over data replication. Applicable to SFSBs only.

- Use buddy replication. By using buddy replication you are not replicating the session data to all nodes but to a limited set of nodes. Can be applicable both to SFSBs and HttpSession.

- Configure replication granularity and replication trigger. You can apply custom session policies to your HttpSession to define when data needs to be replicated and which elements need to be replicated as well. Applicable to HttpSession.

Override SFSB's isModified method

One of the simplest ways to reduce the cost of SFSBs data replication is implementing in your EJB a method with the following signature: public boolean isModified ();

Before replicating your bean, the container will detect if your bean implements this method. If your bean does, the container calls the isModified method and it *only replicates the bean when the method returns true*. If the bean has not been modified (or not enough to require replication, depending on your own preferences), you can return false and the replication will not occur.

If your session does not hold critical data (such as financial information), using the isModified method is a good option to achieve a substantial benefit in terms of performance. A good example could be a reporting application, which needs session management to generate aggregate reports through a set of wizards. Here's a graphical view of this process:

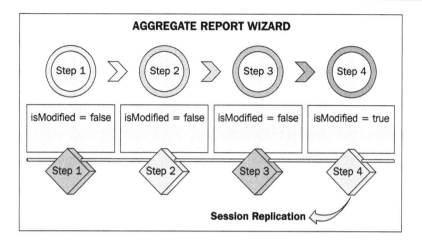

The following benchmark is built on exactly the use case of an OLAP application, which uses SFSBs to drive some session data across a four step wizard. The benchmark compares the performance of the wizard without including isModified and by returning true to isModified at the end of the wizard.

Label	# Samples	Average	Median	90% Line	Min	Max	Error %	Throughput	KB/sec
HTTP Request	50000	2405	2200	3882	220	10369	0,00%	19,7/sec	5,4
TOTAL	50000	2405	2200	3882	220	10369	0,00%	19,7/sec	5,4
				SFSB without isModified					
Label	# Samples	Average	Median	90% Line	Min	Max	Error %	Throughput	KB/sec
HTTP Request	50000	2218	2069	3467	192	8912	0,00%	20,8/sec	6,4
TOTAL	50000	2218	2069	3467	192	8912	0,00%	20,8/sec	6,4
				SFSB setting isModified(true) every four calls					

Ultimately, by using the isModified method to propagate the session data at wider intervals you can improve the performance of your application with an acceptable risk to re-generate your reports in case of node failures.

Use buddy replication

By using buddy replication, sessions are replicated to a configurable number of backup servers in the cluster (also called buddies), rather than to all servers in the cluster. If a user fails over from the server that is hosting his or her session, the session data is transferred to the new server from one of the backup buddies. Buddy replication provides the following benefits:

- Reduced memory usage
- Reduced CPU utilization
- Reduced network transmission

The reason behind this large set of advantages is that each server only needs to store in its memory the sessions it is hosting as well as those of the servers for which it is acting as a backup. Thus, less memory required to store data, less CPU to elaborate bits to Java translations, and less data to transmit.

For example, in an 8-node cluster with each server configured to have one buddy, a server would just need to store 2 sessions instead of 8. That's just one fourth of the memory required with total replication.

In the following picture, you can see an example of a cluster configured for buddy replication:

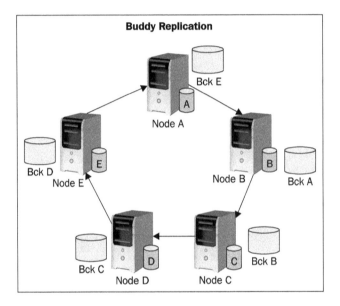

Here, each node contains a cache of its session data and a backup of another node. For example, node A contains its session data and a backup of node E. Its data is in turn replicated to node B and so on.

In case of failure of node A, its data moves to node B which becomes the owner of both A and B data, plus the backup of node E. Node B in turn replicates (A + B) data to node C.

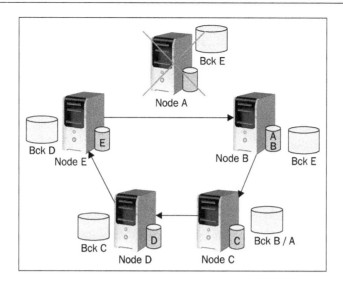

In order to configure your SFSB sessions or HttpSessions to use buddy replication
you have just to set to the property `enabled` of the bean `BuddyReplicationConfig`
inside the `<server>/deploy/cluster/jboss-cache-manager.sar/META-INF/`
`jboss-cache-manager-jboss-beans.xml` configuration file, as shown in the next
code fragment:

```
<property name="buddyReplicationConfig">
        <bean
class="org.jboss.cache.config.BuddyReplicationConfig">

        <property name="enabled">true</property>

        . . .

        </bean>
</property>
```

In the following test, we are comparing the throughput of a 5-node clustered web
application which uses buddy replication against one which replicates data across
all members of the cluster.

Label	# Samples	Average	Median	90% Line	Min	Max	Error %	Throughput	KB/sec
HTTP Requ...	150000	187	169	239	163	1439	0,00%	65,3/sec	51,4
TOTAL	150000	187	169	239	163	1439	0,00%	65,3/sec	51,4
Web application benchmark using buddy replication									
Label	# Samples	Average	Median	90% Line	Min	Max	Error %	Throughput	KB/sec
HTTP Requ...	150000	200	176	291	167	1591	0,00%	50,0/sec	41,3
TOTAL	150000	200	176	291	167	1591	0,00%	50,0/sec	41,3
Web application benchmark with full cluster replication									

In this benchmark, switching on buddy replication improved the application throughput of about 30%. No doubt that by using buddy replication there's a high potential for scaling because memory/CPU/network usage per node does not increase linearly as new nodes are added.

Advanced buddy replication

With the minimal configuration we have just described, each server will look for one buddy across the network where data needs to be replicated. If you need to backup your session to a larger set of buddies you can modify the numBuddies property of the BuddyReplicationConfig bean. Consider, however, that replicating the session to a large set of nodes would conversely reduce the benefits of buddy replication.

Still using the default configuration, each node will try to select its buddy on a different physical host: this helps to reduce chances of introducing a single point of failure in your cluster. Just in case the cluster node is not able to find buddies on different physical hosts, it will not honour the property ignoreColocatedBuddies and fall back to co-located nodes.

The default policy is often what you might need in your applications, however if you need a fine-grained control over the composition of your buddies you can use a feature named *buddy pool*. A buddy pool is an optional construct where each instance in a cluster may be configured to be part of a group- just like an "exclusive club membership".

This allows system administrators a degree of flexibility and control over how buddies are selected. For example, you might put two instances on separate physical servers that may be on two separate physical racks in the same buddy pool. So rather than picking an instance on a different host on the same rack, the BuddyLocators would rather pick the instance in the same buddy pool, on a separate rack which may add a degree of redundancy.

Here's a complete configuration which includes buddy pools:

```
<property name="buddyReplicationConfig">
    <bean class="org.jboss.cache.config.BuddyReplicationConfig">

        <property name="enabled">true</property>
        <property name="buddyPoolName">rack1</property>
        <property name="buddyCommunicationTimeout">17500</property>

        <property name="autoDataGravitation">false</property>
        <property name="dataGravitationRemoveOnFind">true</property>
        <property
name="dataGravitationSearchBackupTrees">true</property>
```

```
        <property name="buddyLocatorConfig">
            <bean
class="org.jboss.cache.buddyreplication.NextMemberBuddyLocatorConfig"
>

                <property name="numBuddies">1</property>
                <property name="ignoreColocatedBuddies">true</property>
            </bean>
        </property>
    </bean>
</property>
```

In this configuration fragment, the buddyPoolName element, if specified, creates a logical subgroup and only picks buddies who share the same buddy pool name. If not specified, this defaults to an internal constant name, which then treats the entire cluster as a single buddy pool.

If the cache on another node needs data that it doesn't have locally, it can ask the other nodes in the cluster to provide it; nodes that have a copy will provide it as part of a process called **data gravitation**. The new node will become the owner of the data, placing a backup copy of the data on its buddies.

The ability to gravitate data means there is no need for all requests for data to occur on a node that has a copy of it; that is, any node can handle a request for any data. However, data gravitation is expensive and should not be a frequent occurrence; ideally it should only occur if the node that is using some data fails or is shut down, forcing interested clients to fail over to a different node.

The following optional properties pertain to data gravitation:

- autoDataGravitation: Whether data gravitation occurs for every cache miss. By default this is set to false to prevent unnecessary network calls.

- DataGravitationRemoveOnFind: Forces all remote caches that own the data or hold backups for the data to remove that data, thereby making the requesting cache the new data owner. If set to false, an evict is broadcast instead of a remove, so any state persisted in cache loaders will remain. This is useful if you have a shared cache loader configured. (See next section about Cache loader). Defaults to true.

- dataGravitationSearchBackupTrees: Asks remote instances to search through their backups as well as main data trees. Defaults to true. The resulting effect is that if this is true then backup nodes can respond to data gravitation requests in addition to data owners.

Buddy replication and session affinity

One of the pre-requisites to buddy replication working well and being a real benefit is the use of session affinity, also known as **sticky sessions** in HttpSession replication speak. What this means is that if certain data is frequently accessed, it is desirable that this is always accessed on one instance rather than in a "round-robin" fashion as this helps the cache cluster optimise how it chooses buddies, where it stores data, and minimises replication traffic.

If you are replicating SFSBs session, there is no need to configure anything since SFSBs, once created, are pinned to the server that created them.

When using HttpSession, you need to make sure your software or hardware load balancer maintain the session on the same host where it was created.

By using Apache's mod_jk, you have to configure the workers file (workers. properties) specifying where the different node and how calls should be load-balanced across them. For example, on a 5-node cluster:

```
worker.loadbalancer.balance_workers=node1,node2,node3,node4,node5
worker.loadbalancer.sticky_session=1
```

Basically, the above snippet configures mod_jk to perform round-robin load balancing with sticky sessions (sticky_session=1) across 5 nodes of a cluster.

Configure replication granularity and replication trigger

Applications that want to store data in the HttpSession need to use the methods setAttribute to store the attributes and getAttribute to retrieve them. You can define two kind of properties related to HttpSessions:

- The replication-trigger configures when data needs to be replicated.
- The replication-granularity defines which part of the session needs to be replicated.

Let's dissect both aspects in the following sections:

How to configure the replication-trigger

The replication-trigger element determines what triggers a session replication and can be configured by means of the `jboss-web.xml` element (packed in the `WEB-INF` folder of your web application). Here's an example:

```
<jboss-web>
   <replication-config>
      <replication-trigger>SET</replication-trigger>
   </replication-config>
</jboss-web>
```

The following is a list of possible alternative options:

- `SET_AND_GET` is conservative but not performance-wise; it will always replicate session data even if its content has not been modified but simply accessed. This setting made (a little) sense in AS 4 since using it was a way to ensure that every request triggered replication of the session's timestamp. Setting `max_unreplicated_interval` to 0 accomplishes the same thing at much lower cost.

- `SET_AND_NON_PRIMITIVE_GET` is conservative but will only replicate if an object of a non-primitive type has been accessed (that is, the object is not of a well-known immutable JDK type such as Integer, Long, String, and so on.) This is the default value.

- `SET` assumes that the developer will explicitly call `setAttribute` on the session if the data needs to be replicated. This setting prevents unnecessary replication and can have a major beneficial impact on performance.

 In all cases, calling `setAttribute` marks the session as dirty and thus triggers replication.

For the purpose of evaluating the available alternatives in performance terms, we have compared a benchmark of a web application using different replication-triggers:

Label	# Samples	Average	Median	90% Line	Min	Max	Error %	Throughput	KB/sec
HTTP Request	200000	237	97	808	7	2744	0,00%	165,6/sec	45,1
TOTAL	200000	237	97	808	7	2744	0,00%	165,6/sec	45,1

Replication trigger: SET_AND_NON_PRIMITIVE_GET (default)

Label	# Samples	Average	Median	90% Line	Min	Max	Error %	Throughput	KB/sec
HTTP Request	200000	149	9	379	4	3557	0,00%	205,1/sec	55,9
TOTAL	200000	149	9	379	4	3557	0,00%	205,1/sec	55,9

Replication trigger: SET (50% items in session modified)

Label	# Samples	Average	Median	90% Line	Min	Max	Error %	Throughput	KB/sec
HTTP Request	200000	124	22	324	2	4262	0,00%	263,8/sec	71,9
TOTAL	200000	124	22	324	2	4262	0,00%	263,8/sec	71,9

Replication trigger: SET (0% items modified)

In the first benchmark, we are using the default rule (SET_AND_NON_PRIMITIVE_GET). In the second we have switched to SET policy, issuing a setAttribute on 50% of the requests. In the last benchmark, we have formerly populated the session with the required attributes and then issued only queries on the session via the getAttribute method.

As you can see the benefit of using the SET replication trigger is obvious, especially if you follow a read-mostly approach on non-primitive types. On the other hand, this requires very good coding practices to ensure setAttribute is always called whenever a mutable object stored in the session is modified.

How to configure the replication-granularity

As far as what data needs to be replicated is concerned, you can opt for the following choices:

- SESSION indicates that the *entire session* attribute map should be replicated when any attribute is considered modified. Replication occurs at request end. This option replicates the most data and thus incurs the highest replication cost, but since all attributes values are always replicated together it ensures that any references between attribute values will not be broken when the session is deserialized. For this reason it is the default setting.

- ATTRIBUTE indicates that *only attributes* that the session considers to be potentially modified are replicated. Replication occurs at request end. For sessions carrying large amounts of data, parts of which are infrequently updated, this option can significantly increase replication performance.

- FIELD level replication only *replicates modified data fields* inside objects stored in the session. Its use could potentially drastically reduce the data traffic between clustered nodes, and hence improve the performance of the whole cluster. To use FIELD-level replication, you have to first prepare (that is bytecode enhance) your Java class to allow the session cache to detect when fields in cached objects have been changed and need to be replicated.

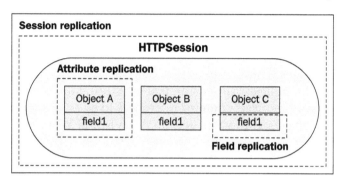

In order to change the default replication granularity, you have to configure the desired attribute in your jboss-web.xml configuration file:

```
<jboss-web>
    <replication-config>
        <replication-granularity>FIELD</replication-granularity>
        <replication-field-batch-mode>true</replication-field-batch-
mode>
    </replication-config>
</jboss-web>
```

In the above example, the replication-field-batch-mode element indicates whether you want all replication messages associated with a request to be batched into one message.

Additionally, if you want to use FIELD level replication you need to perform a bit of extra work. At first you need to add the @org.jboss.cache.pojo.annotation. Replicable annotation at class level:

```
@Replicable
public class Person { ... }
```

If you annotate a class with @Replicable, then all of its subclasses will be automatically annotated as well.

Once you have annotated your classes, you will need to perform a post-compiler processing step to bytecode enhance your classes for use by your cache. Please check the JBoss AOP documentation (http://www.jboss.org/jbossaop) for the usage of the aoc post-compiler. The JBoss AOP project also provides easy to use ANT tasks to help integrate those steps into your application build process.

As proof of concept, let's build a use case to compare the performance of ATTRIBUTE and FIELD granularity policies. Supposing you are storing in your HttpSession an object of Person type. The object contains references to an Address, ContactInfo, and PersonalInfo objects. It contains also an ArrayList of WorkExperience.

 A prerequisite to this benchmark is that there are no references between the field values stored in the Person class (for example between the contactInfo and personalInfo fields), otherwise the references will be broken by ATTRIBUTE or FIELD policies.

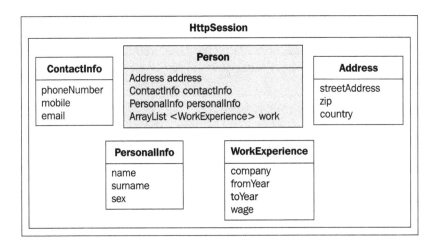

By using the SESSION or ATTRIBUTE replication-granularity policy, even if just one of these fields is modified, the whole Person object need to be retransmitted. Let's compare the throughput of two applications using respectively the ATTRIBUTE and FIELD replication-granularity.

Label	# Samples	Average	Median	90% Line	Min	Max	Error %	Throughput	KB/sec
HTTP Requ...	20000	215	80	658	5	2556	0,00%	180,8/sec	49,5
TOTAL	20000	215	80	658	5	2556	0,00%	180,8/sec	49,5

HTTP Session Attribute Replication

Label	# Samples	Average	Median	90% Line	Min	Max	Error %	Throughput	KB/sec
HTTP Requ...	20000	164	65	440	5	1923	0,00%	206,4/sec	59,2
TOTAL	20000	164	65	440	5	1923	0,00%	206,4/sec	59,2

HTTP Session Field Replication

In this example, based on the assumption that we have a single *dirty* field of Person' class per request, by using `FIELD` Replication generate a substantial 10% gain.

Tuning cache storage

Cache loading allows JBoss Cache to store cached data in a persistent store and is used mainly for HttpSession and SFSB sessions. Hibernate and JPA on the other hand, have already their persistence storage in the database so it doesn't make sense to add another storage.

This data can either be an overflow, where the data in the persistent store has been evicted from memory. Or it can be a replication of what is in memory, where everything in memory is also reflected in the persistent store, along with items that have been evicted from memory.

The cache storage used for web session and EJB3 SFSB caching comes into play in two circumstances:

- Whenever a cache element is *accessed*, and that element is not in the cache (for example, due to eviction or due to server restart), then the cache loader transparently loads the element into the cache if found in the backend store.

- Whenever an element is *modified*, *added* or *removed*, then that modification is persisted in the backend store via the cache loader (except if the `ignoreModifications` property has been set to true for a specific cache loader). If transactions are used, all modifications created within a transaction are persisted as well.

Cache loaders are configured by means of the property `cacheLoaderConfig` of session caches. For example, in the case of SFSB cache:

```
<entry><key>sfsb-cache</key>
    <value>
        <bean name="StandardSFSBCacheConfig"
class="org.jboss.cache.config.Configuration">
        . . . . .
    <property name="cacheLoaderConfig">
```

```
<bean class="org.jboss.cache.config.CacheLoaderConfig">
    <property name="passivation">true</property>
    <property name="shared">false</property>
    <property name="individualCacheLoaderConfigs">
      <list>
        <bean
class="org.jboss.cache.loader.FileCacheLoaderConfig">
          <property
name="location">${jboss.server.data.dir}${/}sfsb</property>
<property name="async">false</property>
          <property name="fetchPersistentState">true</property>
          <property name="purgeOnStartup">true</property>
          <property name="ignoreModifications">false</property>
          <property
name="checkCharacterPortability">false</property>
        </bean>
      </list>
    </property>
  </bean>
      . . . ..
</entry>
```

The `passivation` property, when set to true, means the persistent store acts as an overflow area written to when data is evicted from the in-memory cache.

The *shared* attribute indicates that the cache loader is shared among different cache instances, for example where all instances in a cluster use the same JDBC settings to talk to the same remote, shared database. Setting this to true prevents repeated and unnecessary writes of the same data to the cache loader by different cache instances. The default value is false.

Where does cache data get stored?

By default, the Cache loader uses a filesystem implementation based on the class `org.jboss.cache.loader.FileCacheLoaderConfig`, which requires the `location` property to define the root directory to be used.

If set to true, the `async` attribute read operations are done synchronously, while write (**CRUD** - Create, Remove, Update, and Delete) operations are done asynchronously. If set to false (default), both read and writes are performed synchronously.

Should I use an async channel for my Cache Loader?

When using an async channel, an instance of `org.jboss.cache.loader.AsyncCacheLoader` is constructed which will act as an asynchronous channel to the actual cache loader to be used. Be aware that, using the `AsyncCacheLoader`, there is always the possibility of dirty reads since all writes are performed asynchronously, and it is thus impossible to guarantee when (and even if) a write succeeds. On the other hand the `AsyncCacheLoader` allows massive writes to be written asynchronously, possibly in batches, with large performance benefits. Checkout the JBoss Cache docs for further information `http://docs.jboss.org/jbosscache/3.2.1.GA/apidocs/index.html`.

`fetchPersistentState` determines whether or not to fetch the persistent state of a cache when a node joins a cluster and conversely the `purgeOnStartup` property evicts data from the storage on startup, if set to true.

Finally, `checkCharacterPortability` should be false for a minor performance improvement.

The `FileCacheLoader` is a good choice in terms of performance, however it has some limitations, which you should be aware of before rolling your application in a production environment. In particular:

1. Due to the way the `FileCacheLoader` represents a tree structure on disk (directories and files) traversal is "inefficient" for deep trees.

2. Usage on shared filesystems such as NFS, Windows shares, and others should be avoided as these do not implement proper file locking and can cause data corruption.

3. Filesystems are inherently not "transactional", so when attempting to use your cache in a transactional context, failures when writing to the file (which happens during the commit phase) cannot be recovered.

As a rule of thumb, it is recommended that the `FileCacheLoader` not be used in a highly concurrent, transactional. or stressful environment, and, in this kind of scenario consider using it just in the testing environment.

As an alternative, consider that JBoss Cache is distributed with a set of different Cache loaders which can be used as alternative. For example:

- The JDBC-based cache loader implementation that stores/loads nodes' state into a relational database. The implementing class is `org.jboss.cache. loader.JDBCCacheLoader`.

- The `BdbjeCacheLoader`, which is a cache loader implementation based on the Oracle/Sleepycat's BerkeleyDB Java Edition (note that the BerkeleyDB implementation is much more efficient than the filesystem-based implementation, and provides transactional guarantees, but requires a commercial license if distributed with an application (see `http://www.oracle.com/database/berkeley-db/index.html for details`).

- The `JdbmCacheLoader`, which is a cache loader implementation based on the JDBM engine, a fast and free alternative to BerkeleyDB.

- Finally, `S3CacheLoader`, which uses the Amazon S3 solution (Simple Storage Solution `http://aws.amazon.com/`) for storing cache data. Since Amazon S3 is remote network storage and has fairly high latency, it is really best for caches that store large pieces of data, such as media or files.

When it comes to measuring the performance of different Cache Loaders, here's a benchmark executed to compare the File CacheLoader, the JDBC CacheLoader (based on Oracle Database) and Jdbm CacheLoader.

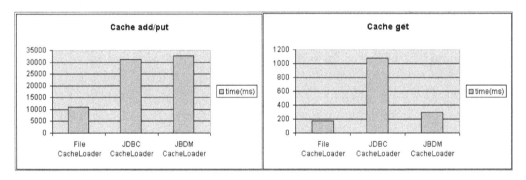

In the above benchmark we are testing cache insertion and cache gets of batches of 1000 Fqn each one bearing 10 attributes. The File CacheLoader accomplished the overall best performance, while the JBDM CacheLoader is almost as fast for Cache gets.

The JDBC CacheLoader is the most robust solution but it adds more overhead to the Cache storage of your session data.

Summary

Clustering is a key element in building scalable Enterprise applications. The infrastructure used by JBoss AS for clustered applications is based on JGroups framework for the nodes inter-communication and JBoss Cache for keeping the cluster data synchronized across nodes.

- **JGroups** can use both UDP and TCP as communication protocol. Unless you have network restriction, you should stay with the default UDP that uses multicast to send and receive messages.

    ° You can tune the transmission protocol by setting an appropriate buffer size with the properties `mcast_recv_buf_size`, `mcast_send_buf_size`, `ucast_recv_buf_size`, and `ucast_send_buf_size`. You should as well increase your O/S buffer size, which need to be adequate to accept JGroups' settings.

- **JBoss Cache** provides the foundation for robust clustered services.

- By configuring the **cacheMode** you can choose if your cluster messages will be synchronous (that is will wait for message acknowledgement) or asynchronous. Unless you need to handle cache message exceptions, stay with the asynchronous pattern, which provides the best performance.

- Cache messages can trigger as well cluster replication or cluster invalidation. A cluster replication is needed for transferring the session state across the cluster while invalidation is the default for Entity/Hibernate, where state can be recovered from the database.

- The cache concurrency can be configured by means of the `nodeLockingScheme` property. The most efficient locking schema is the MVCC, which reduces the cost of slow, or synchronization-heavy schemas of Pessimistic and Optimistic schemas.

- Cache replication of sessions can be optimised mostly in three ways:

    ° By overriding the `isModified` method of your SFSBs you can achieve a fine-grained control over data replication. It's an optimal quick-tuning option for OLAP applications using SFSBs.

    ° **Buddy replication** is the most important performance addition to your session replication. It helps to increase the performance by reducing memory and CPU usage as well as network traffic. Use buddy replication pools to achieve a higher level of redundancy for mission critical applications.

- ° Clustered web applications can configure **replication-granularity** and **replication-trigger**:

  - ° As far as the replication trigger is concerned, if you mostly read immutable data from your session, the SET attribute provides a substantial benefit over the default SET_AND_PRIMITIVE_GET.

  - ° As far as replication granularity is concerned, if your sessions are generally small, you can stay with the default policy (SESSION). If your session is larger and some parts are infrequently accessed, ATTRIBUTE replication will be more effective. If your application has very big data objects in session attributes and only fields in those objects are frequently modified, the FIELD policy would be the best.

Tomcat Web Server Tuning

8

7th Circle of Hell: Suicide. In this ring are the architects who were unable to see beyond their nose, guilty of increasing the Web thread count, instead of fixing a bottleneck in the EJB classes.

Earlier in client-server computing, each application had its own client program and it worked as a user interface and needed to be installed on each user's personal computer.

An upgrade to the server part of the application would typically require an upgrade to the clients installed on each user workstation, adding to the support cost and decreasing productivity.

As the World Wide Web and the Internet gained popularity, so did the desire to set up applications virtually accessible from everywhere. This gave rise to a new paradigm where the browser became a popular medium for accessing enterprise applications, thus eliminating the need to install any library on the client machine.

However, one of the consequences of this shift of paradigm was that this new computing model depends entirely on the availability of the server delivering the front-end layer. Thus, a misconfigured Web server configuration might have a fatal impact on the whole system.

For the purpose of our narration, we have dedicated two chapters to Web applications: the optimal configuration of the Web server, which is covered in this chapter and how to write fast and efficient applications on the JBoss Web server, which will be covered in *Chapter 9, Tuning Web applications on JBoss AS*.

More in detail, we will now start discussing the following topics:

- A short introduction to JBoss Web server and its core configuration files.

- How to configure the Connector element, which is the key element of the Web server performance.

- How to get the best results from modules, like `mod_jk`, which allow fronting JBoss Web server with Apache Web server.

JBoss Web server basics

JBoss AS ships by default with an embedded Web server, which is behind the scenes the open source Web server **Apache Tomcat** (`http://tomcat.apache.org`). The Web server is deployed as a **Service ARchive** (`.sar`) module and can be found in different locations depending on the release of the application server:

JBoss AS Release	Web server location
4.x	`<server>/deploy/jboss-web.deployer`
5.x and 6.x	`<server>/deploy/jbossweb.sar`

The main configuration file of JBoss Web server is `server.xml`, which contains the basic configuration and is located at the root of your Service ARchive. Each Web application is in turn deployed with a configuration file (named `web.xml`), which defines per-application settings. If you need to share your application settings with other applications, you can fill in your configuration in the `context.xml` file, which is located at the same level as `server.xml`.

The key elements for tuning the Web server are the **Connectors**, which are used to collect incoming traffic from specific protocols. A quick look at the `server.xml` configuration file reveals that two Connector elements are set up by default in every installation:

- An HTTP 1.1 Connector, used to receive requests coming from the HTTP protocol. This connector is normally adopted by applications running on a standalone installation of JBoss Web server.

- An AJP 1.3 Connector, used to receive requests arriving from the Apache JServ Protocol. This connector is used in architectures where an Apache Web server (communicating through `mod_jk` or `mod_proxy` libraries) fronts JBoss Web server.

Whatever type of Connector is used by your application, the proper configuration of its resources is the groundwork for achieving good performance in your dynamic web applications. That's what we will learn in the next section.

Configuring Connectors for optimal performance

The built-in Connector configuration contains a bare two elements section, which relies largely on default values:

```
<Connector protocol="HTTP/1.1" port="8080" address="${jboss.bind.
address}"
          connectionTimeout="20000" redirectPort="8443"
maxThreads="300" />


<Connector protocol="AJP/1.3" port="8009" address="${jboss.bind.
address}"
          redirectPort="8443" />
```

In order to configure your JBoss Web server for optimal results, you need to pay attention to the following key properties:

Parameter	Meaning
minSpareThreads	The minimum number of threads always kept alive, the default is 25.
maxThreads	The maximum number of request processing threads to be created by this Connector, which therefore determines the maximum number of *simultaneous* requests that can be handled. If not specified, this attribute is set to 200.
acceptCount	The maximum queue length for incoming connection requests when all possible request processing threads are in use. Any requests received when the queue is full will be refused. The default value is 100.
maxIdleTime	The maximum time an idle thread will be available in the application server before being terminated. The default value is 60000 (60 seconds).

These are the default thread attributes used by the Web server planned for small/medium loads. If you want your web applications to survive the challenge of heavy traffic, then you have no choice but to customize your Connector configuration. For example, in order to allow a maximum of concurrent 300 requests, then the following configuration would fit in:

```
<Executor name="tomcatThreadPool" namePrefix="catalina-exec-"
        maxThreads="300" minSpareThreads="15" maxIdleTime="60000"
acceptCount="100" />
```

```
        <Connector executor="tomcatThreadPool" port="8080"
    protocol="HTTP/1.1" address="${jboss.bind.address}"
                connectionTimeout="20000"
                redirectPort="8443" />
```

> If you are new to Tomcat 6.0 configuration, you might have noticed the new **Executor** element. As a matter of fact, the new 6.x release of Tomcat Web server (embedded in the application server since release 4.2 of JBoss AS) use a shared Executor element to define one or more named thread pools.
>
> The thread pool configuration can thus be defined in the Executor element and later referenced in the Connectors, using the `executor` attribute.

With this example configuration, if the number of concurrent requests is greater than the `maxThreads` attribute (300), they are stacked up to the configured `acceptCount` attribute. Any further simultaneous requests will receive *Connection refused* errors, until resources are available to process them.

When some of the HTTP threads become idle for over the `maxIdleTime` (`60000` ms), the Web server starts terminating the threads up to the `minSpareThreads` attribute (`15`).

As you can imagine, setting the correct number of threads generates a trade-off in several areas (performance/memory/CPU). Applications using a high number of spare threads will certainly reduce the costly operation of creating new threads. The reverse of the coin is that, using lots of threads can easily make your application CPU-bound due to excessive context-switching and will require more memory to be managed. However, you can try to mitigate this problem by introducing a reduced thread stack, using the `-Xssn` JVM parameter.

The only safe way to find out the configuration "sweet spot" is by load testing your application and analyzing the outcome. The next section will show you how.

How do you calculate the threads for your application?

`maxThreads` sets the limit on maximum simultaneous requests that can be supported by the server. No more than this number of threads is created. As we said, the default value, which is 200, is just fine for small to medium traffic sites. High traffic sites can process several hundreds or even thousands of requests concurrently, so you should consider setting a value *between 200 and 1000*.

A quick rule of thumb for calculating the value of `maxThreads` is to multiply `200 * CPU`, so for example, if we assume a quad core machine, we could push that value to 800, +/- depending on RAM and other machine specs.

If you are on the edge, however, an approximation would not be enough and it's important that you find out the most correct value for your threads configuration.

For this purpose, let's open the JMX-console. The attribute we are interested in can be located in the `jboss.web` domain. By digging into the domain you should have a look at the `name=http-127.0.0.1-8080,type=ThreadPool` Mbean. This MBean contains some attributes, which are related to the web thread pool:

Attribute	Meaning
currentThreadsBusy	The number of threads which are serving requests at this time.
currentThreadCount	The total number of threads which are running.

The attribute, which is most meaningful to us, is `currentThreadsBusy`, which is however related to a fixed time window.

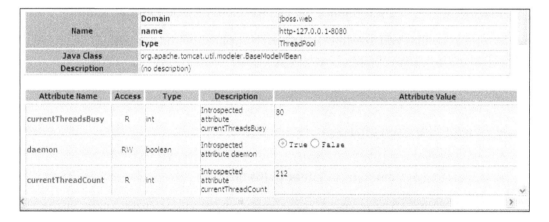

In the preceding screenshot, we're observing a **currentThreadCount** of **212**, which means that 212 concurrent users are being served. As we did for other pools, we need to poll for the MBean value during the load test. The simplest way to achieve this is by means of the twiddle command line utility:

```
twiddle -s localhost get "jboss.web:name=http-127.0.0.1-
8080,type=ThreadPool" currentThreadsBusy
```

```
currentThreadCount=212
```

 Replace the name attribute value with the host/port combination of your HTTP server. Also, if you need to inquire on a different Connector protocol, just insert it before the host address, like in the following example:

```
twiddle -s localhost get "jboss.web:name=ajp-127.0.0.1-
8009,type=ThreadPool" currentThreadsBusy
```

A concrete example

Understanding the dynamics of the Web server performance can be better understood with a simple example. The mock-up application we want to test is straightforward and does not involve any legacy system: as a matter of fact, we would like to measure nothing else but the raw performance of the Web server; other factors which might influence the test were not included in this example.

So, let's suppose that you are delivering a web application made up of JSP/Servlets each one taking approximately 15-30 ms to be served.

The application is deployed on JBoss AS 5.1.0, which is hosted on the following hardware/software configuration:

- 4 Intel CPU Xeon dual core
- 16 GB RAM
- Operating System: Linux Fedora 12 (64 bit)
- JVM 1.6 update 20

As for every benchmark, the suggested strategy is to load test the application first with the default configuration, which allows 200 concurrent users. The following is the graph benchmark supposing a range of concurrent users between 50 and 500:

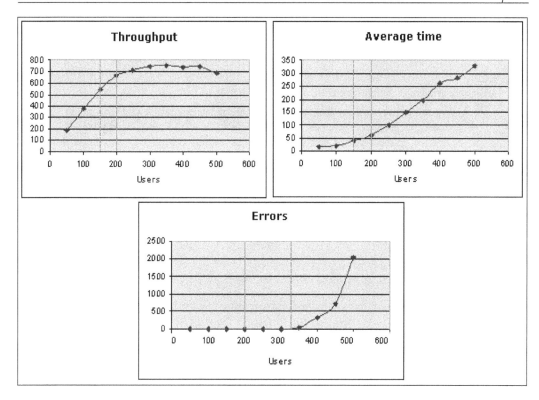

The upper left graph displays the throughput of the application as the range of users varies. The right one shows the average time spent in processing the single page and the bottom one traces the amount of errors on the whole range of requests.

As you can see, the highest throughput (KB/sec) grows *linearly* until the number of concurrent users approaches the maximum number of concurrent users (200), which are marked by the contiguous vertical line. The dashed line shows exactly the point where the line modifies its trend. This happens at about 75% of the concurrent users, so the default configuration would be ideal for a load of 150 users.

The same behavior is observed with the average time, which increases proportionally up to 150 users; above this limit the time spent in serving dynamic pages starts to grow exponentially.

The outcome of errors (which are connection refused), on the other hand, becomes evident when the Web server is not able to accept any more requests: with the default configuration the Web server is able to serve 200 concurrent requests and set aside 100 (due to the `acceptCount` parameter). This is confirmed by the graph, which starts plotting errors when users exceed 300.

Best practice

As a general rule, measure the `currentThreadsBusy` attribute and set `MaxThreads` to the following value:

`Optimal MaxThreads = (currentThreadsBusy * 1.25)`

Then again measure your Web application performance and compare the throughput. If you still cannot find a satisfying throughput you need to extend your search to other areas like I/O or CPU, which could potentially invalidate your correct `MaxThread` setting.

The long life of Web threads

We have just learnt that, as you request dynamic pages to the JBoss Web container, a thread is picked up from the pool (or created when needed) to serve the request. One thing you should be aware of is that Web threads do not end their job in the Servlet/JSP tier but they are used as well to drive the user call through the EJB tier.

Let's see first a sample use case where the user invokes an EJB from a standalone client. The following graph displays the **Threads** section of VisualVM along with a snippet from the thread dump:

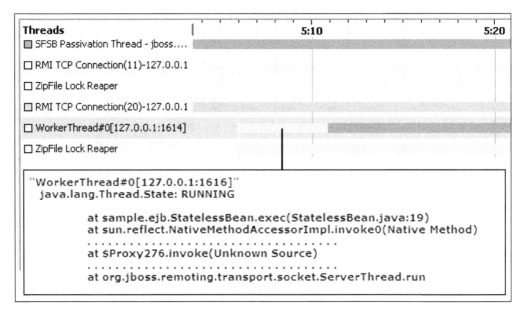

As you can see, when the client invokes the EJB, the call is propagated by means of the Remoting framework and a **WorkerThread** is picked up (or created when necessary) to contact the pool of stateless EJB.

On the other hand, when the same call is initiated by means of a Web tier, which acts as bridge between the user and the EJB tier, the same HTTP thread is used both to execute the Servlet's `service` method and to cross the boundaries of EJB proxies, up to the stateless bean.

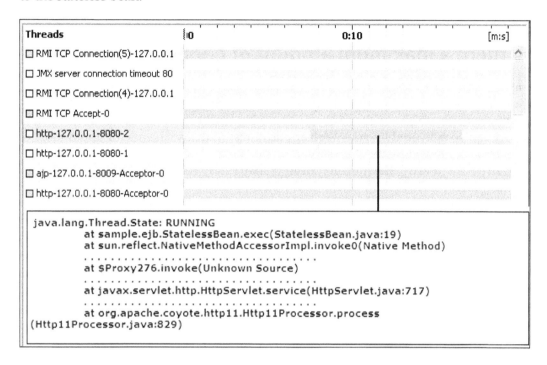

The consequence of this is that you need to pay special attention to your Web threads configuration as they can channel your initial request to deeper tiers of your application. Therefore, a bottleneck in your EJB tier will be directly propagated through your Web tier causing an inflation of Web threads needed to serve new requests.

A common mistake by myopic administrators is to limit the analysis to the Web tier, concluding that the right cure to your application is just to increase the `MaxThreads` parameter. The price of this mistake will be striking: by adding more and more threads to your application, your CPU will soon be stuffed, consumed by continuous context switches. More threads will require even more memory and more memory will in turn trigger garbage collector cycles, which will further slow down your application.

If you tend to lie, then you can propose to your boss to buy larger, and more expensive hardware to roll your application in production. If you are a nice guy, you will rather analyze the whole application stack and fix the bottleneck in the EJB tier. And don't forget to stress to your management that lots of money could have been lost, if they contacted the wrong person to fix this application.

Is there a maximum amount of connections the Web server can handle?

Granted that you need to control the number of threads required by your Web application, you might be wondering if there is a limit to the number of connections which can be delivered by your Web applications. Actually, the maximum number of connections allowed by the Web server depends partly on the amount of hardware resources (RAM being the most important factor) and on the type of system you are running (32bit – 64 bit).

As you know, if you are running a 32-bit system, any process is limited to 2 GB of user space. As each thread by default consumes 256 KB of virtual space, just for filling the stack frames, we have a theoretical limit of 8192 threads. We said theoretical because we need contiguous memory space; for example, on 32-bit Windows systems, because of scattered memory allocations, you will hardly be able to allocate over 5000 threads.

Besides system process limits, a much more frequent bottleneck is the number of sockets allowed by the operating system. This limit is however configurable.

To increase the OS limit under Linux you can use the `ulimit` command. The command `ulimit -aS` displays the current limit (default 1024), and `ulimit -aH` displays the hard limit (above which you need to modify your kernel parameters in /proc and reboot your Linux machine).

The file descriptor limit can be increased using the following procedure:

1. Edit /etc/security/limits.conf and add the lines:

   ```
   *         soft      nofile    1024
   *         hard      nofile    65535
   ```

2. Edit /etc/pam.d/login, adding the line:

   ```
   session required /lib/security/pam_limits.so
   ```

3. The system file descriptor limit is set in `/proc/sys/fs/file-max`. The following command will increase the limit to 65535:

```
echo 65535 > /proc/sys/fs/file-max
```

4. You should then be able to increase the file descriptor limits using:

```
ulimit -n unlimited
```

   The above command will set the limits to the hard limit specified in `/etc/security/limits.conf`.

On the other hand, Solaris users will need to tune the `rlim_fd_max` parameter to set up the maximum number of opened file descriptors (sockets, files, or pipes). For example, supposing you want to set this limit to 8192, add the following command to `/etc/system` and reboot:

```
set rlim_fd_max = 8192
```

This value should be enough for small/medium sites, but you might consider increasing it to a higher value for heavily loaded sites.

To increase the OS limit under HPUX, you can use the "sam" administration interface. Go to the 'Kernel Configuration' page, then through to 'Configurable Parameters'.

There you can configure the two key attributes which are:

- `nfile` — the maximum number of files that can be open system-wide simultaneously at any given time.
- `ninode`—max number of open inodes

You can check the current limits by running the following command:

```
sysdef | egrep "NAME|ninode|nfile|maxfiles_lim"
```

To increase the OS limits under a Windows platform you have to hack a bit on the Windows Registry. We suggest reading carefully this resource to learn more about it: `http://support.microsoft.com/kb/196271`.

Using Apache Portable Runtime

Apache Tomcat can use **Apache Portable Runtime** to provide superior scalability, performance, and better integration with native server technologies. Apache Portable Runtime is a highly portable library that is at the heart of Apache HTTP Server 2.x. APR has many uses, including access to advanced IO functionality (such as `sendfile`, `epoll`, and `OpenSSL`), OS level functionality (random number generation, system status, and so on), and native process handling (shared memory, NT pipes, and Unix sockets).

The latest APR library can be downloaded from the JBoss site at this address: `http://www.jboss.org/jbossweb/downloads/jboss-native-2-0-9.html`.

Installing the library is a trivial task; provided that you have downloaded the correct libraries for your OS, it's just a matter of uncompressing the downloaded archive into the JBoss home folder. (A troubleshooting wiki can however be read here: `http://community.jboss.org/wiki/HowToAddAprToJBoss`).

Once started, the application server will look for native libraries in its `LIBRARY_PATH`, if found you will see the following message on the console:

INFO [AprLifecycleListener] Loaded Apache Tomcat Native library 1.1.20.

INFO [AprLifecycleListener] APR capabilities: IPv6 [false], sendfile [true], random [true].

INFO [Http11AprProtocol] Initializing Coyote HTTP/1.1 on http-127.0.0.1-8080

For the purpose of testing, we have benchmarked the jmx-console with and without the APR library on a two processor Linux box. The following are the numbers we have reported:

Label	# Samples	Average	Median	90% Line	Min	Max	Error %	Throughput	KB/sec
HTTP Request	500000	407	244	1081	3	3497	0,00%	198,7/sec	130,7
TOTAL	500000	407	244	1081	3	3497	0,00%	198,7/sec	130,7

Jmx-console benchmark without APR

Label	# Samples	Average	Median	90% Line	Min	Max	Error %	Throughput	KB/sec
HTTP Request	500000	325	190	835	3	3842	0,00%	229,7/sec	150,6
TOTAL	500000	325	190	835	3	3842	0,00%	229,7/sec	150,6

Jmx-console benchmark with APR

By turning on the APR library, you will be able to use advanced features like the sendfile native function, which avoids separate read and send operations, and buffer allocations.

However, some platforms might have broken sendfile support that the build system did not detect, especially if the binaries were built on another box and moved to such a machine with broken sendfile support. In particular, our lab tests have shown, for the same load test, that on an XP box the standard configuration outperformed the APR-patched installation by about 10%.

For this reason we advise the reader to stay away from the APR installation on a Windows platform, unless you have a solid proof that your web application will benefit from it.

Integrating JBoss Web server with Apache Web server

We have shown how to optimize the configuration of JBoss Web server assuming a standalone configuration. In real world cases, however, application servers are usually not the first line of access to your applications; a quite common scenario is the Web server Apache placed in front of your JBoss AS/Tomcat Web server. Why? Mainly for the following set of reasons:

- Serving static pages with Apache reduces the load on the application server while improving the throughput of static pages. As a matter of fact Apache can transparently cache your static assets, including css, JavaScript, and images.

- Furthermore, using Apache in front of your application server increases the security of your Intranet private data: in fact, by putting Web server on a computer host inserted as a "neutral zone" (between a company's private network and the internet) gives the applications hosted on JBoss/Tomcat the capability to access company private data, while securing the access to other private resources.

- Ultimately, a Web application managed by Apache Web server can benefit from a large set of modules that can be plugged in at will (think for example about mod_rewrite, which is the "Swiss Army Knife" of URL manipulation).

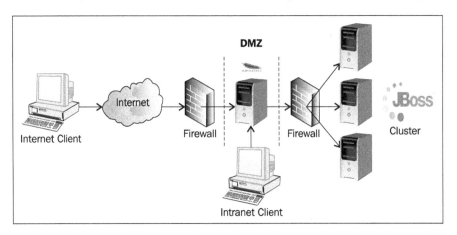

By using this architecture, which fronts JBoss nodes with an Apache Web server (or whatever Web server is capable of redirecting the communication to JBoss), a native library is needed to handle the communication between Apache and JBoss Web server.

You have three possible ways to connect Apache with JBoss Web server:

One very popular choice among developers is mod_jk (http://tomcat.apache.org/connectors-doc/), which has reached the stable release 1.2.30. The advantage of using mod_jk is that it provides advanced load balancer and node failure detection. On the other hand, it requires a separate module to build and maintain.

Another viable alternative is Apache's advanced mod_proxy set of modules (http://httpd.apache.org/docs/2.2/mod/mod_proxy.html) that can be run through both AJP and HTTP protocol. The advantage of using mod_proxy is that it comes as part of the standard Apache 2.2+ distribution. Conversely mod_proxy has not got all the advanced clustering features mod_jk has, like for example support for domain model clustering.

Ultimately, if you need a fine-grained control for your communication channel and dynamic configuration of httpd workers, you might consider trying mod_cluster (http://jboss.org/mod_cluster), which will be part of the JBoss AS 6 distribution.

One question which might arise is how does this architecture impacts on performance, compared with a standalone configuration?

As usual there is not a unique answer. If you proxy all of the requests to JBoss/Tomcat then performance is likely to decrease. If Apache's httpd server handles some requests (for example, all the static content which can be easily cached) then you will probably see some benefit.

We have set up a benchmark comparing a standalone JBoss AS configuration with an Apache-JBoss configuration. In this benchmark, we have evaluated the difference when serving a static page through Apache's Web server and through JBoss embedded Web server.

Label	# Samples	Average	Median	90% Line	Min	Max	Error %	Throughput	KB/sec
HTTP Requ...	500000	44	4	14	2	3962	0,00%	1093,2/sec	7200,8
TOTAL	500000	44	4	14	2	3962	0,00%	1093,2/sec	7200,8

Apache http server benchmark serving 10Kb static page

Label	# Samples	Average	Median	90% Line	Min	Max	Error %	Throughput	KB/sec
HTTP Requ...	500000	105	10	302	4	3662	0,00%	746,4/sec	4916,5
TOTAL	500000	105	10	302	4	3662	0,00%	746,4/sec	4916,5

JBoss http server benchmark serving 10Kb static page

As you can see from this benchmark, Apache http server is about 30% faster at delivering static content. This benchmark was executed on a Solaris 4 CPU environment; reproducing the same test on a Windows server, however, it taught us a different story with Apache Web server running about 40% slower than its JBoss Web server counterpart.

Definitively, as there are so many low-level knobs, which impact the performance of Apache native libraries, it is very likely that you could achieve different results in your applications. The only way to know for sure the impact of a 2-layer Web server architecture is to test it in your environment with realistic load and usage pattern.

Load testing Apache-JBoss connectivity

In the previous section, we mentioned the list of options available to front JBoss Web server with Apache server. We also described some advantages and disadvantages of each module. However how do they compare in terms of performance?

We have constructed a sample benchmark based on a 10 KB JSP page, performing some basic request/session snooping. In the first benchmark, we have tested the Web application with a JBoss standalone installation. Next, we have fronted JBoss Web server with Apache 2.2 server using three different modules: `mod_jk`, `mod_proxy_ajp`, and `mod_proxy_http`. We have collected the following numbers:

Label	# Samples	Average	Median	90% Line	Min	Max	Error %	Throughput	KB/sec
HTTP Requ...	500000	82	1	1	0	9033	0,00%	921,9/sec	1221,5
TOTAL	500000	82	1	1	0	9033	0,00%	921,9/sec	1221,5

JBoss Web server standalone

Label	# Samples	Average	Median	90% Line	Min	Max	Error %	Throughput	KB/sec
HTTP Requ...	500000	376	3	19	1	52100	0,36%	324,9/sec	430,2
TOTAL	500000	376	3	19	1	52100	0,36%	324,9/sec	430,2

JBoss Web server fronted by mod_jk

Label	# Samples	Average	Median	90% Line	Min	Max	Error %	Throughput	KB/sec
HTTP Requ...	500000	121	1	3	0	18502	0,00%	541,4/sec	721,5
TOTAL	500000	121	1	3	0	18502	0,00%	541,4/sec	721,5

JBoss Web server fronted by mod_proxy_ajp

Label	# Samples	Average	Median	90% Line	Min	Max	Error %	Throughput	KB/sec
HTTP Requ...	500000	127	1	3	0	17645	0,00%	511,2/sec	672,2
TOTAL	500000	127	1	3	0	17645	0,00%	511,2/sec	672,2

JBoss Web server fronted by mod_proxy_http

As you can see, the results are quite different: in particular, `mod_jk`, tested with the default configuration, was roughly *three times slower* than JBoss Web server standalone, exhibiting some sporadic errors as well. Conversely, Apache's `mod_proxy` libraries showed better performance both using `mod_proxy_ajp` module (`mod_proxy_ajp.so`) and `mod_proxy_http` (`mod_proxy_http.so`).

So we might conclude that `mod_proxy` is definitively faster then `mod_jk`? Well, that's not always the case.

We should account for two facts: at first this benchmark was based just on one hardware configuration (that's the same as exposed in the *A concrete example* section). In order to ascertain which module is definitely faster, you should verify these assumptions with different kinds of hardware too. Secondarily, JBoss Web server connectivity can be further tuned by tweaking the default modules configuration.

In particular, `mod_jk` configuration makes no assumption about your existing hardware or potential load, so therefore, it is often not adequate for a heavy load.

For example, one of the major issues is to synchronize the maximum number of concurrent connections between Apache and Tomcat/JBoss AS. If those two configuration parameters differ, usually with Tomcat having a lower configured number of connections, you will be faced with the preceding sporadic connection errors dumped in the log files. If the load gets even higher, your users will start receiving `HTTP 500 server errors` even if your hardware is capable of dealing with the load.

We have already learnt how to properly configure the maximum number of connections with Tomcat/JBoss AS—what about Apache? Setting the number of maximum connections with Apache web server depends on the **Multi-Processing Module (MPM)** used. The following is a sample table, which resumes it:

Multi-Processing Module (MPM)	Configuration parameter
Prefork	MaxClients
Worker	MaxClients
WinNT	ThreadsPerChild
Netware	MaxThreads

Which MPM module provides the best performance?

The prefork MPM forks off a number of identical Apache processes, while the worker creates multiple threads. In general, prefork is better on systems with one or two processors where the operating system is better geared towards time slicing between multiple processes. On a system with a *higher number of CPUs* the worker's threading model will probably be more effective.

In nearly all cases, the `MaxClients` directive is the key for increasing server performance, as it controls that maximum number of simultaneous connections Apache can handle. However, the way `MaxClients` get calculated differs from one module to another. Check Apache docs for further details: `http://httpd.apache.org/docs/2.2/mod/mpm_common.html`.

Determining which MPM module is used on your Apache's installation is quite easy: just feed the `-V` option to the httpd shell command:

```
httpd -V
Server version: Apache/2.2.16
Server built:   Jul 30 2010 16:15:37
Server's Module Magic Number: 20051115:24
Server loaded:  APR 1.4.2, APR-Util 1.3.9
```

```
Compiled using: APR 1.4.2, APR-Util 1.3.9

Architecture:    64-bit

Server MPM:      Prefork
```

. . . .

In this example, having ascertained that you are using the prefork module, you should modify your Apache's configuration file, `httpd.conf`. Supposing you have allowed 500 `MaxThreads` on Tomcat, then adapt the Apache configuration the following way:

```
<IfModule prefork.c>
   StartServers         8
   MinSpareServers      5
   MaxSpareServers     20
   MaxClients         500
   MaxRequestsPerChild  4000
</IfModule>
```

Another thing that could improve `mod_jk`'s communication process is setting communication timeouts. Some of the issues observed when `mod_jk` is under heavy load (degradation of performance and the system becoming unresponsive) can arise because there are no connection timeouts specified to take care of orphaned connections, no error handling properties defined in `workers.properties`, and no connection limits set in Apache and Tomcat.

This issue needs to be fixed both in Tomcat's `server.xml` and in `mod_jk`'s `worker.properties`.

The main concern with `server.xml` is setting the `connectionTimeout`, which sets the `SO_TIMEOUT` property of the underlying socket. So when a connection in Tomcat hasn't had a request in the amount of time specified by `connectionTimeout`, then the connection dies off. This is necessary because if the connection isn't closed there will be an inflation of threads which can over the time hit the `maxThreads` count in Tomcat. Then Tomcat will not be able to accept any new connections.

A `connectionTimeout` of 60000 (1 minute) is usually a good number to start out with:

```
<Connector port="8009"
           address="${jboss.bind.address}"
           emptySessionPath="true"
           enableLookups="false"
           redirectPort="8443"
           protocol="AJP/1.3"
           maxThreads="200"
           connectionTimeout="60000" />
```

There may be a situation where the connections are not being recycled fast enough, in this instance the `connectionTimeout` could be lowered to 30000 (30 seconds).

Now it's time to also fix the `mod_jk` configuration file: this can be done by means of the `connect_timeout/prepost_timeout` properties, which allows detection that the Tomcat connection has been closed and preventing a retry request. Since release 1.2.27 of `mod_jk`, the properties used to establish a connection timeout are `ping_mode` and `ping_timeout` like in the following configuration snippet:

```
#Configuring workers.properties:
worker.list=loadbalancer,status
worker.template.port=8009
worker.template.type=ajp13
worker.template.lbfactor=1

#if not using 1.2.27 please specify connect_timeout=10000
#and prepost_timeout=10000 as an alternative
worker.template.ping_timeout=1000
worker.template.ping_mode=A
worker.template.socket_timeout=10

#It is not necessary to specify connection_pool_timeout if you are
running the worker mpm
worker.template.connection_pool_timeout=60

#Referencing the template worker properties makes the workers.
properties shorter and more concise
worker.node1.reference=worker.template

worker.node1.host=192.168.1.1
worker.node2.reference=worker.template
worker.node2.host=192.168.1.2
worker.loadbalancer.type=lb
worker.loadbalancer.balance_workers=node1,node2
worker.loadbalancer.sticky_session=True
worker.status.type=status
```

`Ping_mode` and `ping_timeout`, are used to handle probing a connection for errors and `connection_pool_timeout` which must be set to equal `server.xml`'s `connectionTimeout` when using the prefork MPM. When these two values are the same, after a connection has been inactive for x amount of time, the connection in `mod_jk` and Tomcat will be closed at the same time, preventing a half-closed connection.

There exist many other useful optimizations, but these depend on the environment and web application in use. See `http://tomcat.apache.org/connectors-doc/reference/workers.html` for details on all available `mod_jk` properties.

mod_cluster to the rescue?

We want to conclude this section with a small note about `mod_cluster`. `Mod_cluster` is a new httpd-based load balancer. Like `mod_jk`, `mod_cluster` uses a communication channel to forward requests from httpd to one of a set of application server nodes. Unlike `mod_jk`, `mod_cluster` leverages an additional connection between the application server nodes and httpd.

The application server nodes use this connection to transmit server-side load balance factors and lifecycle events back to httpd using a custom set of HTTP methods, known as the **Mod-Cluster Management Protocol (MCMP)**. This additional feedback channel allows `mod_cluster` to offer a level of intelligence and granularity not found in other load balancing solutions.

There are not many statistics about `mod_cluster` on the web so all in all we were curious to know how this library performed under heavy load. So here's a benchmark performed using the same pattern employed in the previous benchmark:

Label	# Samples	Average	Median	90% Line	Min	Max	Error %	Throughput	KB/sec
HTTP Requ...	500000	102	1	2	1	17172	0,00%	561,8/sec	745,7
TOTAL	500000	102	1	2	1	17172	0,00%	561,8/sec	745,7

JBoss Web server fronted by mod_cluster

The performance of `mod_cluster` is pretty much the same as Apache's `mod_proxy` and this should be no surprise at all as much of the Apache-JBoss Web server communication is based on `mod_proxy`.

However, `mod_cluster` provides innovative load balancing features like dynamic registration of AS instances and context mountings, pluggable policies for calculating the load balance factors, and many others (You can find advanced `mod_cluster` design documentation at this URL: `http://community.jboss.org/wiki/ModClusterDesign`).

At the end of this journey through Apache-JBoss connectivity, we have arranged the most important points in the following table. You can use it as a guide for deciding which module is best suited to the needs of your project:

Module	Advantage	Disadvantage
mod_jk	Advanced load balancer. Advanced failure node detection.	Out-of-the box not tuned configuration. Complex module configuration (need a separate module to build and maintain).
mod_proxy	Out-of-the box good performance. Simple module configuration (No need for a separate module.)	Basic load balancer Does not support domain model clustering
mod_cluster	Good performance. Fine-grained control for your communication channel and dynamic configuration of httpd workers.	Newer project, with smaller community of users.

Last tips before rolling JBoss Web server in production

Once that you are ready to roll in production your web application on JBoss Web server/Tomcat you should consider making some changes from the default configuration, which is just fine when you are using the Web server for developing. These properties can be set as the init parameter of the core JspServlet class which handles JSP to Servlet translation:

```
<servlet>
<servlet-name>jsp</servlet-name>
<servlet-class>org.apache.jasper.servlet.JspServlet</servlet-class>
  <init-param>
   <param-name>development</param-name>
   <param-value>false</param-value>
  </init-param>
  <init-param>
   <param-name>checkInterval</param-name>
   <param-value>0</param-value>
  </init-param>
  <init-param>
   <param-name>trimSpaces</param-name>
   <param-value>true</param-value>
  </init-param>
    <init-param>
   <param-name>genStringAsCharArray</param-name>
   <param-value>true</param-value>
  </init-param>
</servlet>
```

The following table describes the meaning of these parameters:

Parameter	Value
development	Used to disable on access checks for JSP pages compilation. Set this to `false` in production.
checkInterval	Sets the time in seconds between checks to see if a JSP page (and its dependent files) needs to be recompiled. Default 0 seconds
trimSpaces	Can be used to remove useless bytes from the response. Set this to `true` as a minor performance optimization
genStringAsCharArray	Takes care to generate slightly more efficient char arrays. Set this to `true`.

Summary

In this chapter, we have learnt how to configure optimally the embedded JBoss Web server, which is behind the scenes of the well-known Tomcat Web server.

- The default JBoss Web server configuration is fit for a Web application with little or medium traffic. In order to carry high loads the Web configuration needs to be appropriately tuned.
    - The `MaxThreads` parameter of `server.xml` is the most important parameter as it determines the maximum number of concurrent connections allowed. A good rule of thumb is setting it at about 25% more of the `currentBusyThreads` property of your Web server Thread Pool.
    - The minimum number of threads always kept alive are controlled by the `MinSpareThreads` attribute.
    - By setting an appropriate value of `maxIdleTime`, you can reduce the number of threads used by your applications at idle time.
    - Setting the correct number of threads to be used greatly influences the performance of your application. Too few threads will require costly threads creation (low `MinSpareThreads` property) or might cause connection refused (low `MaxThreads` and `acceptCount` properties). Too many threads will make your application CPU-bound and might potentially exhaust your memory.

- The Apache Portable Runtime Connector provides advanced IO functionality and native process handling which can greatly enhance the performance of your web applications. Best results have been observed on Unix platforms.

- Hardware capabilities and kernel configuration can actually limit the number of connections released by the Web server. The default kernel configuration is usually targeted at Web applications with small or moderate traffic.

- Fronting a JBoss Web server with Apache or any other Web server can be useful to take advantage of the Web server native modules. It can be required for security policies.

- Before rolling your Web applications in production don't forget to set up the `development` property to false of the `JspServlet` class. Also `checkInterval` should accordingly be set to 0 seconds. Minor optimizations can be achieved by setting `trimSpaces` and `genStringAsCharArray` to `true`.

Tuning Web Applications on JBoss AS

9th Circle of Hell: Betrayal. In this circle resides the author of this book, guilty of having once ported an application from JBoss AS to Oracle Weblogic Server, in exchange for 30 pieces of silver.

The last chapter of this book teaches the reader how to write fast and efficient web applications on the JBoss web server. From a bird's eye view, all web applications can be roughly divided into two broad areas:

- Business-to-Consumer (B2C) applications, where the user interacts with legacy systems by means of an interface, usually a browser. The archetype of a B2C application is engineered using dynamic web pages (JSP/Servlets) and/or frameworks based on a component-driven UI design model (JSF).

- Business-to-Business (B2B) applications: They typically require exchange of information between businesses and their legacy systems. Common examples of B2B application are web services, which are a common paradigm to integrate heterogeneous systems.

Following this simple distinction, we have split this chapter into two main sections. In the first one, we will discuss tuning B2C web applications, focusing on the performance of different frameworks available. In the second part of this chapter, we will talk about web service performance tuning, which can ultimately determine how fast your B2B apparatus will respond.

Choosing a framework for your web applications

The new era of web applications has introduced a number of frameworks designed to aid in rapid development. But, no matter what your preferred language is, finding a suitable framework is not usually an easy task.

When it comes to adopting a new technology, many of the decision points are *organizational* and not developer driven. When an organization intends to adopt an application-development framework, it is typically looking to accomplish three things:

- Address the complexities of some lower-level application architecture
- Reduce the amount of code developers have to write (also known as "productivity")
- Allow developers to focus on "business logic"

In the landscape of Java technologies, **Model View Controller** (MVC) frameworks have been the most popular choice in the web development arena for years, exhibiting strong features of the concept of a *separation of concerns*. This can be accomplished by structuring the **Model** to deal with the business domain objects, the **Controller** to handle request processing and the **View**, which renders the model into a form suitable for interaction, typically a user-interface element.

The following image depicts the basic interaction between the main MVC components:

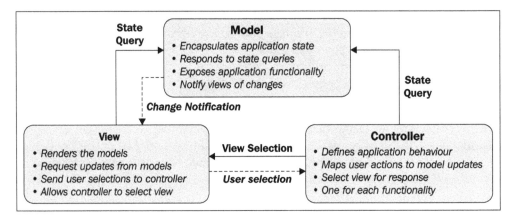

The biggest advantage of using MVC frameworks is that, because of the logic separation of concerns, future enhancements, and other maintenance, the code base should be very easy and should be reusable as well.

Unfortunately, as for all technologies which match their hype, some defects started to become evident to developers. In particular, the biggest complain is that MVC frameworks, like Struts for example, will tightly couple your application to the framework interfaces. As a matter of fact, Struts uses `ActionForm` and `Action` interfaces to mediate between the Model and the View. This makes it awkward to test your application, which needs a server runtime environment accessible. The second main disadvantage is related to the difficulty of managing the details of HTTP requests and responses, which is error prone and needs to follow a complex path (Controller-Model-View) even for simple actions.

The **Java Server Faces** framework was designed during a period of big changes in the community of Java developers where a growing number of people agreed that Java Enterprise technology was getting over complicated. JSF eases the development of Graphical User Interfaces (GUI) for web applications allowing developers to work with extensible user interfaces like buttons, textboxes, checkboxes, and so on. These components are no more bound to HTTP request but to simple events in the form of Java methods, thus greatly simplifying web application programming.

On the wave of the success of JSF technologies, many companies started to produce JSF-component libraries, which offer a large set of custom components to cover most of the application requirements in a reasonably easy way. The JBoss team, for example, developed the **RichFaces** library (`http://jboss.org/richfaces`), which offers a broad set of built-in widgets and components and a vast community of users.

This new level of interactivity, however, does carry a price and today it's not rare to see in JSF forums some complaints about, guess what, the performance of the "new" compared with the performance of the "old". Maybe people have discovered that not all that glitters is gold?

Comparing framework performance

One day you might be asked at a job interview "Which framework would you use for best performance?" That's a tough question, which requires some additional input to produce a comprehensive answer. However, should you have plain Servlet/JSP on one checkbox and JSF on another, be sure to go for the first option.

Why is JSF slower than plain Servlet/JSP stuff? If you think about it, when you request a simple JSP page, the client makes an HTTP request for the page, and the server responds with the page translated into HTML. As a result, a single path is executed to render the content to the output stream. The following image depicts this simple process:

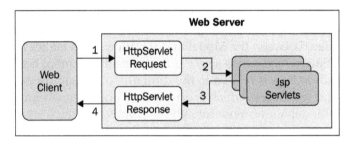

On the other hand, a Java Server Faces page is represented by a tree of UI components, called a View. When a client makes a request for the page, a complex life cycle starts. During the life cycle, the JSF implementation must build the View while considering the state saved from a previous submission of the page. When the client submits a page, the JSF implementation must perform several tasks, such as validating the data input of components in the View and converting input data to types specified on the server side. The JSF implementation performs all these tasks as a series of steps in the life cycle. The following image will give you an idea of the complexity of the JSF life cycle.

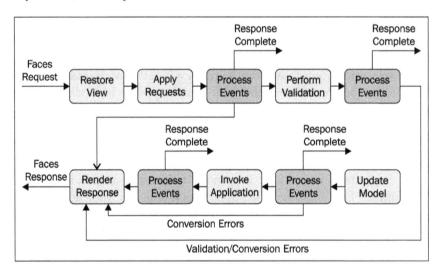

Although the JSF lifecycle is hardly set in stone (you can change the order of execution by skipping phases or leaving the lifecycle altogether), customizing the lifecycle of JSF is s a non-trivial task and a deep understanding of the JSF architecture is required to get it right.

So where do we go after this preamble? Chiefly to one point: To evaluate web frameworks not just on the basis of productivity and cool widgets but also with performance in mind. In the following sections, we will compare the performance of two common web tasks, displaying tabular and hierarchical data, using different approaches.

The numbers we will collect do not represent, as usual, a definitive truth since they are dependant on the type of application tested, on the kind of hardware used, and finally on the release of the component library used. What we will try to establish is *an order of magnitude* among several approaches, which must be a part of your wealth of knowledge.

The performance of tabular data

The HTML table is one of the most common constructs in a web application. Besides its usefulness when laying out components on a page, a table can display rows of data from a collection.

Trying to gather the most popular alternatives, we will consider these three possible options to iterate over the data:

*   Use a Servlet/JSP-based solution
*   Use a JSF solution, running the Mojarra JSF 1.2 implementation.
*   Use the RichFaces 3.3 component library with the Mojarra JSF 1.2 implementation

In our test, we will suppose that the user needs to browse a table containing 10 columns and 50 rows.

The first, barebone solution, will require just to iterate through the collection of elements created on the server side:

```
<c:forEach var="bean" items="${list}">
      ${bean.column1}
      ${bean.column2}
   . . . . . . . . . . . .
</c:forEach>
```

The corresponding benchmark, built upon a total of 250 concurrent users, follows here:

Label	# Samples	Average	Median	90% Line	Min	Max	Error %	Throughput	KB/sec
HTTP Requ...	50000	261	9	931	5	5037	0,00%	100,1/sec	574,8
TOTAL	50000	261	9	931	5	5037	0,00%	100,1/sec	574,8

Jsp/Servlet Table Benchmark

The second benchmark uses JSF's **dataTable** built-in UI component:

```
<h:dataTable value="#{list}"
   styleClass="myStyle"
      rowClasses="odd,even"
var="bean">
. . . . . . . . .
```

And here's the corresponding outcome, from JMeter:

Label	# Samples	Average	Median	90% Line	Min	Max	Error %	Throughput	KB/sec
HTTP Requ...	50000	965	406	2760	20	10255	0,00%	41,3/sec	286,0
TOTAL	50000	965	406	2760	20	10255	0,00%	41,3/sec	286,0

JSF Mojarra 1.2 dataTable Benchmark

Finally, we will test a `rich:dataTable`, powered by the JBoss Richfaces 3.3 suite:

```
<rich:dataTable value="#{list}"
      styleClass="myStyle"
      rowClasses="odd,even"
   var="bean">
. . . . . . . . . . . .
```

This is the last benchmark produced:

Label	# Samples	Average	Median	90% Line	Min	Max	Error %	Throughput	KB/sec
HTTP Requ...	50000	1565	845	4114	30	15062	0,00%	29,6/sec	805,6
TOTAL	50000	1565	845	4114	30	15062	0,00%	29,6/sec	805,6

Richfaces 3.3 dataTable Benchmark

The numbers we have collected tell us that a simple JSP solution is about 2.5 times faster than the Mojarra's JSF 1.2 implementation and over 3 times faster than the RichFaces 3.3 library.

What this benchmark does not tell us is that JSF experienced developers will surely complete a reporting GUI in less time than using a JSP/Servlet approach because you don't have to write lots of repetitive code to read the request and deliver the response. Besides this, JSF-centric libraries offer a wide array of built-in useful features. These features include, but are not limited to, column sorting, pagination for large record sets, and a logical grouping of data.

As you can see, the choice of the technology for delivering the frontend introduces a trade-off between productivity and faster execution. You should decide on a per-case basis what the best is for you. For example, reports requiring the highest possible throughput should be delivered with a low-level technology like JSP/Servlets. Also, if you can afford to use JSF for designing your tables, always use the basic `h:dataTable` component, unless you need some specific properties of the `rich:dataTable`.

In the end, if you are happy with `rich:dataTable` performance, try to keep its structure as simple as possible; for example, avoid nesting rich components like `rich:tooltip` inside it. They can slow down page rendering significantly especially on Internet Explorer.

The performance of rich tree

Displaying hierarchical data is a common requirement for many web applications. Possible usage includes, for example, file system browsing, enterprise organization path, and, network domain browsing.

The JSF specification does not include any standard tree component, so you need to extend your JSF implementation with a component library. In our case, we will test JBoss's `RichFaces` tree component.

The sample tree we will benchmark will be built using a depth of 5 x 5 x 20 elements, summing up a total of 500 elements in the tree. For this purpose, the tree will be at first loaded with some data and then fully expanded.

Here's the RichFaces' benchmark outcome:

Label	# Samples	Average	Median	90% Line	Min	Max	Error %	Throughput	KB/sec
HTTP Requ…	50000	15206	15089	20211	546	41199	0,00%	4,1/sec	1839,8
TOTAL	50000	15206	15089	20211	546	41199	0,00%	4,1/sec	1839,8

RichFaces 3.3.3 Tree Benchmark

The average amount of time needed for each test was about 15 seconds, with a load of 250 concurrent users. Since we have skimmed any legacy systems interaction from this test, the amount of time is just spent in loading the set of elements, displaying the tree and fully expanding it.

A quick analysis of Eclipse's profile view reveals that the server-side methods account only for a few milliseconds for building the tree, as shown in the following image:

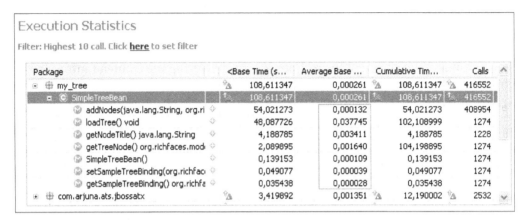

What this simple analysis suggests is that most of the time is spent through the JSF lifecycle and, in particular, in the rendering phase which displays visually the component on the screen.

As a comparison, we will test a simple JavaScript solution, which has got a minimal set of API to create, expand, and collapse the tree (http://destroydrop.com/javascripts/tree/).

This is the same test, built using the same kind of tree:

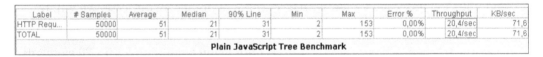

Label	# Samples	Average	Median	90% Line	Min	Max	Error %	Throughput	KB/sec
HTTP Requ...	50000	51	21	31	2	153	0,00%	20,4/sec	71,6
TOTAL	50000	51	21	31	2	153	0,00%	20,4/sec	71,6

Plain JavaScript Tree Benchmark

It's evident from this benchmark that the pure JavaScript solution works on another order of magnitude, taking just milliseconds to complete.

Should you then avoid using a rich tree? Well, from the performance point of view, the answer seems obvious. You might use a rich tree for a small set of data, possibly static data, where the user does not expand/collapse large tree structures.

One thing you might try to improve the performance of your rich:tree is switching to an Ajax-based communication, thus an Ajax request is sent when you trigger an action on the tree (see the next section to learn more about Ajax framework).

The same benchmark, executed with `<rich:tree switchType="ajax" . . . />` produces this result, which exhibits a rich 10 percent gain in the average execution time and throughput:

Label	# Samples	Average	Median	90% Line	Min	Max	Error %	Throughput	KB/sec
HTTP Requ...	50000	14606	14509	19911	546	41199	0,00%	4,5/sec	1934,8
TOTAL	50000	14606	14509	19911	546	41199	0,00%	4,5/sec	1934,8

RichFaces 3.3.3 Tree Benchmark switchType="ajax"

An additional performance saving can be gained by introducing a caching strategy like Hibernate second-level cache. (Please refer to *Chapter 6, Tuning the Persistence Layer,* to learn how to structure Hibernate caches in your application).

Increasing the performance of JSF and RichFaces

Until now, we have covered two common components, which are part of almost any web application. Unfortunately there is no magic switch which can improve dramatically the performance of single JSF UI components. However, some general best practices do exist to accelerate the whole JSF lifecycle. We can group them roughly into three areas:

- Configuring JSF state saving efficiently
- Using Ajax support to reduce the cost of page rendering and data transmission
- Loading external files (JavaScript/CSS) efficiently

Configuring JSF state saving efficiently

One of the most important settings, affecting the performance and the memory used by JSF UI components, is where to save the session state. You can opt between saving the state in the **server** (the default), which provides better performance, or saving it in the **client** which reduces the memory footprint, at the cost of a loss of performance.

Besides this, by using server-session state, you can have control over the **serialization** process, which is mandated by the JSF specification, to keep the application state consistent through the JSF lifecycle. Thus, the suggested guideline is to leave to the default (server) session-state saving:

```
<context-param>
    <param-name>javax.faces.STATE_SAVING_METHOD</param-name>
```

```
        <param-value>server</param-value>
    </context-param>
```

We have benchmarked the dataTable example (from the previous section) using the two different session-state saving methods. As a result, the server-state saving method produced a 15 percent higher throughput:

Label	# Samples	Average	Median	90% Line	Min	Max	Error %	Throughput	KB/sec
HTTP Requ...	50000	1231	720	2964	30	12360	0,00%	29,6/sec	966,9
TOTAL	50000	1231	720	2964	30	12360	0,00%	29,6/sec	966,9

RichFaces 3.3.3 STATE_SAVING_METHOD: server

Label	# Samples	Average	Median	90% Line	Min	Max	Error %	Throughput	KB/sec
HTTP Requ...	50000	217	182	524	34	609	0,00%	25,6/sec	924,6
TOTAL	50000	217	182	524	34	609	0,00%	25,6/sec	924,6

RichFaces 3.3.3 STATE_SAVING_METHOD: client

If you find excessive memory usage, you can limit the amount of Views to be stored in the session:

```
    <context-param>
        <param-name>org.apache.myfaces.NUMBER_OF_VIEWS_IN_SESSION</param-name>
        <param-value>20</param-value>
    </context-param>
```

An additional performance hit can be achieved by setting the compression and serialization of the state in the session to false:

```
    <context-param>
        <param-name>org.apache.myfaces.COMPRESS_STATE_IN_SESSION</param-name>
        <param-value>false</param-value>
    </context-param>

    <context-param>
        <param-name>org.apache.myfaces.SERIALIZE_STATE_IN_SESSION</param-name>
        <param-value>false</param-value>
    </context-param>
```

The above optimizations cannot be used when saving the state to the client:

```
    <context-param>
        <param-name>javax.faces.STATE_SAVING_METHOD</param-name>
        <param-value>client</param-value>
    </context-param>
```

You can, however, specify a different serialization factory for your application, like **org.apache.myfaces.JbossSerialFactory**, which delivers better performance:

```
<context-param>
    <param-name>org.apache.myfaces.SERIAL_FACTORY</param-name>
    <param-value>org.apache.myfaces.JbossSerialFactory</param-value>
</context-param>
```

Benchmarking our application using **JbossSerialFactory** showed a better performance for our application using client state saving. The performance, however, is still inferior to the server state saving method:

Label	# Samples	Average	Median	90% Line	Min	Max	Error %	Throughput	KB/sec
HTTP Requ...	50000	1366	797	3398	34	14015	0,00%	26,4/sec	954,7
TOTAL	50000	1366	797	3398	34	14015	0,00%	26,4/sec	954,7

RichFaces 3.3.3 serialization using JbossSerialFactory

In order to install JbossSerialFactory on your application, please refer to the following link, which documents all the necessary steps: http://wiki.apache.org/myfaces/Performance.

Using Ajax to speed up your JSF applications

One of the major upgrades of JSF 2 release is the addition of **Ajax** support for UI components. By using Ajax development techniques, web applications can retrieve data from the server asynchronously in the background without interfering with the display and behavior of the existing page. This leads to an increase in interactivity with the website and a boost in performance, since only a portion of the web page can now be updated as a consequence of users' actions.

One of the main advantages in using JBoss's `RichFaces` component library is Ajax-native support for its UI's components. For example, if you need to limit the part of the web page which needs to be updated, you can do it by means of the **reRender** attribute.

In the following code snippet, we are requesting a partial rendering of the web page by means of the update command button, which will re-draw just the info `panelGrid`:

```
<a4j:commandButton value="update" reRender="info"/>
...
<h:panelGrid id="info">
    ...
</h:panelGrid>
```

A closely related feature is the **ajaxSingle** attribute, which allows sending only a reduced set of attributes for processing, instead of the whole form attributes:

```
<a4j:commandButton action="#{bean.save}" value="Click Me"
ajaxSingle="true"/>
```

Another area where you could expect some performance hits are **Ajax filters**. In an Ajax request, a filter is required for correct functioning of the partial page refreshes. You can define a filter in your application's web.xml with the following XML fragment:

```
<filter>
  <display-name>RichFaces Filter</display-name>
    <filter-name>richfaces</filter-name>
    <filter-class>org.ajax4jsf.Filter</filter-class>
</filter>
```

What this filter does is to *tidy* all HTML responses so that they are valid XHTML (thus XML compliant). This is needed as dynamic DOM updates in the browser need correct XML.

Parsing HTML is, however, a CPU and time-consuming operation. So, you should use the most efficient parser available. RichFaces has a few parsers built in. The default one is based on a **Tidy** parser but it is quite slow. The **Neko** parser is considerably faster and can be used by setting the following context params:

```
<context-param>
        <param-name>org.ajax4jsf.xmlparser.ORDER</param-name>
        <param-value>NEKO</param-value>
</context-param>
<context-param>
        <param-name>org.ajax4jsf.xmlparser.NEKO</param-name>
        <param-value>.*\..*</param-value>
</context-param>
```

The following image shows a benchmark, which compares an Ajax-driven form submission using the default Tidy parser and the Neko parser:

Label	# Samples	Average	Median	90% Line	Min	Max	Error %	Throughput	KB/sec
HTTP Requ...	50000	124	12	398	9	1940	0,00%	79,1/sec	260,8
TOTAL	50000	124	12	398	9	1940	0,00%	79,1/sec	260,8

RichFaces 3.3.3 Tidy parser Benchmark

Label	# Samples	Average	Median	90% Line	Min	Max	Error %	Throughput	KB/sec
HTTP Requ...	50000	53	11	155	9	942	0,00%	87,8/sec	289,7
TOTAL	50000	53	11	155	9	942	0,00%	87,8/sec	289,7

RichFaces 3.3.3 NEKO parser Benchmark

Be aware that the Neko parser requires that the application's markup code is strictly verified. Code that is not strictly verified can cause a number of errors and corrupt layouts when used with the Neko filter.

A last configuration tweak for the `RichFaces Filter` can be applied by setting its **forceparser** parameter to `false`. With this setting, just Ajax requests will be tidied, thus speeding all other requests.

```
<filter>
<display-name>RichFaces Filter</display-name>
<filter-name>richfaces</filter-name>
<filter-class>org.ajax4jsf.Filter</filter-class>
<init-param>
      <param-name>forceparser</param-name>
      <param-value>false</param-value>
</init-param>
</filter>
```

Speeding up CSS and JavaScript file loading

As you can see from a quick inspection of a rich web page, lots of CSS and JavaScript files are used to produce the intriguing GUI. JavaScript, unfortunately, has a dark side to it that not many people are aware of. It causes the browser to stop everything that it's doing until the script has been downloaded, parsed and executed.

Some browsers, for example Google's Chrome or even IE8, can load files in parallel so that two smaller JavaScript files might load more quickly than one massive file. In most cases, however, you should configure your application to load the external file with a single external call. This can be done by means of the RichFaces's **LoadStyleStrategy** parameter:

```
<context-param>
  <param-name>
    org.richfaces.LoadStyleStrategy
  </param-name>
  <param-value>ALL</param-value>
</context-param>
```

Be aware that when using the `ALL` load strategy, you need to turn off script compression to get it working.

```
<context-param>
    <param-name>
```

```
        org.ajax4jsf.COMPRESS_SCRIPT
    </param-name>
    <param-value>false</param-value>
</context-param>
```

 If you need a JSP compliant library for arranging your JavaScript and CSS resources, you might consider having a look at the **pack:tab** library (`http://www.ohloh.net/p/packtag`). This is a JSP-Taglib that minifies, compresses, and combines resources (like JavaScript and CSS) and caches them in memory or in a generated file. It works transparent to the user/developer and the compressing algorithms are pluggable.

Tuning web services

The other broad category of web applications includes web services, which is a typical B2B technology. Web services have deeply changed the landscape of B2B services by introducing a common transport protocol for network communication, which before was left to different kinds of adapters and plugins provided by the single application server.

How do web services actually bridge different systems? Web services use XML as the standard for exchanging data across disparate systems. Specifically, the XML content needs to be converted to a format that is readable by the Java application and vice versa. **Data binding** is the process that describes the conversion of data between its XML and Java representations.

The current standard for designing web services is **JAX-WS**, which uses **Java Architecture for XML Binding** (JAXB) to manage all of the data binding tasks. Specifically, JAXB binds Java method signatures and WSDL messages and operations, and allows you to customize the mapping while automatically handling the runtime conversion. This makes it easy for you to incorporate XML data and processing functions in applications based on Java technology without having to know much about XML.

The following image shows the JAXB data-binding process:

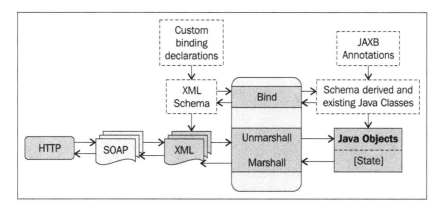

The core process, which allows the translation of XML into Java Objects and vice versa, is known as marshalling and unmarshalling. As with all libraries dealing with XML, they are CPU-intensive operations, which can easily become a performance bottleneck. Thus, most of your tuning efforts should be directed at reducing the graph of Java Objects to be converted into XML.

Difference between serialization and marshalling

Marshalling and serialization are loosely synonymous in the context of remote procedure call, but semantically different as a matter of intent.

Serialization is a general technique for converting objects to sequences of bits that can be transported to a different VM. Serialization is used by EJB to transport objects from the client JVM to the server JVM.

Marshalling, on the other hand, means bundling up parameters for a remote method call. Under SOAP, marshalling uses a much more complex approach, translating parameters to XML.

Performance of web services

Until now we have spoken about web services as complex stuff because of the inherently intricate process of marshalling and unmarshalling and the network latency to move SOAP packets. However, how do web services perform? As single tests are not very indicative, we will compare the performance of a web service with the equivalent operation executed by an EJB.

The web service will be in charge of executing a task on a legacy system and returning a collection of 500 objects. We will deploy our project on JBoss 5.1.0, which uses the default **JBossWS native stack** as JAX-WS implementation.

You have several options available to benchmark your web services. For example, you could create a simple web service client in the form of a JSP/Servlet and use it to load-test your web application. Alternatively, you can use a Web Service SOAP Sampler, which is built-in in your JMeter collection of samplers.

Just right-click from your **Thread Group** and choose **Add | Sampler | Web Service (SOAP) Request**.

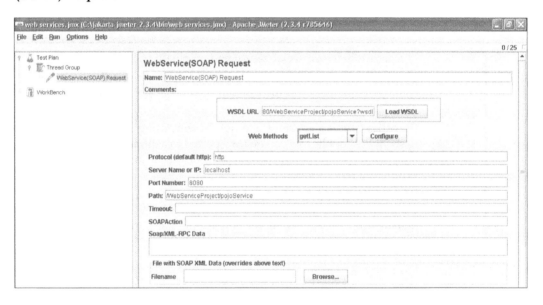

You can either configure manually all the settings, which are related to the web service or, simply, let JMeter configure them for you by loading the WSDL (Choose **Load WSDL button**). Then pick up the method you want to test and select **Configure** which automatically configures your web service properties.

Our benchmark will collect 50000 samples from our web service. Here's the resulting JMeter aggregate report:

Label	# Samples	Average	Median	90% Line	Min	Max	Error %	Throughput	KB/sec
HTTP Requ...	50000	1089	855	2722	15	8392	0,00%	17,2/sec	4,8
TOTAL	50000	1089	855	2722	15	8392	0,00%	17,2/sec	4,8
Web service Benchmark - 500 records fetched									

The web service requires an average of about 1 second to return, exhibiting a throughput of 17/sec.

Smart readers should have noticed another peculiarity from this benchmark in that there is a huge difference between the **Min** and **Max** value. This is due to the fact that JBossWS performs differently during the first method invocation of each service and the following ones, especially when dealing with large WSDL contracts.

During the first invocation of the service lots of data is internally cached and reused during the following ones. While this actually improves the performance of subsequent calls, it might be necessary to limit the maximum response time. By setting the `org.jboss.ws.eagerInitia` `lizeJAXBContextCache` system property to `true`, both on the server side (in the JBoss start script) and on the client side (a convenient constant is available in `org.jboss.ws.Constants`) JBossWS will try to eagerly create and cache the JAXB contexts before the first invocation is handled.

The same test will be now executed using an EJB layer, which performs exactly the same job. The result is quite different:

Label	# Samples	Average	Median	90% Line	Min	Max	Error %	Throughput	KB/sec
HTTP Requ...	50000	129	6	447	5	4409	0,00%	142,6/sec	37,7
TOTAL	50000	129	6	447	5	4409	0,00%	142,6/sec	37,7
Stateless EJB Benchmark - 500 records fetched									

As you can see, the EJB was over eight times faster than the web service for the most relevant metrics. This benchmark is intentionally misusing web services just to warn the reader against the potential risk of a flawed interface design, like returning a huge set of data from a collection.

Web services are no doubt a key factor in the integration of heterogeneous systems and have reached a reasonable level of maturity; however they should be not proposed as the right solution for everything, just because they use a standard protocol for exchanging data.

Even if web services fit in perfectly in your project's picture, you should be aware of the most important factors, which influence the performance of web services. The next section gathers some useful elements, which should serve as wake-up call at the early phase of project designing.

Elements influencing the performance of web services

The most important factor in determining the performance of web services are the characteristics of the XML documents, which are sent and returned by web services. We can distinguish three main elements:

- Size: The length of data elements in the XML document.
- Complexity: The number of elements that the XML document contains.
- Level of nesting: Refers to objects or collections of objects that are defined within other objects in the XML document.

On the basis of these assumptions, we can elaborate the following performance guidelines:

You should design **coarse-grained web services**, that is services which perform a lot of work on the server and acknowledge just a response code or a minimal set of attributes.

The amount of parameters passed to the web service should be as well skimmed to the essential in order to reduce the size of outgoing SOAP messages. Nevertheless, take into consideration that XML size is not the only factor that you need to consider, but also network latency is a key element. If your web services tend to be chatty, with lots of little round trips and a subtle statefulness between individual communications, they will be slow. This will be slower than sending a single larger SOAP message.

Developers often fail to realize that the web service API call model isn't well suited to building communicating applications where caller and callee are separated by a medium (networks!) with variable and unconstrained performance characteristics/latency.

For this reason, don't make the mistake of fragmenting your web service invocation in several chunks. In the end the size of the XML will stay the same but you will pay with additional network latency.

Another important factor, which can improve the performance of your web services, is caching. You could consider caching responses at the price of additional memory requirements or potential stale data issues. Caching should be also accomplished on web services documents, like the **Web service description language (WSDL)**, which contains the specifications of the web service contract. It's advised to refer to a local backup copy of your WSDL when you are rolling your service in production as in the following example:

```
@WebServiceClient(name = "ExampleWebService", targetNamespace =
"http://www.packtpub.com/", wsdlLocation = "http://127.0.0.1:8080/
ExampleWebService/helloWorld?wsdl")
```

At the same time, you should consider caching the instance that contains the web service port. A **web service port** is an abstract set of operations supported by one or more endpoints. Its name attribute provides a unique identifier among all port types defined within the enclosing WSDL document.

> In short, a port contains an abstract view of the web service, but acquiring a copy of it is an expensive operation, which should be avoided every time you need to access your Web service.

```
// Class variables
POJOWebService pojoService;
. . . . . .
// Cache it in a class variable
pojoService = pojo.getPOJOWebServicePort();
```

The potential threat of this approach is that you might introduce in your client code objects (the proxy port), which are not thread safe, so you should synchronize their access or use a pool of instances instead. An exception to this rule is the **Apache CXF** implementation, which documents the use cases where the proxy port can be safely cached in the project FAQs: http://cxf.apache.org/faq.html.

Reducing the size of SOAP messages

Reducing the size of the XML messages, which are sent across your services, is one of the most relevant tuning points. However, there are some scenarios where you need to receive lots of data from your services; as a matter of fact, the Java EE 1.5 specifications introduce the **javax.jws.WebService** annotation, which makes it quite tempting to expose your POJOs as web services.

The reverse of the coin is that many web services will grow up and prosper with inherited characteristics of POJOs like, for example:

```
@WebService
  .  .  .  .  .
@WebMethod
  public List<MyPOJO> getList(int arg1)      {
  .  .  .  .  .
}
```

If you cannot afford the price of rewriting your business implementations from scratch, then you need to reduce at least the cost of this expensive fetch.

A simple but effective strategy is to override the default binding rules for Java-to-XML Schema mapping using JAXB annotations. Consider the following class Person, which has the following fields:

```
public class Person {

  String name;
  String address;
  String city;
  String state;
  int postcode;
  String country
  .  .  .  .
}
```

When you are returning a sample instance of this class from a web service, you will move across the network this 460 bytes SOAP message:

```
<env:Envelope xmlns:env='http://schemas.xmlsoap.org/soap/envelope/'>
  <env:Header />
  <env:Body>
  <ns2:getListResponse xmlns:ns2='http://www.packtpub.com/'>
  <return>
    <item>
      <name>John and Jane Doe</name>
      <address>100 Main Street</street>
      <city>Anytown</city>
      <state>NY</state>
      <postcode>12345</postcode>
      <country>USA</country>
    </item>
    <!-- other items -->
  </return>
```

```
</ns2:getListResponse>
</env:Body>
</env:Envelope>
```

As you can see, lots of characters are wasted in XML elements which could conveniently be replaced by attributes, thus saving a good quantity of bytes:

```
@XmlRootElement
public class Person {

    @XmlAttribute
    String name;

    @XmlAttribute
    String address;

    @XmlAttribute
    String city;

    @XmlAttribute
    String state;

    @XmlAttribute
    int postcode;

    @XmlAttribute
    String country
    . . . .

}
```

The corresponding XML generated is 380 bytes, about 18 percent smaller than the default XML prepared by the JAXB parser:

```
<env:Envelope xmlns:env='http://schemas.xmlsoap.org/soap/envelope/'>
    <env:Header />
    <env:Body>
    <ns2:getListResponse xmlns:ns2='http://www.packtpub.com/'>
    <return>
        <item name="John and Jane Doe" address="100" city="Anytown" state
    ="NY" postcode="12345" country="USA">
        </item>
        <!-- other items -->
    </return>
</ns2:getListResponse>
</env:Body>
</env:Envelope>
```

If we try to issue again our initial benchmark, using custom JAXB annotations, the reduced size in the SOAP message is reflected in a higher throughput:

Label	# Samples	Average	Median	90% Line	Min	Max	Error %	Throughput	KB/sec
HTTP Requ..	50000	855	1134	1346	31	8435	0,00%	24,2/sec	6,0
TOTAL	50000	855	1134	1346	31	8435	0,00%	24,2/sec	6,0

Web service Benchmark - 500 records fetched –XML Content optimization

Compressing attribute text

One of the most powerful features of JAX-RPC web services is the **Handler chain** mechanism. A Handler can be used to modify a SOAP request or response message at the client and the server side. A Handler class is tied to the service endpoint and can be configured to intercept the SOAP message and perform various operations on it.

A comprehensive guide to install and deploy Handlers with the JBossWS platform can be found here: `http://community.jboss.org/wiki/JBossWS-UserGuide`.

A Handler extends the **GenericSOAPHandler** interface and is commonly used for performing aspect-oriented activities on the SOAP message like logging or encrypting. However, it can also be used to compress the content of the web service attributes. Showing a complete code example of this is out of the scope of this book, however, in a nutshell, compressing the web service body requires reading the **SOAPBodyElements** in the `handleInbound(MessageContext msgContext)` method and send them compressed through the `handleOutbound(MessageContext msgContext)`. Depending on the efficiency of the compression algorithm, you can expect a performance benefit due to the reduced size of the SOAP payload.

Faster JBossWS provider

JBossWS project provides a **JAX-WS** web service stack compatible with the Java EE 5 standard. The JBossWS framework is quite flexible as you can use three different kinds of web services implementations:

- **JBossWS Native**: This is the JBossWS web service framework integrating the original JBossWS native stack that has been developed in the past few years.

- **JBossWS CXF**: This is the JBossWS web service framework integrating the Apache CXF web service stack. It is the default web service framework in release 6.x of the application server.

- **JBossWS Metro**: This is the JBossWS web service framework integrating the GlassFish Metro Web Service stack.

Releases 4.x and 5.x of the application deliver the JBossWS native stack as the default
JAX-WS implementation. However, it is worth trying different providers to see
which one can achieve the best performance for your web services. This is what we
will do in the next sections.

At first, you need to download the additional providers from the JBossWS download
page: `http://www.jboss.org/jbossws/downloads.html`.

Installing a new web services stack is quite easy and follows the same procedure
for all web services stacks. Just drop a file named `ant.properties` in the `home`
`directory` of your web services stack. The file needs to contain information
about your `JBOSS_HOME` directory, for example:

```
jboss510.home=C:\\jboss-5.1.0.GA
jbossws.integration.target=jboss510
```

Then, launch the ant make file adding as an argument the release where the web
services libraries will be installed:

```
ant deploy-jboss510
```

We will now compare the web services providers with three different kinds of
payloads: small (5 KB), medium (50 KB) and large (500 KB). The first implementation
tested will be the default **JBossWS native stack**. Here's the benchmark aftermath:

Label	# Samples	Average	Median	90% Line	Min	Max	Error %	Throughput	KB/sec
HTTP Requ...	50000	492	160	1005	23	7710	0,00%	34,1/sec	11,1
TOTAL	50000	492	160	1005	23	7710	0,00%	34,1/sec	11,1
JBossWS native Benchmark - small payload									
Label	# Samples	Average	Median	90% Line	Min	Max	Error %	Throughput	KB/sec
HTTP Requ...	50000	666	184	1854	33	10462	0,00%	26,3/sec	8,6
TOTAL	50000	666	184	1854	33	10462	0,00%	26,3/sec	8,6
JBossWS native Benchmark - medium payload									
Label	# Samples	Average	Median	90% Line	Min	Max	Error %	Throughput	KB/sec
HTTP Requ...	50000	5060	4450	9425	157	20345	0,00%	4,7/sec	1,5
TOTAL	50000	5060	4450	9425	157	20345	0,00%	4,7/sec	1,5
JBossWS native Benchmark - large payload									

As you can see, the throughput of the JBossWS native implementation stays in the range between 26-34/sec for small or medium payloads. When using large payloads the throughput decreases to just 4.7/sec with an average of 5 seconds per request.

We will now repeat the test with **Apache CXF stack**:

Label	# Samples	Average	Median	90% Line	Min	Max	Error %	Throughput	KB/sec
HTTP Requ...	50000	14	8	10	7	810	0,00%	98,2/sec	32,1
TOTAL	50000	14	8	10	7	810	0,00%	98,2/sec	32,1

Apache CXF Benchmark - small payload

Label	# Samples	Average	Median	90% Line	Min	Max	Error %	Throughput	KB/sec
HTTP Requ...	50000	44	10	84	9	3887	0,00%	87,0/sec	28,4
TOTAL	50000	44	10	84	9	3887	0,00%	87,0/sec	28,4

Apache CXF Benchmark - medium payload

Label	# Samples	Average	Median	90% Line	Min	Max	Error %	Throughput	KB/sec
HTTP Requ...	50000	1029	568	2735	44	13513	0,00%	19,1/sec	6,2
TOTAL	50000	1029	568	2735	44	13513	0,00%	19,1/sec	6,2

Apache CXF Benchmark - large payload

The result of this benchmark shows a consistent boost in all main metrics, revealing a throughput **from** 2.8 to 4 times higher. Besides this, Apache CXF stacks also exhibit a minor decrease in performance as the payload increases. The transition from a 5 KB XML size to a 500 KB reduces the throughput to 1/5 while the JBossWS native implementation reduced the throughput to 1/7.

The following graph completes our analysis with the **Glassfish Metro** benchmark:

Label	# Samples	Average	Median	90% Line	Min	Max	Error %	Throughput	KB/sec
HTTP Requ...	50000	7	4	8	3	1175	0,00%	101,7/sec	33,2
TOTAL	50000	7	4	8	3	1175	0,00%	101,7/sec	33,2

Glassfish Metro Benchmark - small payload

Label	# Samples	Average	Median	90% Line	Min	Max	Error %	Throughput	KB/sec
HTTP Requ...	50000	31	9	39	8	1518	0,00%	94,6/sec	30,9
TOTAL	50000	31	9	39	8	1518	0,00%	94,6/sec	30,9

Glassfish Metro Benchmark - medium payload

Label	# Samples	Average	Median	90% Line	Min	Max	Error %	Throughput	KB/sec
HTTP Requ...	50000	972	336	2672	42	14760	0,00%	19,3/sec	6,3
TOTAL	50000	972	336	2672	42	14760	0,00%	19,3/sec	6,3

Glassfish Metro Benchmark - large payload

This benchmark sets a new record for all three tests, with very interesting performance numbers when dealing with small/medium-sized SOAP messages. The average response time for small payloads (which is just 7 ms) indicates clearly that this web service stack adopts internally caching algorithms to store the structure of the web service definition (WSDL). The time spent for small payloads using this stack can be as low as the mere network latency.

The wisdom behind these benchmarks

At the end of this test, we can draw some conclusions. As far as performance is concerned, the Apache CXF and Glassfish metro stack seem definitely superior to the default JBossWS native stack. GlassFish Metro scored the highest overall throughput, while Apache CXF seemed to be the one which scales better as payload increases.

Nevertheless, this test cannot say a definitive word about which web service stack is actually the fastest. There are still too many factors to compare, for example the performance of the security API or encryption metrics. Also these numbers are likely to change as the web service releases are upgraded.

What we can certainly argue with these statistics is that, if you have performance goals in your web service project, then you should seriously evaluate Apache CXF and Glassfish Metro stack. Setting up an alternate JBoss AS server configuration with another web service implementation, as we showed, is quite trivial so just benchmark before rolling in production with the default implementation.

Summary

In this chapter, we have covered in detail how to deliver fast web application modules. In the first part of the chapter we have discussed the best tactics to deliver a fast web application, covering the following topics:

- Earlier MVC web applications are intrinsically coupled with a set of interfaces and require lots of tedious and repetitive code to deal with low-level request and response objects. On the other hand, because of their shorter lifecycle they deliver fast responses.

- On the other hand, developers with a sound knowledge of JSF technology, can build highly flexible web applications in a much shorter time, at the price of a more complex (and thus slower) runtime lifecycle.

  - Producing a tabular set of data is a common requisite of every web application. By using a plain JSP/Servlet approach you can achieve the best performance hit. Using JSF's Mojarra 1.2 implementation was about 2.5 times slower in our lab tests. The RichFaces component library added an additional 20 percent slow down. The dataTable and rich:dataTable, however, are highly customizable and can mitigate the additional overhead by rendering a small dataset and using pagination.

- If you are going to render a set of hierarchical data by means of a tree, be aware that a JSF solution might impact performance. You are advised to stay on a low-level technology like JavaScript, if you have lots of data in the tree. Depending on the type of hardware and the browser used, as little as 500 records in a tree can produce a significant slow down in your JSF tree.

- JSF performance can, however, be enhanced by setting the `javax.faces.STATE_SAVING_METHOD` to server. If using client-state saving method you are advised to use `org.apache.myfaces.JbossSerialFactory` as a serialization factory.

  - Ajax technology can greatly enhance the performance of your web applications by limiting the area of the page to be reloaded and reducing also the amount of data to be sent for processing.

  - The **reRender** attribute can be used to define the UIComponent, which is affected by page reloading. The **ajaxSingle** attribute when set to `true` can limit the amount of parameters sent by the view.

  - Ajax partial page refresh requires a Servlet Filter, which adapts the content of the HTML page. If your application's markup code is strictly verified, the **NEKO** parser yields the best performance results.

In the second part of this chapter, we have discussed B2B components, namely web services, and how to improve their performance.

- The performance of web services is strongly dependant on the size of the SOAP packet sent during the communications. You can reduce the packet size by overriding the default binding rules for Java-to-XML schema mapping using JAXB annotations; for example defining class fields as XML attributes instead of XML elements.

- Another element you should consider is caching, which could be applied both on the web service contract (WSDL) and, with some restrictions, on the web service port, in order to cache the abstract view of the web service.

- Finally, before rolling your web services in production, you should evaluate the available web services stacks. Basically, you can opt for three different web service stacks:
    - ° JBossWS Native, which is the default JBoss 5.x web service stack
    - ° JBossWS CXF, which integrates the Apache CXF web service stack
    - ° JBossWS Metro, which integrates the GlassFish Metro web service stack.
- From a performance point of view, Apache CXF and GlasshFish showed a much better throughput than JBossWS Native. The former one (JBossWS CXF) is the default JBoss Web service stack in the 6.x releases.

A Tuned Mind

At the end of this long journey, we have covered many aspects of performance tuning. One of the hardest tasks when writing this book was describing a complex process like tuning in the most practical way, without sacrificing too much theory. As a matter of fact, most people like to think that performance tuning is nothing but a silver bullet which can be shot at any time. Frustrated by tight deadlines and intense pressure to reach their goals, they misunderstand the precise role of performance in the software lifecycle.

Some quick tips do exist and this book has not been parsimonious at showing a great deal of them; but they are there just to enhance the performance of a well-written and designed application or to mitigate the effect of bottlenecks we do not have any control on it.

The real secret behind a lighting fast application is a *good tuning methodology*, which starts right when application requirements are defined and continues until its last mile, when the application is rolled in production. We are certainly aware that this is a questionable statement as many architects *deliberately exclude* the tuning methodology from any design strategy. We do not claim that our choices are better than other's. What we do believe is that, without a special virtue called *flexibility*, architects will have a hard time to survive these turbulent years.

A flexible architect re-uses his/her wealth of experience, including both successes and failures. At the same time, the flexible architect is open to new suggestions and can fearlessly and strategically adapts his/her mind.

As time passes, inevitably some of the tips presented in this book will go stale and new great instruments will appear on the market. In the end, what (we dare to say) will stay the same is that good performance is not accidental; it takes planning, expertise, and plenty of testing. It needs that, when you define your performance requirements, you won't be satisfied with a generic "fast" word from your customers but pretend an *exact* measure of your performance goals and build a plan to support them. Without all these things, tuning is almost a bet. And you know that if you are a frequent better, you are also a frequent loser.

Index

Symbols

A

B

C

J

K

KeepAliveTime parameter 102
key attributes
  nfile 239
  ninode 239
Key Generator 99

L

loadLeaf() method 186
load testing, with JMeter
  complex test plan, creating 48-50
  JMeter, running as shell 51
  listener, creating 46, 47
  sampler, creating 45
  test plan, building 44
  thread group, creating 44
lock striping 211
logging 114
Logging information 115
logging strategy
  AsynchAppender, using 117
  fastest appender 115, 116
  log threshold, increasing 119
  PatternLayout, using 118
  selecting 115
log levels
  about 115
  DEBUG 115
  ERROR 115
  FATAL 115
  INFO 115
  TRACE 115
  WARN 115

M

Mail Service 99
marshalling 267
MaximumPoolSize parameter 102
MaximumQueueSize parameter 102
max-pool-size element 105
max-pool-size, JDBC connection pool
  calculating 106, 107
MCMP 248
MDB 138

memory requirements, JBoss AS release 5.x
  97
Message Driven Bean. *See* MDB
MessageProducer class 149
method
  setDisableMessageID 149
  setDisableMessageTimeStamp 149
Microcontainer kernel 96
middleware tuning 20
MinimumPoolSize parameter 102
min-pool-size attribute 105
minSpareThreads attribute 232
mod_cluster
  mod_cluster, module 249
  mod_jk, module 249
  mod_proxy, module 249
Mod-Cluster Management Protocol. *See*
  MCMP
Model View Controller. *See* MVC
monitor tab, JBoss AS 5.1.0 server 31
MPM
  about 245
  module, selecting 245
  Netware 245
  Prefork 245
  WinNT 245
  Worker 245
multicast UDP socket 197
Multi-Processing Module. *See* MPM
MVC
  about 254, 255
  Controller 254
  Model 254
  View 254
MVCC
  features 211
  using, with session data 211

N

n+1 problem 170
Neko parser 264
new space 62
numBuddies property 216

O

object retrieval, optimizing
  data fetched amount, limiting 170, 171
  fetch join 171
  Hibernate queries speeding up, batches
      used 172, 173
  join fetches, combining with paging 172
  named queries, using 173, 174
old generation 62
on-demand deployment 99
Online Transaction Processing 159
operating system tools
  for Unix users 54
  for Window users 52
  Manage Engine 54
  Process Explorer 54
  System Explorer 54
operating system tuning 20
**optimal min-pool-size, JDBC connection
      pool**
  calculating 106, 107
OutOfMemory errors 80
  handling 82
  large Java objects creation, avoiding 80, 81
  memory leak, finding in code 83-85

P

parallel collector, garbage collectors
  about 74
  working 74
parallel compaction 75
passivation property 224
PatternLayout 118
performance
  about 9
  preface 7
  Response Time 9
  Throughput 10
performance monitor 52, 53
performance test
  baseline, establishing 15, 16
  configuring 18
  data, analyzing 17
  data, collecting 16, 17
permanent space 62
POJO-based kernel 97

Prepared Statements
  using 108-110
profiler snapshots
  about 34
  collecting 34, 35
profiler tab, JBoss AS 5.1.0 server 33
property, data gravitation
  autoDataGravitation 217
  DataGravitationRemoveOnFind 217
  dataGravitationSearchBackupTrees 217
Protocol stack configuration
  TCP protocol stacks 198
  TCP transport configuration, defining 198
  UDP transport configuration 197
Protocol stack, JGroups
  configurable attributes 205
  cryptic configuration 202, 203
  optimizing 201
prstat utility 55
purgeOnStartup property 225

Q

Quartz Scheduler 99
query cache
  about 180
  using 181
  versus entity cache 181-183
QueryHint annotation 181

R

Regions 77
Remoting framework 140
reRender attribute 263
Response Time 9
RichFaces library
  LoadStyleStrategy parameter 265

S

scalability
  about 10
  horizontal scalability 11
  vertical scalability 11
scientific tuning 23
Seam libraries 99

Thank you for buying
JBoss AS 5 Performance Tuning

About Packt Publishing

Packt, pronounced 'packed', published its first book "*Mastering phpMyAdmin for Effective MySQL Management*" in April 2004 and subsequently continued to specialize in publishing highly focused books on specific technologies and solutions.

Our books and publications share the experiences of your fellow IT professionals in adapting and customizing today's systems, applications, and frameworks. Our solution based books give you the knowledge and power to customize the software and technologies you're using to get the job done. Packt books are more specific and less general than the IT books you have seen in the past. Our unique business model allows us to bring you more focused information, giving you more of what you need to know, and less of what you don't.

Packt is a modern, yet unique publishing company, which focuses on producing quality, cutting-edge books for communities of developers, administrators, and newbies alike. For more information, please visit our website: www.packtpub.com.

About Packt Open Source

In 2010, Packt launched two new brands, Packt Open Source and Packt Enterprise, in order to continue its focus on specialization. This book is part of the Packt Open Source brand, home to books published on software built around Open Source licences, and offering information to anybody from advanced developers to budding web designers. The Open Source brand also runs Packt's Open Source Royalty Scheme, by which Packt gives a royalty to each Open Source project about whose software a book is sold.

Writing for Packt

We welcome all inquiries from people who are interested in authoring. Book proposals should be sent to author@packtpub.com. If your book idea is still at an early stage and you would like to discuss it first before writing a formal book proposal, contact us; one of our commissioning editors will get in touch with you.

We're not just looking for published authors; if you have strong technical skills but no writing experience, our experienced editors can help you develop a writing career, or simply get some additional reward for your expertise.

JBoss Tools 3 Developers Guide

ISBN: 978-1-847196-14-9   Paperback: 408 pages

Develop JSF, Struts, Seam, Hibernate, jBPM, ESB, web services, and portal applications faster than ever using JBoss Tools for Eclipse and the JBoss

1. Develop complete JSF, Struts, Seam, Hibernate, jBPM, ESB, web service, and portlet applications using JBoss Tools

2. Tools covered in separate chapters so you can dive into the one you want to learn

3. Manage JBoss Application Server through JBoss AS Tools

JBoss RichFaces 3.3

ISBN: 978-1-847196-88-0   Paperback: 320 pages

Enhance your JSF web applications using powerful AJAX components

1. Build a new RichFaces JSF project in minutes using JBoss RichFaces with JBoss Seam and Facelets

2. Customize the look-and-feel of your JSF applications with Skinnability

3. Integrate AJAX into your applications without using JavaScript

4. Create, customize, and deploy new skins for the RichFaces framework using the powerful plug'n'skin feature

Please check **www.PacktPub.com** for information on our titles

JBoss Drools Business Rules

ISBN: 978-1-847196-06-4   Paperback: 304 pages

Capture, automate, and reuse your business processes in a clear English language that your computer can understand.

1. An easy-to-understand JBoss Drools business rules tutorial for non-programmers

2. Automate your business processes such as order processing, supply management, staff activity, and more

3. Prototype, test, and implement workflows by themselves using business rules that are simple statements written in an English-like language

4. Discover advanced features of Drools to write clear business rules that execute quickly

JBoss AS 5 Development

ISBN: 978-1-847196-82-8   Paperback: 416 pages

Develop, deploy, and secure Java applications on this robust, open source application server

1. A complete guide for JBoss developers covering everything from basic installation to creating, debugging, and securing Java EE applications on this popular, award-winning JBoss application server

2. Master the most important areas of Java Enterprise programming including EJB 3.0, web services, the security framework, and more

3. Starts with the basics of JBoss AS and moves on to cover important advanced topics with the help of easy-to-understand practical examples

Please check **www.PacktPub.com** for information on our titles

www.ingramcontent.com/pod-product-compliance
Lightning Source LLC
Chambersburg PA
CBHW080354060326
40689CB00019B/4001